THE MANAGEMENT OF INFORMATION FROM ARCHIVES

SECOND EDITION

MICHAEL COOK

Gower

First edition published 1986 by Gower Publishing Company Limited
Third edition published by

Gower Publishing Limited
Gower House
Croft Road
Aldershot
Hampshire GU11 3HR
England

Gower
Old Post Road
Brookfield
Vermont 05036
USA

British Library Cataloguing in Publication Data
Cook, Michael, 1931–
    The management of information from archives. – 2nd ed.
    1.Archives – Management
    I.Title
    025.1 '7 '14

    ISBN 0 566 07993 3

Library of Congress Cataloging-in-Publication Data
Cook, Michael, 1931–
    The management of information from archives / Michael Cook. – 2nd ed.
        p.   cm.
    Includes bibliographical references and index.
    ISBN 0–566–07993–3
    1. Information storage and retrieval systems–Archival material.
2. Cataloging of archival material–Data processing. 3. Archival materials
–Data processing. 4. Archives–Automation–Management.
5. Archives–Administration.   I. Title
CD971.C66   1999
025'.00285–dc21   98–32250
                                                                CIP

Typeset in Great Britain by Saxon Graphics Ltd, Derby
Printed at the University Press, Cambridge

CONTENTS

LIST OF FIGURES

PREFACE

Like all my other writings on archives and records management, this book is intended to provide a summary of the most important areas of professional practice. This is a discipline that attracts many who have not trained for it, and who wish to understand it as part of a wider knowledge of document or information management. I hope that this exposition will be useful for these. However, in writing it I had in mind a text for the use of students preparing for their first-entry qualification and consequently their initial step towards professional registration.[1] In particular, the students most immediately in mind are those preparing for the Master's degree in Archives Records and Administration at LUCAS, the Centre for Archive Studies at the University of Liverpool.

This degree course (in its various manifestations) has a history going back to 1947. The archives staff at Liverpool are celebrating 50 years of this work. A great deal has happened in that time, and the changing syllabus of the degree course is witness to this. The original idea, put forward by historians, was that archivistics was mainly about the techniques of the auxiliary sciences to history, chiefly palaeography and diplomatics. Over time, this aspect has, as one would expect, been increasingly overshadowed by management aspects, and by the concepts and technologies of information management. Nevertheless, the original subjects of study are still strong, and it is only recently that options have been allowed that have removed the compulsory knowledge of the Latin language. This book, I hope, represents the central body of professional knowledge that is taught in archival training, in its current form.

It is important to point out some of the subjects that are not dealt with in this study. The most pressing of these is conservation, a subject

---

[1] Registration as an archivist is managed by the Society of Archivists: application should be made to the Registrar, care of the society at its offices at 40 Northampton Road, London EC1R 0HB.

that is increasingly prominent in society generally, in the information community in particular, and is occupying a greater role in training courses. Nevertheless, broadly speaking, the view taken in this book is that conservation and preservation is not necessarily central to archives work. All branches of information work have both current and retrospective aspects. One can manage and use the information carried by archival media in the same way as one can do this with books and documents, that is, without considering the long-term preservation of the media. All the same, the ultimate survival of the best materials as part of the common heritage remains an underlying need of society, and therefore the physical basis for this activity should remain a legitimate subject of study and research. Similarly, the equipping and provisioning of an archives service is not dealt with here, nor is the marketing of archival expertise (nowadays often termed 'advocacy').

Another increasingly important subject not centrally dealt with here is the management and use of records and archives held in electronic form. This very important topic merits a book of its own. In any case, the state of this art is still somewhat in flux. Administrators in both public and private sectors are beginning to be aware of the problems caused by the computer revolution. The initial task is to make their perception more precise and to convince policy-makers that they need to set up the necessary administrative machinery.

This book attempts to assimilate the newly adopted international standards for archival description and for authority work in archives. These documents have been adopted by the archival community during the 1990s and, remarkably, have been generally received with acceptance and welcome over the boundaries of national and language tradition. Not all of the consequences of the general adoption of these standards have yet become obvious. This book attempts to bring some of them out, but there are many changes still to come.

Michael Cook
Liverpool University Centre for Archive Studies

ACKNOWLEDGEMENTS

There are very many people who deserve thanks for their help, either general or specific, in these linked projects. Since they cannot all be mentioned, I would like to record particular thanks to these colleagues: Caroline Williams and Sarah Westwood at LUCAS; Margaret Procter, Simon Wilson and Edmund King at the Liverpool University Archives; Patricia Methven and the members of the Professional Methodology Panel of the Society of Archivists; Susan Healy and several other members of the staff of the Public Record Office; Anne Thurston, Piers Cain, Elizabeth Box and other members of the International Records Management Trust (and through them, the members of staff of the Ghana Records Administration and of the Department of Library and Archives Studies of the University of Ghana). Copyright material held in the Public Record Office is reproduced by permission of the Controller of Her Majesty's Stationery Office.

LIST OF ABBREVIATIONS

AACR2	Anglo-American Cataloguing Rules
AMC	Archives and Manuscripts Control
APPM	Archives, Private Papers and Manuscripts
ARMA	Association for Records Managers and Administrators
BAS	British Antarctic Survey
BBC	British Broadcasting Corporation
BSI	British Standards Institution
CCF	Common Communications Format
CRG	Classification Research Group
DP	Data Protection (legislation)
DTD	Document Type Definition
EAD	Encoded Archival Description
ESRO	East Sussex Record Office
EU	European Union
FAQs	frequently asked questions
FOI	Freedom of Information (legislation)
HMC	Royal Commission on Historical Manuscripts (London)
HMT	historical manuscripts tradition
HTML	Hypertext Mark-up Language
ICA	International Council on Archives
IRMT	International Records Management Trust
ISAAR(CPF)	International Standard Archival Authority Record for Corporate Bodies, Persons and Families
ISAD(G)	General International Standard for Archival Description
ISBD	International Standard Book Description
IT	information technology
KWAC	Keyword Alongside Context
KWIC	Keyword In Context
KWOC	Keyword Out of Context
LCSH	Library of Congress Subject Headings

MAD2	*Manual of Archival Description* (British standard for archival description) 2nd edn
MARC	Machine-Readable Catalogue
MDA	Museum Documentation Association
MIS	management information system
NBM	non-book materials
NCA	National Council on Archives
NRA	National Register of Archives
NUCMC	National Union Catalog of Manuscript Collections
OCLC	Online Computer Library Center
OPAC	Online Public Access Catalogue
PAT	public archives tradition
PRO	Public Record Office, London
PRONI	Public Record Office of Northern Ireland
RAD	Rules for Archival Description
RGO	Royal Greenwich Observatory
RLG	Research Libraries Group
RLIN	Research Libraries Information Network
RM	records management
RMG	Records Management Group, Society of Archivists
SDI	selective dissemination of information
SGML	Standard Generalized Mark-up Language
SHIC	Social History and Industrial Classification
SQL	Structured Query Language
SRG	Special Repository Group
SRO	Scottish Record Office
TEI	Text Encoding Initiative
Unesco	United Nations Educational, Scientific, and Cultural Organization
WLN	Western Libraries Network

CHAPTER

1

ARCHIVAL MANAGEMENT IN AN INFORMATION CONTEXT

This book describes the management of information derived from archival media. There are already several books on archives administration and rather fewer on records management. In both fields, the literature has taken its starting-point from the existing practice of an archives or records management service. In most cases this was one of the large national archives services: the British Public Record Office in the case of Sir Hilary Jenkinson,[1] the National Archives of the USA in the case of T.R. Schellenberg.[2] W. Benedon[3] was the first influential writer on records management, and wrote from the point of view of a large American manufacturing company. Reacting to the work of these authorities, the present author[4] brought out a manual of archives and records management which was based on the experience of smaller organizations, an experience which could more easily be translated to fit the needs and practices of the majority of people faced with problems in managing their records and archives.

Since these beginnings, a substantial literature has appeared, and the original standpoint of the various authors is now much less obvious. Good examples are the Fundamentals series of the Society of American Archivists,[5] and the excellent practical guide produced by the Australian Society of Archivists.[6] We have now reached a stage where both archives and records management can be seen as distinct but interrelated disciplines, independent of the traditions and preoccupations of any one institution. However, very few authors have attempted to bring together the two branches of records and of archives management.[7]

The experience and background of the early writers led them to approach the problem of explaining the administration of records or archives in basically the same way in all cases. They described the work and materials they were accustomed to, added an analysis of the underlying problems, and a superstructure of theory, and produced the whole as a kind of complete and self-justifying system. This method of treatment had the advantage, as it was perceived by most of the people involved, that it tended to emphasize the differences between archive and library techniques and systems.

Some time during the late 1950s – after T.R. Schellenberg's momentous tour of Australia in 1954, and the appearance of the Grigg Report in the same year[8] – there emerged a new school of archives management. The protagonists of this school, which included a number of important writers – F.B. Evans[9], Ernst Posner[10], Michael Roper[11] and Schellenberg himself – claimed to have perceived a new dynamism in the movement for the preservation and exploitation of archives. The feeling of the time was that archive administration had been lifted away from a rather dusty and antiquarian past in which it had largely acted as a support to historical studies. Instead it had been brought into a present in which the discipline was the direct servant of current administration and of the public.

In this new school of thought, emphasis passed away from the conservation of ancient materials, and from the study of historical interpretation, towards the provision of information in planning and government. The good management of current and recent records linked closely with this, ensured the inflow of new archives from modern activities, and provided large economies in records storage as well as improvements in administration. Seen against the background of modern trends in historical and social research, in which increasing numbers of researchers seek access to recent records, the modern school of archival theorists gave the necessary literary and theoretical backing to the spread of archives services and institutions which, encouraged by Unesco[12] and the International Council on Archives,[13] was a feature of the 1960s and 1970s.

NEW DEVELOPMENTS

In the 1990s archivists have begun to synthesize the archival literature of several countries and languages. Notable among these are Luciana Duranti, who has linked the traditions of Italy and Canada in a very fruitful way,[14] and Fernanda Ribeiro, writing from Portugal, who has produced a restatement of archival theory and practice drawing widely on European and American experience.[15] North American colleagues are also actively investigating many of the difficult details: Terry Cook's re-examination of archival appraisal,[16] and Hugo Stibbe's study, drawing on Australian sources, of the use of access points in archives may be mentioned.[17] From the International Congress on Archives held in Beijing in 1996, there is an increasing input from Chinese colleagues, that may be expected to become more influential over time. We are undergoing a rapid period of change and redirection.

In the meantime there had been important developments in the world of information service. Information science came into existence as a discipline associated with a set of particular practices and techniques. It made a relatively rapid conquest of librarianship: most university departments of library studies changed their names to become departments of library and information studies, or the like, during the 1970s. Computers and their effects spread rapidly, and library and documentation services got used to new habits such as centralized cataloguing and access to online databases. Information management began to establish itself as an aspect of the management of companies.

The spread of this particular movement into the world of archives was slower and incomplete. For largely historical reasons, the training of archivists is usually in separate establishments, and most archives services of any size are managed separately and very differently from the parallel library and information services. Despite this isolation, there were influences at work, and today the world of archive administration is becoming gradually more open to ideas from the world of the other information services. This openness is especially obvious in the field of records management. Penetration by technology is a part of the reason for the spread of new ideas, but this has been slow to reach many parts of the profession, and even now is far from complete.

We are, in the 1990s, experiencing the effects of yet another wave of new approaches and technologies. In this also, archivists and records managers are feeling the effects of changes generated elsewhere, and operating powerfully in society. The most obvious feature is the change in attitude towards any public service: these now have to give much greater effort to demonstrating their accountability to their funding bodies and to their users, and to showing how they can deliver 'value for money'. In itself, this is a beneficial change, for there is little doubt that this profession, like others, had contained a certain quality of self-satisfaction, and a tendency not to look urgently at planned outcomes. Other aspects of the change are not so useful, particularly the constant erosion of resources and the increasing tendency to merge archives services into larger units. The merger of records management into information management is a similar development, but carries with it more advantages than disadvantages.

This short survey of attitudes illuminates one interesting feature, which is that archives administration was always regarded as a branch of management, and not – even in the early days – as an auxiliary science of history, comparable with palaeography. The academic study of archival materials, their interpretation and associated technologies might perhaps be given the title of archivistics, which is a translation of a term common in languages of Latin origin. The management of archives, however, is clearly one of the many kinds of management employed in the running of large organizations today. To manage archives or records, it is not only necessary to have some knowledge of the aims and techniques of management generally, but also to share in its attitudes and ethos.

Archivists and records managers need to be able to use most of the common methods of management, and particularly they must be able to:

○   provide leadership for their team
○   secure and deploy resources
○   be accountable to funding agencies, line management and public scrutiny
○   cost all aspects of their operation
○   recruit and retain qualified staff, and support career development for them
○   apply all relevant human resources regulations.

After this, it is necessary to add one further observation. The management styles and techniques that are appropriate for running an archives service are not the same as those suitable for running a profit-making business. The model for a large archives service would be more appropriately derived from a collegiate structure (where professional colleagues are broadly equal collaborators) than from a pyramidal structure (where a small number of directors issue instructions to a larger number of workers). Archives services can only run well where there is a general diffusion of expert knowledge throughout the team, and a necessary consequence of this is that responsibility should be delegated to team members as far as possible, according to their capacity. Where records management is concerned, it is not so easy to generalize, but a common and good pattern is similar: a small team sharing expertise and responsibility works better within the context of a larger organization than an autocratically directed workforce.[18]

The first edition of this book, which appeared in 1986, was a response to the new influences, and claimed to be different from previous manuals of professional practice. In many ways the actual practices described have not changed all that much from those which were common in previous times. It was the standpoint that had changed, and with that standpoint a profound change in attitudes and values –

changes in techniques as well, which are derived from newly evaluated goals and objectives. The new edition has to assimilate more, and perhaps even more profound, changes of attitude and perception, since it has to accommodate the new ideas of what might be called the Thatcher period together with the rapid march of the new technologies. Its aim is to reassess the theory and practice of archives and records management, viewing them from the standpoint of processors and suppliers of information, as part of a developed and effective information management service, operating within the constraints and with the declared objectives that are acceptable in the modern world.

In 1986, the information professions had recently adopted the concept of planned national information systems, in which the library, archives and documentation services would be developed integrally in accordance with a national plan: Jamaica was taken as an example of how this would operate in the relatively simple structures of a small country.[19] In accordance with this development plan, the Jamaica Archives Service had instituted a large-scale records management system.[20] This was based on a capacious records centre in central Kingston, with a staff of records analysts who would, with a network of clerical support, manage the records produced in the various government ministries. In developing countries, records management of this kind is particularly valuable, since not only does it economize on resources, but it renders useful the information that is locked up in the files (often the unmanageable and irretrievable files) of government departments.[21] At the same time, the libraries which had been developed by specialist ministries were being built up to include technical documentation services. To an outsider it was strikingly obvious that the lack of close co-ordination between these two developments, records management and the specialized documentation centres, was a considerable drawback. The scheme would be vastly improved if these two strands could be brought together and a common reporting channel set up. The umbrella under which this could be done would inevitably be labelled information management.

Since that time, the lessons to be learnt from early attempts at integrated national information planning have become clearer, and we have been able to refine our view of what roles these services should play in society. The experience of Jamaica has now been extended, in one way or another, to many other countries and situations. Soon after the appearance of the first edition of this book, the establishment of what is now the International Records Management Trust (IRMT), brought about the large-scale Management of Public Sector Records in Commonwealth Countries Project.[22] This influential project, backed by a number of development-aid funding organizations (including the United Nations) in different countries, has led to significant new developments and has provided a clear model for extension to new areas of the world.

The work of the trust has enabled us also to clarify our ideas about what the purpose and role of this area of work should be:

1. Good records management is a necessity for the successful working of a democratic state subject to the rule of law.
2. It underpins the rights and duties of citizens, holds governments and public authorities to account, facilitates development and makes the implementation of sound planning possible.

Archives form a necessary part of this work, and a total records management view would be impossible without this aspect. This perspective on records and archives management is probably most clearly demonstrated in the context of developing countries, but the same principles have been adopted and declared by the heads of national archives services in the European Union.[23]

The practical successes and the declared principles of the IRMT are cases of clear progression from our situation in 1986. In other respects, it is not easy to report progress. In most countries, the various branches of the information industry continue to operate separately: the movement towards planned integrated national information systems proved broadly unworkable. Movements towards harmonizing training courses between the professions have not been widely taken up. The reasons for these failures are not easy to distinguish, but probably the most important factor is simply that of vested interest and the handing-on of received traditions through training institutions.

Nevertheless, records managers and archivists find themselves members of an increasingly diversified profession. These two branches are themselves becoming more distinct, although interpenetration between them remains a strong feature. Both groups are now present in growing numbers in a wider range of organizations. Whereas a generation ago the great majority of archivists worked in central or local government, now the spread of employment covers all sectors of society: commercial and manufacturing businesses, higher education and research institutes, heritage bodies, museums and private enterprises, large and small organizations. Records management is now a recognized activity in all sorts of organizations, although it should be admitted that, at least in terms of the formal recognition of the phrase, its absence from organizations of all types is also striking. Professional associations exist for both groups (with a significant overlap of membership) and are themselves larger and more formally administered than before.

From the end of the 1980s the two professions began to apply significant resources and interest to the development of common standards. British archivists, records managers and users combined to establish the National Council on Archives (NCA), under the umbrella of which an outline national policy for archives was issued in 1996.[24] The general standard for the constitution and legal status of repositories[25] dates from this time. The first British attempt at a standard for archival description (MAD2) was published in 1990,[26] paralleling work that had been proceeding in North America during the previous decade.[27] This was further developed by an international commission, leading to the adoption of a basic international standard for description, ISAD(G).[28] Work on authorities then began to receive a higher priority, and in this area the International Standard Archival Authority Record for Corporate Bodies, Persons and Families (ISAAR(CPF)) was adopted in 1996, and the NCA's authority for personal and corporate names soon followed. In this case, too, there was considerable activity in other parts of the world. These developments are quite new in the history of these branches of the information professions. It is one of the main purposes of this book to examine these standards and suggest how they may be integrated into an effective archives or records management service.

DEFINITIONS

What are archives? A reassessment of the subject of their management had better begin with its most basic definition.

The earlier writers, in defining archives, picked out two principles which they saw as the important distinguishing points. These were, first, that archives were information-bearing media which had been generated by an organization in the course of its business, and which had turned out to be worth keeping, and secondly, that these archives had been selected by some means or other from a larger body of media produced by the same process, but which had not passed the selection test, and much of which was not worth keeping in the long or very long term. The components of this large group are, in principle, called 'records'.[29] Both archives and records form part of the transactions they record.

This seems a useful and clear distinction, although it is not one that has been used consistently. Some records managers have criticized it, because of the assumption that is implicit in it, that records must necessarily pass, over time, from one state to the other. In modern administration, it is more likely that records and archives must be seen as stages in a continuum, and that archivists and records managers must collaborate in managing them at all points along this continuum.[30]

In the light of these definitions, archives and records can be seen to have some properties that mark them off from materials which look similar but which are handled by different people: technical documentation (whether published or not), and manuscripts or non-book materials in libraries. The important thing about archives and records is that, having been created in the course of business, it is natural that they should be administered by a service which is part of, or at any rate responsible to, the creating organization. Every complex organization generates records and archives, and needs to manage them to its own advantage. A records management service, therefore, aims to control and exploit the records and the information they contain, for the benefit of the creating organization. An archives service also exercises administrative functions, either within the larger organization that has created the records, or by delegation from it.

Since libraries are organizations they, too, generate records and archives, but these are not the same as the manuscripts or other non-book materials which the library may collect from external sources. Collecting manuscripts is not the same as exercising the duty of archival management, delegated by a creating organization. There is a real distinction. Unfortunately it is one that has been exaggerated by people who have an interest (whether justifiable or not) in maximizing the differences in technique and function between library services and archives services. But the distinction nevertheless is real, and has given rise to the view that the handling of manuscript materials must be divided into two quite distinct traditions, named by one writer[31] as the public archives tradition (PAT) and the historical manuscripts tradition (HMT). Certainly there is a clear logical distinction between institutions whose primary function it is to service the archives of their employing body (generally, but not always, a government), and those whose function is to collect materials from the world outside. Most archives institutions, in fact, combine these functions at least to some extent, but there is a gulf of principle and practice between them. It is one of the purposes of this book to examine and evaluate this distinction, and if possible to find ways to reconcile the two approaches.

An impartial observer may find it difficult, in practice, to see where the difference between archives and manuscripts lies. An archives service of the public archives kind manages the records (the raw material from which it draws the archives) of its employing body. A manuscript library under the historical manuscripts tradition acquires particular items by collecting them through a more or less arbitrary system of marketing, or on loan. The programme of collection may be very systematic and based upon surveys of the materials that fall within the terms of the programme, but the materials themselves may differ less than the method by which they are acquired. On the one hand, a public archives service may well hold items acquired originally from outside the organization (by purchase, even). On the other hand, the manuscripts acquired by a library may exhibit archival characteristics. They may actually be the archives of an organization that has disposed of them: in this case one may say that the library is exercising delegated functions, although the delegation is implicit. It is quite normal for archives services to exercise some at least of the functions of a manuscript (or even of a more general) library; and it is quite normal, nowadays, for a manuscript library to enter into service relationships with an organization which covers the management of archives. Although the two traditions do exist, and should be described distinctly, it is not possible to separate them in a discussion of how to manage archival materials.

Manuscripts are controlled and catalogued under rules of bibliographic description generated from within the world of library science; in particular by Chapter 4 of the Anglo-American Cataloguing Rules (AACR2), or by a set of instructions intended to replace this.[32] These rules have so far been regarded as inappropriate by most archivists. One of the objectives of this book is to seek to extend the application of the descriptive methods suggest by MAD2 until they meet the boundaries of AACR2's effective application.

The discussion has led us to a point where we can begin to consider new definitions. As we have seen, an essential feature of archives is that they are materials acquired under some form of delegation: the archives service is carrying out functions which are natural to the archival management of the originating body. But the chain that links that body with the eventual custodial service may be obscure. However, no custodian will trouble to keep an object unless it has a clearly perceived value – if possible, a value that can be quantified and compared with the costs of preservation. In some cases this value resides in the physical qualities of the archives, which may be intrinsically valuable as objects; but in most cases archives are kept because the information they contain is the valuable element about them. They are primary sources; and the situation of mankind is such that primary sources are an essential part of the information stock. There will never be a time when a proportion of people is not engaged in researching primary sources in order to process information for more general use.

Of course, there are many different kinds of primary sources, and there are also gradations of 'primaryness', which sometimes make it hard to distinguish clearly between primary and secondary documentation. To the user, the distinction would not necessarily be of great interest. Researchers using primary materials are concerned to evaluate the trustworthiness and even the meaning of their source. To do this, they must learn the circumstances of its origin: they must know something about its custodial history. The original context is important, as are features of the document's diplomatics – significant marks on it, the formulas of its wording, or its shape and colour. The authenticity of the materials is tested by reference to provenance and format. After an evaluation of these, the only important thing about the source is its relevance to the enquiry in hand, and of this the user is the best judge. Users will select the most relevant materials for their enquiry, they will select them from all available sources, and they will subject them to tests of authenticity and validity.

It appears from this that the differences between archival materials and other information media are of interest primarily to those who have to manage them, and much less to users. If this is true (at least in general), two conclusions can be drawn. First, the strength of the distinction that has traditionally been maintained between archives transferred to an archives service from within the organization, and primary materials received from other sources (the distinction between official and non-official archives) may be reduced. Of course, it is still necessary to preserve a record of the provenance and custodial history of an archive, but not to insist that different points of origin imply different informational values.

Secondly, archival material can be evaluated as a source as against other sources available in the same institution. What is distinctive about the archives is the circumstances of their origin, not the quality of the information they carry (which may be great or little, as with other media). The definition of archives can therefore concentrate on their origin within the creating agency. Archives are information-bearing media which have been generated from within the organization; library and documentation materials are information-bearing media that were originally acquired from outside the organization.

A definition such as this places archives services firmly in the context of other information services. Libraries administer information held in materials bought in from outside (mainly books and journals); documentation centres manage materials also acquired from outside, but through specialist channels (mainly technical reports and papers); specialized repositories manage technically different media (such as film, videotape, audio recordings, electronic datasets and other non-book or non-paper materials). Together these services provide, maintain and exploit the information stock of an organization or of a community. In terms of the full information picture, each type of service is dependent on the others, and users appreciate this. It would be natural if the management practices of the three sectors could be co-ordinated, and should approximate to each other, and it would be natural if the various branches of the profession of information management should be more closely integrated in their work and in their training.

A definition that speaks of the internal generation of materials still leaves unresolved the distinction between archives services that are departments of the creating organization, and those that are external collecting agencies. At the extremes, these two types will presumably always remain distinct from each other. The Public Record Office (PRO) will never resemble the Manuscripts Division of the British Library much more than it does now. Nevertheless, the archival nature of much of the holdings of the collecting services gives validity to the notion of delegated archival management. Most archives services exercise these delegated powers in relation to material acquired from outside. The definition can still stand, but with one important proviso, which is that archives services may (or should) appraise the material they accept with an eye to the completion of their information holdings. Like libraries, and like documentation centres, archives services seek to acquire holdings which add up to a full and relevant information stock.

To sum up, archives may be defined as information media that have been generated from within the organization, and the management of which has been delegated to a specialist service. The purpose of this delegation is the preservation of the materials and the exploitation of the information in them.

This definition is new, but it does not displace the older definitions, which stressed appraisal and custody. Archives are also records which have been selected and kept because of their long-term values. Nor does it disturb the practice of archives administration or records management. This practice has an established tradition which includes a fairly well understood terminology. This should be used by practitioners, as the terms and concepts involved describe systems which have been proven through experience and which are distinct from practices common in the other information professions. Thus it is important to speak of the arrangement and description of archives, and not of their classification and cataloguing: there are important principles behind these terms.

On the other hand, if archives are perceived as belonging to the universe of information media, then the terminology and practices of information management and retrieval will apply to them as much as to any other information service. The new approach signalled by the new definition will have its effect by helping to incorporate archives services into the framework of information services, and by helping to introduce or develop technically similar practices in the exploitation of information.

COMMUNICATION THEORY

There is one other way in which the strengthening of the information-supply concept has changed the attitude of at least some archivists to their work. This is the perception that archival management resembles other information work in obeying the basic principles of information theory. The Shannon-Weaver model of the communication process, originally developed in connection with telephony, but later applied to librarianship,[33] appears to apply just as well to archives (see Figure 1.1).

In this model, the assumption has been made that the source message is the archive itself. Logically, this assumption is inadequate, for the true source is the mind of the person who originally generated the material. This component has been omitted in this case, because the author of an archival document is not an author in the same way as the writer of a book. It is the event documented by the archive which is the true source, an event in which many persons probably participated, and in which the document itself had an integral part. It is simpler to begin the communication model with the existence of the archive.

The message is encoded for transmission to the receiver by the characters used in the recording process: the archive has a certain physical and diplomatic shape which allows it to carry the message by means of symbols. The channel is the document produced and the system which provides a passage from originator to user. The decoder is the act of reading it, an act that may involve technical interpretative skills.

Below the top line of the model appears a second, alternative, line in which there are secondary encoders, decoders and a store. This represents the archive service itself, which provides a second (actually the principal) channel. It carries out a second encoding, which is the finding aid system. The user has to decode this, employing whatever aids are available: specialist knowledge, guides to users, and other assistance provided by the service. The finding aids are kept in a store, from which they have to be retrieved.

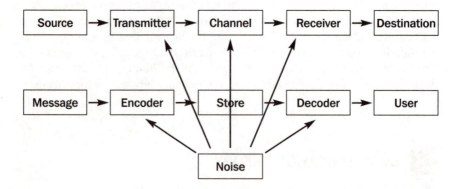

Figure 1.1   A model of the communication process within an archives service

Noise represents any of the many factors that stand in the way of full understanding of the original message by users. The most important of these is the tendency in finding aid systems to retrieve the wrong documents in answer to a request, or to fail to retrieve some of the right documents.[34] When a user obtains all the relevant information that there is in the system, with nothing redundant or irrelevant, then noise is at a minimum.

The Shannon-Weaver model is now some 50 years old, and in any case was devised to explain a very simple system of communication in which information is shown as flowing in a linear way. Usually things are more complicated than this, and there have been many elaborations since its appearance. In particular, there is often feedback, in which the flow of information is reversed. These models can be supplemented by others elaborated by the study of semiotics, which help us to examine what goes on when messages are transferred. Pierce's model, as in Figure 1.2, is relevant to work in archives and records.[35]

This model recognizes that an information user may has direct knowledge of the object that is being signified, as well as of the sign that signifies it. Users will then interpret the information presented to them by allowing these two types of information to interact. It is interesting that this influential and modern school of thought has developed systems of thinking so immediately appropriate to archives.

Discussion of these models and the theories behind them has shown that archives administration does conform to the same general principles as do other information services, and that there are important differences of principle which are due to the special nature of the materials, the service and the relationship of both. If archives services should, in ideal circumstances, be planned in society in relation to the development of overall information services, then it must be accepted that they have their own resources and techniques. These must be maintained and perfected, and not subsumed in the general resources and procedures.

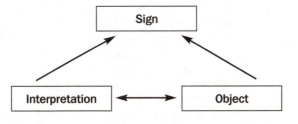

Figure 1.2   Semiotic model of message transfer

The chapters that follow set out to describe and explain the practices of records and archives management in the light of an enhanced emphasis on the provision of information as a commodity to a body of users. It is not intended to repeat well understood information, or to give a commentary on uncontroversial practices, nor is it intended that the terminology or concepts of information science should be presented in a way that will seem outlandish to managers or users of archives. As we advance into the information age, both of these will find it increasingly necessary to rely on concepts, theories and terminology that can be clearly understood within the specialist area.

To a degree, the archivists' terms of art will have to be understood also by the users. For that reason, as well as for general convenience, the term 'user' has been employed, in most contexts throughout the book, in a very general sense. It includes all types of user, even those who are internal users: archivists who are seeking access to materials in their care, members of staff of the employing organization who wish to access information for the support of current activities, professional researchers in pursuit of information to support a report on a clearly defined area of enquiry, and unskilled members of the public seeking relatively undefined or vague information for their own use.

NOTES

1. Jenkinson, C.H. (1922), *A Manual of Archive Administration*, 1st edn (2nd edn revd 1965), London: Lund Humphries.
2. Schellenberg, T.R. (1956), *Modern Archives, Principles and Techniques*, Chicago: University of Chicago Press.
3. Benedon, W. (1969), *Records Management*, Berkeley: California State University Press.
4. Cook, M. (1977), *Archives Administration*, Folkestone: Dawson.
5. Wilsted, T. and Nolte, W. (1991), *Managing Archival and Manuscript Repositories*, Chicago: Society of American Archivists. Other publications in the Archival Fundamentals Series cover the understanding of archives, selection and appraisal, arrangement and description, preservation, reference services and a glossary.
6. Ellis, J. (ed.) (1993), *Keeping Archives*, 2nd edn revd, Sydney: Thorpe in association with the Australian Society of Archivists Inc.
7. An exception is Cook, M. (1993), *Information Management and Archival Data*, London: Library Association Publishing.
8. The Grigg Report (1954), *Report of the Committee on*

Departmental Records, (Cmd. 9163), London: HMSO.

9. Evans, F.B. (1970), 'Modern Concepts of Archives Administration and Records Management', *Unesco Bulletin for Libraries*, **24**, 242–7.
10. Posner, E. (1964), *American State Archives*, Chicago: University of Chicago Press.
11. Roper, M. (1972), 'Modern Departmental Records and the Record Office', *Journal of the Society of Archivists*, **4**, 400–12.
12. Evans, F.B. (1983), *Writings on Archives Published by and with the Assistance of Unesco: a RAMP Study*, Paris: Unesco.
13. International Council on Archives, handlist of publications issued annually by its secretariat in Paris. See in particular, *Proceedings of the Round Table on Archives*, twice every four years from 1954.
14. Duranti, L. (1989–92), 'Diplomatics: New Uses for an Old Science', *Archivaria*, **28** (1989), 7–27; **29** (1989–90), 4–17; **30** (1990), 4–20; **31** (1990–91), 10–25; **32** (1991), 6–24; **33** (1991–92), 6–24.
15. Da Silva, A., Ramos, J., Ribeiro, F. and Real, M.L. (1998), *Arquivistica: teoria e práctica de uma ciência da informação*, Porto: Arquivo Municipal do Porto.
16. Cook, T. (1992), 'Mind over Matter: Towards a New Theory of Archival Appraisal', in B.L. Craig, *The Archival Imagination: Essays in Honour of Hugh A. Taylor*, pp. 38–70, Ottawa: Association of Canadian Archivists.
17. Stibbe, H. (1992), 'Implementing the Concept of Fonds: Primary Access Point, Multilevel Description and Authority Control', *Archivaria*, **34**, 109–37.
18. 'We went round in a team: someone from the information sciences team, someone from IT, and me, and the results from that were phenomenal ... ': 'Jean Samuel, Records Manager of the Year 1996', *Records Management Bulletin*, **81**, August 1997, 13.
19. National Council on Libraries, Archives and Documentation Services (1978), *Plan for a National Documentation, Information and Library System for Jamaica*, Kingston, Jamaica: Government Printer.
20. Government of Jamaica (1981), *Records Management Handbook: Disposition of Government Records*, Kingston: Office of the Prime Minister, Jamaica Archives and Records Department.
21. Rhoads, J.B. (1983), *The Role of Archives and Records Management in National Information Systems: a RAMP Study*, Paris: Unesco.
22. International Records Management Trust, Institute of Commonwealth Studies, London.
23. Tyacke, S., van den Broek, J. and Steendam, E. (1995), 'Archives in a Democratic State', *Journal of the Society of Archivists*, **16**, 133–8.

24. 'An Archives Policy for the United Kingdom: Statement of Principles and Policy Objectives', prepared by the National Archives Policy Liaison Group, National Council on Archives, 1996.

25. Royal Commission on Historical Manuscripts (1997), *A Standard for Records Repositories*, 2nd edn, London: HMSO.

26. Cook, M. and Procter, M. (1989), *Manual of Archival Description*, 2nd edn, Aldershot: Gower.

27. Hensen, S.L. (1989), *Archives, Personal Papers and Manuscripts: a Cataloging Manual for Archival Repositories, Historical Societies and Manuscripts Libraries*, 2nd edn, Chicago: Society of American Archivists; Bureau of Canadian Archivists (in progress), *Rules for Archival Description*, Ottawa.

28. International Council on Archives, Ad Hoc Commission on Archival Description (1992), *ISAD(G): Standard General Archival Description*, Ottawa: National Archives of Canada.

29. Sources for these definitions are summarized in Cook, M. (1977), *Archives Administration*, pp. 1–11, Folkestone: Dawson.

30. McKemmish, S. and Piggott, M. (1994), *The Records Continuum: Ian Maclean and Australian Archives First Fifty Years*, Sydney: Ancora Press in association with Australian Archives.

31. Berner, R.C. (1983), *Archival Theory and Practice in the United States: a Historical Analysis*, Seattle: University of Washington.

32. In practice today, this means Hensen, S.L. (1989), *Archives, Personal Papers and Manuscripts: a Cataloging Manual for Archival Repositories, Historical Societies and Manuscripts Libraries*, 2nd edn, Chicago: Society of American Archivists.

33. Foskett, A.C. (1982), *The Subject Approach to Information,* 4th edn, p. 6, London: Clive Bingley.

34. The operation of these retrieval characteristics is well illustrated by Ribeiro, F. (1996), 'Subject Indexing and Authority Control in Archives', *Journal of the Society of Archivists*, **17**, 27–54.

35. Fiske, J. (1988), *Introduction to Communication Studies*, London: Routledge.

ARCHIVES SERVICES: THEIR GENERAL NATURE, STRUCTURE AND FUNCTION

To illustrate the nature and functions of an archives service in a national or international context, a brief survey of some of the types of institution concerned with archival management may be useful. Although its immediate context is that of a developed western country, and specifically Britain, an effort has been made to take into account the experience of other countries of different resources and traditions, and of international co-operation. The underlying aim of this chapter is to establish a model, or series of models, which may help to sharpen the picture of what an archives service should be, and how it might be structured in order to achieve the best results.[1]

If we look around the world at the various kinds of archives service that can be seen there, we may observe that there are some distinct categories into which these services can fall. The most fundamental distinction that can be made is the one already explained in Chapter 1 – that between archives services that are dedicated to the management of archives derived from a single creating organization, this being the organization that also supports the archives service itself, and those that set themselves to collect archival materials that were generated outside their employing bodies. It has sometimes been questioned whether the same principles apply to both categories. In real life most archives services combine these two functions at least to some extent, probably all must bear in mind the possibility of operating in other traditions, and so in the analysis that follows the distinction is ignored.

Among the archives services that mainly follow the first model, first, there are government archives services. Most prominent among these will be the national archives. Within the boundaries of the state there are provincial or local archives of various sorts, including city or municipal archives. These services may be termed territorial, because the service they offer is (a) public and (b) covers a specified territorial area. Secondly, there are specialist archives services, serving a particular organization and hence specializing in the documentation of a particular activity or subject.

A third distinction may be noted between archives services that are institutions or services in their own right, and those that are departments of a larger service. A possible fourth distinction is between archives services that manage other materials than archives or share in other services as well, and those that are restricted to one specialized activity. Many archives services fall into more than one of these categories, or have other individual features. This makes it difficult to set up precise models for describing the programmes and activities that might be suitable for them.

The international model that is being proposed by the IRMT as suitable for a wide range of countries is that there should be a unified central records administration, responsible for all records management work in the national government, and containing within itself the national archives as a specialist department.

■ NATIONAL INSTITUTIONS

The national archives ought in any country to be the main specialist institution in the archives field. In many parts of the world, the national archives is a unitary service, situated among the central departments of government. It will be linked with the services that manage the records and recording systems of government, perhaps within the framework of a single directorate or service. Within this context it will be charged with the management of the processes that translate the most important records into archives. However, in practice the functions of the national archives may often be discharged by a group of separate services. In many countries the archives of the ministry of foreign affairs or of the armed services are often administered separately, and there is frequently a different system for managing archives of private or non-government origin that are of national importance. In the discussion that follows, these separate services are assumed to be included in the term 'national archives'.

One would expect the national archives to have custody of the fundamental documents of state, such as the constitution or founding charter, if there is such a thing. It would also contain, and receive on a regular basis, the most important and most central of the country's records, those of the legislature, the cabinet or council of ministers, and the courts of law. It is from this central point that the management of the national archives spreads out through the various agencies of government. There are many other series of records that, although less glamorous, are just as fundamental to the functioning of the state and the safeguarding of the rights of its people: these too, after appraisal, should be transferred to the archives under a systematic arrangement.

The IRMT model for a national records administration is the most recent of a series of international models for the establishment and operation of a national archives service.[2] Based upon the experience both of developed and of developing countries, these models have been influential in forming the development plans of several countries in respect of their records and archives services, and therefore there are several case studies of specific applications in particular situations.[3] These studies include specialist archives services and national information services that contain an archival element.

Many countries have institutions that resemble the national archives service of the international models. A good illustration of a central national archives of a modern kind, actively engaged in the management of records of government departments (albeit in this case only of federal government departments) is the *Bundesarchiv* of Germany. Founded only after the end of the Second World War, it has established a reputation for high standards of management and for devoting attention and resources to the exploitation of its information holdings.[4] Outside Europe, another excellent example is that of the Australian Archives,[5] again a federal institution but setting a high standard as a model for other archives services within the country.

Britain does not possess a good example of a national archives service that accords with this model. It is a country with an old tradition of settled and continuous government, and the accumulation of archives over many centuries provides a foundation for archives work that is of great value. For this reason, the three Public Record Offices (the PRO in London, the Scottish Record Office, SRO, and the PRO of Northern Ireland, PRONI) began their careers with publicly recognized work in academic research, and have since retained a high reputation in this sphere. The three PROs are independent of each other. They administer the records of their respective territorial sectors of government, and have developed traditions relating to their methods, the range of institutions whose records they are responsible for, and the perception of their functions and priorities, each of which is quite distinct from those of the others. The PRO is not directly concerned with the development, conduct or standards of archives services outside the strict confines of central government, although it does attempt some liaison, and some oversight of public records (following the legal definition of these) held locally. Both the SRO and PRONI exercise responsibilities in the collection and use of private and local archives. In all three cases there are government departments or institutions that in one way or another are exempt from the supervision of the archives office concerned with their region.

A survey of the central national archives services of a country, however, ought to include those that manage private or non-government archives that have been judged of national importance, and should also include services that provide co-ordination and common access between the various archives services of the country. In Britain this would include the British Library (as a collector of private archives) and the National Register of Archives (as a co-ordinator).

■ LEGISLATION

The international models presuppose that the work and structure of the national archives service will be guided by legislation, and there is also a model for what this legislation should do.[6] The archives law should form part of the legislative framework of the national records administration generally, so that it can serve as a foundation for co-ordinated operation. There should also be a systematic co-ordination between the archives service and the other national information services. The materials for a comparative overview of international archival legislation are easily available, for there is a comprehensive and reasonably up-to-date digest of it, published at regular intervals by the International Council on Archives.[7]

The main purpose of archival legislation is to establish the national archives service and set out its duties and functions. In the case of Britain, this is done by the Public Records Act 1958, which regulates the PRO (actually founded in 1838) and sets out in broad terms the duties of the Keeper of the Public Records. This officer is to 'take all practicable steps for the preservation of records under his charge', and has 'power to do all such things as appear to him necessary or expedient for maintaining the utility of the Public Record Office'.[8] These things are specified only very broadly: they include making indexes and guides to records, issuing publications, regulating conditions of access, making copies of archives, exhibiting them, and making special arrangements for archives that have technically demanding forms. There is no reference to any management function in this list.

The PRO is placed under the responsibility of the Lord Chancellor, a senior minister of the Crown, normally a member of the Cabinet, whose functions in other respects resemble those of president of the senate and minister of justice. In giving responsibility for government archives to this minister, the British government has made an odd choice, for this is neither a minister with central co-ordinating or administrative functions, nor the minister responsible for the nation's information or educational services, the conservation of the heritage, or the conduct of research. The post of Lord Chancellor was historically concerned with the issue and preservation of certain central records of the Crown, which is presumably the reason why this ministry was chosen. This historical link continues to be important because it is the reason why the term 'record', and more technically 'public record', is used in Britain where logically the terms 'archive' and 'central government archive' should be used.

In 1992, following the recently introduced practice whereby self-contained Civil Service units have been separated from the administrative apparatus of central government, the PRO was disengaged from its position as a department within the Lord Chancellor's office, and designated as an executive agency.[9] While continuing to report to the minister through Civil Service channels, and subject of course to audit controls, the PRO is now in a semi-autonomous position. It is no longer constrained by Civil Service procedures, staffing structures or other historical regulatory regimes, but can devise its own strategies for achieving its agreed targets. Outsiders can readily see that one result of these changes has been a change in attitudes, which has been particularly marked in the attitudes expressed towards members of the public coming to use the archives. One test of the efficacy of the new arrangements was posed by the need in 1994–96 to plan and bring into use a major new building at the main site in Kew, near London. This was achieved to a visibly high standard, within budget and on time. This success was in marked contrast to the highly publicized failure of the British Library to do the same thing for its new building, over a much longer period. Few observers would doubt that an important reason for the PRO's relative success here was due to the fact that its staff members could exercise direct control over the planning and building processes. In contradistinction, the British Library, although itself historically an organization distinct from government, was obliged to deal with architects and contractors by acting through officials of more than one ministry.

Legislation may serve to establish and co-ordinate archives services that operate in several fields: central administration, national information systems, education, conservation of the physical heritage, and research. Although in a sense the legislative background is not of primary importance (for British experience certainly shows that it is possible to run an efficient archives service, or any other kind of service, which is not suitably backed by legislation), by framing its legislation suitably it is possible for a government to decide upon and lay down lines of operation for its information services which help them in their development. Traditionally, this would have suggested that an archives law would place the national archives in a central co-ordinating or administrative position in relation to other government departments. This is the idea behind the model proposed by the IRMT. In some cases the drift may have been towards the co-ordination of information services. Looking at the end product in reference and research, some have considered the government department which deals with education and culture to be the proper home for the archives service. Elsewhere other initiatives have been tried.

In some countries, for instance, the government archives service has been placed with the principal archaeological and museum services under the direction of a minister for the heritage. In this case one would expect that activities in this area – collection, research, outreach and conservation – would be well funded, efficiently directed, and form a distinct and valuable part of the government's environmental programme.

Drawing co-operative programmes together into one centrally directed service is an attractive proposition in the abstract, and may lead to substantial achievements in line with the plan. It has one defect in practice, which archivists are particularly aware of. This defect is that parallel services that are subject to a single direction and funding, are in effect direct competitors with each other for resources and priorities. It is often because archives services have so frequently not been part of the directorate of information or libraries (or of museums and heritage) that they have been able to secure the resources to develop fully. Nevertheless, in the late 1990s, a reasonable view must be that the best place for the national archives is close to the services that manage record systems in government. Beyond this, it should be co-ordinated with the other information services. Other situations may be appropriate: the important point is that the best chance of achievement may be when there is a clear goal, established by national government, and directed towards a large area of the public good, such as information, education or heritage.

It is quite common to find that some departments or offices of state are excluded from the system of management of records for which the national archives is responsible. These may often run specialist archives services of their own. This exemption may typically include the department of foreign affairs and the armed forces, both organizations that are commonly rather conscious of the importance of their archives, and of their own independence as institutions. In Britain one of these areas of exclusion is the legislature: the House of Lords Record Office manages the archives of Parliament. Another important specialist archives service is the India Office Library and Records, dealing with the archives inherited from the colonial administration of India.[10] There is no direct institutional link between these and the PRO, and instead recent changes have brought the India Office Library and Records under the umbrella of the national library. In fact, for historical reasons the British Library may be seen as in some ways the principal alternative or secondary national archives of the UK.

It will be argued later that in principle the separate administration of specialist archives services, in certain cases, should be welcomed as a significant accession of resources, rather than deplored as detrimental to the tidiness of overall management by a single service. There is always more work to be done, which may be beyond the resources of one institution; and a generalist organization may sometimes fail to stimulate and support specialist areas of research as much as is needed. Archivists have in the past tended to be over-enthusiastic about centralizing both holdings and services.

Another function of legislation is to define the materials that are to be administered by a national archives service. This is done in Britain by the establishment of a category of 'public records' which are subject to the operation of the public records Acts. Essentially, these are the archives (rather than records) produced by government agencies and transferred to the PRO, or under its control. According to the Public Records Act 1958 (Section 10 and first schedule), public records are:

> administrative and departmental records belonging to Her Majesty whether in the United Kingdom or elsewhere, in right of Her Majesty's Government in the United Kingdom and, in particular,
> (a) records of, or held in, any department of Her Majesty's Government in the United Kingdom, or
> (b) records of any office, commission or other body or establishment whatsoever under Her Majesty's Government in the United Kingdom ...

A list of institutions whose records are to be included in this category is in the schedule to the Act, and this list may be, and has been, amended from time to time, by addition or subtraction, by ministerial order.[11] In the 1990s government policy has tended towards reducing the scope of the public records Acts as far as possible. However, the possibility of amendment in ways like this is a useful feature of archives legislation.

The rather narrow definition of public records has introduced some anomalies, and cannot provide a model for setting out the area of responsibility of a national service. On the one hand, public records are not confined to the records or archives of ministries and departments of central government. Some nationalized agencies, quasi-public bodies and local agencies are included. Thus the records generated by health authorities nation-wide are included, as are those of magistrates, judges and courts. On the other hand, other similar bodies are not brought within the operation of the Act and, as has been seen, the jurisdiction of the PRO itself over the records or archives of central government bodies is restricted in some areas. The Act provides that public records may be held in authorized 'places of deposit', and the PRO has a role in negotiating which and where these are to be. Unfortunately there is little or no coercive power in the provision, and since the PRO has no other co-ordinating duty, its obligation to license places of deposit remains anomalous and difficult to enforce.

The Scottish and Northern Irish Record Offices (and the National Archives of Ireland) derive their existence and powers from Acts specific to their countries, in the case of Scotland much earlier in date than the ruling provisions for England and Wales.[12]

A third area which should be covered by archival legislation is the establishment of an access policy which will define and protect public rights. In the period since 1945, there has been a general tendency in many parts of the world towards greater liberalization of access to government archives.[13] This received a considerable boost when the US government seized and published many series of German government papers after the war, and subsequently adopted a relatively open policy for its own documentation. In the USA this policy was reinforced by a freedom of information law that has been invoked many times, and has notoriously been used to guarantee the transfer of presidential files, papers, electronic messages and telephone recordings to bring them under the control of the National Archives.

Until the beginning of the 1990s it seemed that the countries of the Soviet bloc would remain outside this movement. However, with the collapse of the Soviet system, the release of hitherto inaccessible archives has been a high-profile development. Not only government archives but also those of the former ruling Communist parties have shared in this general release, which has sometimes been chaotic. The reunification of Germany has also led to the integration of the former East German government and party archives into the Western system.[14] In the European Union, the various national archives services have agreed on a convergence that will eventually harmonize the national legislation and practice in regard to access, and to the protection of privacy.[15] In Britain, there have been successive declarations in favour of more openness in government, and these have resulted in the release of some series of archives. The procedure for the release of further series continues, although overall the general result has not been as impressive as might have been expected. The proposed Freedom of Information Act may lead to changes of practice in this rather secretive regime.

It is now widely accepted that archival legislation ought to contain provisions covering the freedom of information (FOI) and data protection (DP). Freedom of information is an established principle of government operation in some countries, such as the USA, Australia and Sweden. From an archival point of view, it is important not only because it affects the public's right of access, but specifically because that right of access is extended to certain series of current records. This in turn is likely to affect the information that is recorded in those series, so that the control of access and the design of the record series is a records management problem.

Data protection is the converse of this. This legislation, introduced everywhere as a result of international agreements on data transfer, is designed to protect individuals from the possible negative effects of personal information about them being held on electronic databases. The usual features of the legislation are that individuals are given a right of access to data referring to themselves, and the right to correct it if it is wrong; databases containing such information are to be controlled, and destroyed when their immediate purpose is fulfilled. There should be provision for retaining certain databases as archives, for long-term research. Here, too, problems of records management are created.[16]

The Data Protection Directive comes into operation in the European Union in 1998, and extends the protection accorded to individuals named in electronic databases to those whose details appear in traditional media. This means that many registers or lists written on paper at various periods may now become subject to the provisions of the legislation. At the time of writing it is not yet clear how the new law will be interpreted, or whether the purpose of preservation for long-term research will be accepted as a legal purpose allowing the retention of personal information. These questions are discussed in more detail in Chapter 9.

OTHER NATIONAL INSTITUTIONS

Archives, including some that come within the category of public records, are also held and managed by a number of other national institutions. In every country it is natural that one of these should be the national library, one of the functions of which is normally to be the principal archive library, or library of record, for the country. Included in this function is usually that of being the library of legal deposit, and the main depository of official publications. Since both of these are important components in the nation's stock of retrospective information, the national library must necessarily play an important part in the overall archival services of a country, irrespective of whether or not this library pursues a policy of collecting manuscript material.

The British Library Department of Manuscripts (now brought within a broader Special Collections Division) has a very large amount of archival material, some of it originating in the departments of central government in past times. The legislative basis of the British Library is quite different from that of the PROs.[17] It does not have powers to administer any group of records or archives, but is regarded as a central repository for archives and manuscripts of national importance, other than those currently being generated by government departments. Acquisition is normally by gift or purchase, and its officers take active steps to discover details of any appropriate materials that might become available. The British Library manuscripts service is an interesting case study, for in the past it has made a serious bid to become the national archives, and although this objective was not achieved officially, it does now employ the largest specialist staff and contains probably the largest accumulation of private archive and manuscript materials of any institution in Britain. Accessions continue to be either actual archives (papers originally generated by some continuing organization, including individuals who held public office) or manuscripts (individual documents of historical or research value) which may or may not once have had an archival relationship with a creating organization.

The British Library is prominent in a large and growing group of academic and research libraries. The overwhelming majority of these hold archives, most actively administer them and all have a professional interest in archives. This interest has grown strongly in the period after 1994, when government funding for archive work in these institutions was significantly increased. In several cases libraries of this type are the official centre for the management of archives of or relating to specified activities. The University of Warwick's oddly named Modern Records Centre, for example, is the centre for archives bearing upon employment and labour.

The British Library began life as a department of the British Museum and it is natural therefore to consider it as one of a group of prestigious national museums, all or most of which have an archival function. The National Maritime Museum, for instance, seeks to acquire the papers (i.e. the personal archive) of admirals and naval personages. The Imperial War Museum looks for the papers of military men of all ranks. The British Museum (Natural History) and the Science Museum take the archives of eminent scientists and innovators in technology. The Tate Gallery acquires the papers of important figures in the world of painting, the Victoria and Albert Museum (whose library is the National Art Library) those of more general artistic relevance.

All museums have both a subject area in which they collect, and a naturally growing archive generated in the course of their research and curatorial activities. Archive material that bears upon their specialist subject is included with the other objects to be collected. The archives that document the existing collection of objects is required as part of the research material of the museum; and the archives arising from the museum's conduct of its business are needed also as part of the research resources of the institution. The museum connection is certainly a most important one for archives, and spreads as much into the field of research and exploitation as into that of conservation.[18]

■ LOCAL ARCHIVES SERVICES

Countries with a centralized national archives service have found that they may be obliged to set up provincial, municipal or local archives services, to manage the archives produced by these branches of government. In France, for instance, there are 101 *départements* and territories, some overseas, in each of which there is a repository building and trained staff under the direction of an officer responsible to the national director in Paris. In the 1980s and 1990s, the French government has pursued a policy of devolution of powers to the regions, in which the archives service has participated; but it remains, by contrast with less organized countries, strongly centralized.[19] This policy may bring France closer to the tradition in Spain or Italy, where there is central control but most of the work is done in regions that have historic roots and considerable autonomy.

In Britain there is a strong tradition of local archives services. These began to be established piecemeal in the years after 1913. Until 1994 it seemed to be an established principle that most local archives would be based upon the oldest local government division, the county. Before that time, all but a very few county councils had come to maintain an archives service, generally known, on the national model, as the county record office.[20] After 1974 there were considerable and continuing changes to the structure of local government. Since there are no legislative or official guidelines for archives services, it was feared that many county record offices would disappear. At the time of writing this fear seems exaggerated, but it is hard to foresee the pattern for these services in the future. Such standards as there are, are almost entirely voluntary. The National Council on Archives was set up on a voluntary basis, to represent the main professional and user bodies. It has issued an outline policy for the development of archives services.[21] Another non-compulsory standard applicable to all local and specialized archives services covers constitution and staffing questions.[22]

Legislative provision for these services is minimal, and has always lagged behind actual practice. They normally carry out two different programmes: they acquire archives from private and non-official sources relevant to their own territorial area, and they administer the archives of the county government itself (or those of whatever local government unit they belong to). Each of these programmes has a different legal underpinning, if that is the word. The external collecting function is permitted by the Local Government (Records) Act 1962, which also allows the provision of public access and outreach facilities. The internal management function is suggested, but hardly more, by the ruling local government Acts. No single minister or government department is responsible for the operation of the whole range of these laws. It is possible that as a result of lobbying and public debate by the professional organizations somewhat different patterns may be emerging in Scotland and Wales.

It is a curious feature that archives services are nearly always weaker in urban areas, particularly the great conurbations, than in the rural areas. There has never been a satisfactory arrangement for overall city government: London is the extreme case, having since 1986 no city government at all. It is not surprising, therefore, that there are no co-ordinated archives services either.[23] There is a historical cause for this urban–rural duality, which arises from the confusion between library and archives services at the local level. City governments have long been accustomed to providing a public library service, which operates, as far as the collection of archives is concerned, under libraries and museums Acts.[24] Such a library would usually possess a public building of some presence and character, and would have an extensive body of users. The public library is interested in providing facilities for access to archives bearing upon the city and its cultural area. Urban library services, therefore, quite often provide the archives facilities for these areas, and it is common for them to display the disadvantages of archives services run by libraries – they are frequently run to lower professional standards (especially standards of resourcing) than those of specialist archives services – and they frequently take little interest in the management of the employing authority's own records. Their tendency to cling to the HMT approach of manuscript curatorship means that traditions of active fieldwork and administrative liaison tend to be weak.

On the other hand, it is frequently observed that rural provinces commonly have well-established archives services, based upon the provincial government authorities. These areas may typically have relatively weak library facilities. Archives services in these regions perhaps show the opposite faults to those of the urban areas: they may neglect the collecting function in favour of the internal management of their employing agency's records; they may have relatively poor standards of reference service and user access, and may have little experience of bibliographic reference services and databases. Rural archives services may in some respects show a tendency to usurp some of the functions of a library service, building up a local collection of printed material, newspapers or memorabilia; or they may tend to usurp some of the functions of a regional museum, by collecting and displaying objects, or even sponsoring oral history or archaeological research.

These cases of confused function show not only what happens when the support and direction given by central government through legislation and regulation is missing, but also that there is a natural tendency for information services to grow together when functional needs and the legitimate demands of the user public are made plain.

The existence of the local record offices, and of their common tradition of work, never yet fully written out but never challenged publicly, means that certain principles have been established. One of the most important of these is that owners of archives, whether private or corporate, have a right to expect that (if they pass appraisal tests) the materials they are responsible for will be preserved and managed at the public expense. In some cases owners may even expect a subsidy in the form of tax relief when they deposit their archives in a record office. Less important, but still significant, is the practice of accepting private or corporate non-official archives on deposit (a form of permanent loan) without the owner having to relinquish ownership. Thirdly, the tradition has grown up that research into archives, except at the national centres, is connected with local studies, and has essentially a territorial link.

SINGLE-PURPOSE ORGANIZATIONS

Every country possesses quasi-governmental single-purpose authorities ('quangos' or para-statals) whose sphere of activity covers the whole geographical area of the country, or at least extends over boundaries wider than any single local government area. In Britain long-established examples are the British Broadcasting Corporation (BBC), or the UK Atomic Energy Authority. Elsewhere in the world, examples may be found covering such activities as public housing, banking or national insurance, among other functions. Over the period since 1980 there has in many places been a systematic policy to create new para-statal bodies and to convert public functions from central or local government to new quangos. In Britain there are now thousands of these bodies, and their work affects nearly every aspect of life. A few of the older bodies are subject to the provisions of the Public Records Acts, but the vast majority are not. A small proportion of the total have set up archives or records management services. The case of the National Health Service is particularly striking: it is subject to the Public Records Acts, but has now distributed many of its management functions to local Hospital Trusts, some of which have decided to employ archivists

The traditions of archives management developed by authorities of this kind are varied, because they naturally reflect the special problems and characteristics of their specialist field. Thus the BBC maintains separate services for written archives, sound recordings and visual recordings. Similarly access facilities, and generally the use made of the archives, reflect the different conditions of each operation. Not much has as yet been published on the work of these archives services, but their experience is likely to be seminal in future developments.[25] This experience militates against the territorial tendency shown in archive development up to the early 1970s (especially when taken in conjunction with the development of archives services in specialist firms, research institutes and universities), and has added greatly to the common experience of treating special physical formats.

Similar to the single-purpose authorities are the research institutes, of which there are a large number. Many are financed by one of the government-funded research councils, although these councils have never exercised any regulatory function in relation to the standards of archive work expected. It is hard to understand this feature, especially since the entire work of a specialist research institute may be directed towards the creation of an archive. For example, the British Antarctic Survey (BAS), based in Cambridge, has the function of compiling data on conditions in Antarctica. This data is managed and made accessible by the BAS archives service, but the financing, staffing and procedures of this service have occurred late in the BAS's existence, and without guidance from any central agency. Another case of a specially outstanding research institute which developed its own archives service was the Royal Greenwich Observatory (RGO). When the RGO was disbanded, provision was made for the archives by depositing them in an existing university repository, but no provision was made for the continuation of the service in related areas of research.

Among research institutes the case of the universities is a special one. As a result of recent changes there are now over a hundred of these, and although finance is channelled to them through central agencies, there is no general guidance from government. Perhaps a third of the universities (mainly those that existed before 1992) have developed archives services, either in connection with a research activity carried on in the same institution, or as one of the academic functions of the university, or as a means of managing their own record resources. In 1994 the university funding councils decided to allow grants for the specific development of archive functions (together with other functions distinct from teaching and research), and there was a huge and rapid increase in the number of people temporarily employed in this work. At this time the beginnings of some central regulation and guidance also appeared, by the emergence of the (semi-voluntary) Archives Sub-committee of the Joint Information Services Committee. This body is at present attempting to set up some common standards of operation, mainly concentrated on the methods and standards used in information technology.[26]

Examples of research-based archives services are the Modern Records Centre at Warwick University, or the Military Archives Centre at King's College London. Archives services based on the general academic functions of a university may be illustrated by the Department of Manuscripts at Nottingham University, or the Borthwick Institute of Historical Research at York University. The third type is not so common, but the oldest universities, including Oxford and Cambridge and their colleges, have archives departments that manage the considerable accumulations of very old archives; a few others, including Liverpool, Imperial College London and Heriot-Watt Universities, have records management services. The majority of university archives services are based within each university's library.[27]

THE PRIVATE SECTOR

Recent years have seen the rapid development of both records management and archives services within commercial or manufacturing firms. Some of these, particularly those within science-based industries such as pharmaceuticals, have a close resemblance to similar services in research institutes. Such firms tend to be in close contact with each other, and the Scientific Archives Group was established to formalize liaison. In other cases the archives are run in close liaison with museum functions, and may be regarded as part of the public relations activity. Elsewhere the main function of the archives service may be to manage either the accumulated backlog of historical papers, or the recent records of the company. Firms that have shown interest in the museum aspect include Marks and Spencers (retail chain stores) and Guinness (brewing). Management of the older archives, of which there is a considerable accumulation, is one of the main concerns of the archives service at Rothschilds (merchant banking). In some cases an important component of the archive holding is provided by the personal or family papers of the firm's pioneering founders, as at Ferranti's. The management of recent records is the main function of many, including, for example, Pilkington Brothers (plate glass manufacture) or Barclays Bank (clearing bank).

It is natural that records management, with its immediate implications for the cost and efficiency of current administration, should be more highly regarded in the private sector than in many public repositories. It is in this area that most rapid development has occurred of recent years, and has led to the formation of the Records Management Society of Great Britain (affiliated to the International Records Management Council). However, in practice most business archives services care for the historical research material and attempt to keep a balance between the two sides of their programmes.

The Business Archives Council exists to stimulate and co-ordinate these activities, and runs an advisory service available to firms and occasional training courses.[28]

PERSONAL ARCHIVES

This brief survey of types of archives service may be concluded by a mention of archives services based upon private papers. All individuals active in public life inevitably compile an archive as they go along. It has always been difficult to define the exact boundary between the rights of the public and of individuals and their families in this field. Politicians and military personnel are at least usually aware that the public has an interest in their material. They may decide to send their papers to join those of Winston Churchill at the Cambridge college founded in his name, or to one of the universities. There are also examples of private archives services run to professional standards. Some of these are based upon the care of ancient documents, such as the archives of the Marquis of Salisbury at Hatfield; and some hold relatively recent papers of national or international importance. An example of the second type is the archive of Earl Mountbatten at Broadlands.[29]

The classic model of an archives service whose function is to conserve and exploit private papers of national importance is provided by the presidential libraries in the USA. These are established and endowed by individual presidents, but are controlled by law and administered by the National Archives. Each presidential library is based upon the archives of a particular president, and seeks to acquire complementary papers from the contemporaries and associates of that president. There are legal provisions that govern the relationship between the private and public papers of national office-holders, and applying the terms of freedom of information legislation to these papers.[30]

In the 1990s the churches have adopted the practice of setting up archives and records services to cover their own administrative needs, and to manage their historic archives. Guided in part by the rules and experience of the Vatican archives, the Catholic Church is in the process of encouraging religious orders and dioceses to undertake at least the minimum work required.[31]

It may be appropriate to add that there appears to be a growing number of freelance archives and records management consultancy agencies. It is generally possible to call in the services of these to solve problems of administration or care either of the older archive material or of current records.

Since a recent survey has listed 1109 archive repositories of one sort or another in Britain, and did not claim to be exhaustive, it may be guessed that there are in reality over 1500, and perhaps as many as 2000, in existence in this one relatively small (but old and crowded) country.[32] The biggest of these repositories may have a professional staff numbering as many as 20 to 30, but the smallest (and there are many of these) will employ only one archivist, perhaps part-time and perhaps also on time-limited contract, with or without clerical or administrative support. Membership of the professional association, the Society of Archivists, was over 1500 at the close of 1997.

Similar conditions, *mutatis mutandis*, may be found in other countries, except that many have a better regulated national service, and have established standards of operation that govern the investment made in local or specialized archives services as well as in the national archives. A good example is provided by the Netherlands. Developing countries have a special need of efficient archives services, since so much of the documentation of their national identity and of their stock of reference data is held in archival form.

CENTRAL CO-ORDINATION AND DIRECTION

It was early realized that some provision must be made, even in the most decentralized state, for private and non-official archives that are of importance to the national heritage. In Britain this was recognized by the setting up of the Royal Commission on Historical Manuscripts (HMC) in 1869.[33] This body in turn established the National Register of Archives (NRA), which has operated since 1945 as a central repository of archival finding aids. Two specialized types of archives have some degree of statutory control, in that they must be registered at the HMC: these are tithe and manorial documents. Otherwise, the NRA database is run entirely on a voluntary basis, and consequently there is no machinery for co-ordinating the format or content of the lists submitted to it. These remain a very varied collection, many thousands in number, supplemented by newspaper reports concerning manuscripts. However the HMC does undertake survey work, publishes a number of finding aids based either upon its own research or upon the material accumulated in the NRA, and has now launched an online index to its holdings and a directory of archives services active in the country.[34]

Another function of the HMC is to advise government about the operation of such regulatory functions as exist in regard to archives. These include the acceptance and disposition of archival accumulations which may be accepted in lieu of tax; and the regulation of exports of archives. Successive Heritage Acts have reinforced these functions but without giving any significant new powers.

■ COMMON ELEMENTS IN MODERN PRACTICE

Most countries can show development of some or all of these archives services in the different sectors, usually in a form that is dictated by the constitutional and legal traditions of the place. Attempts have been made to set out theoretical models that might suggest a framework for archival development, taking into account the various tasks which an archives service might undertake.[35] The outline of a basic structure for an archives service might appear as in Figure 2.1.

In a service of this kind, there might be four categories of professional staff:

1. *Managerial staff*. The chief archivist, deputy and the three departmental heads would form the management team. Ideally, they would be professionally qualified archivists, not only because this background brings understanding of the tasks and nature of the service, but also to provide a satisfying career structure for entrants. Specialist training would be desirable in the case of records management, and necessary in the case of conservation and information technology. Some training in the principles and skills of management is usually regarded as necessary.
2. *Professional staff*. The staff indicated as 'assistants' in the model in fact carry out professional duties. It is they who process the

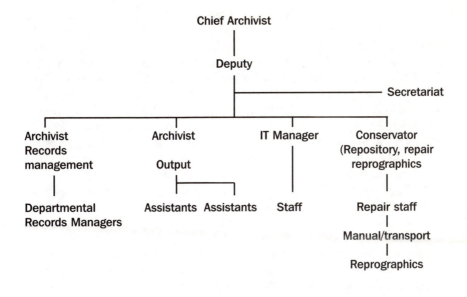

Figure 2.1   Outline organization chart of an archives service

material – that is, they arrange and describe archives, and do all the other practical work processes needed to keep and use the material. In a large archives service, therefore, the more senior of these members of staff (at least) will be professionally qualified archivists, who supervise paraprofessionals (in this case it would be more usual to call them 'assistant archivists').

3. *Paraprofessional staff.* In smaller archives services, the departmental heads supervise paraprofessionals directly. It is clear that paraprofessional staff (the usual designation would be 'archives assistants') have an essential role. Those noted as departmental records managers may also be considered as belonging to this category.

4. *Technical staff.* Specialist and technical staff include conservators, and those who maintain reprographic services. These often include microfilm, photography, various methods of printing, and operating information technology.

In addition to these categories, there will be a need for clerical and support staff.

The nature of the training required for each of the professional categories of staff has also been outlined in an international model.[36] Professional staff should be graduates who have completed specialized training in an archives school, and have complied with the appropriate career development provisions of their professional association: in Britain, this means working towards and then maintaining their status as Registered Archivists. Paraprofessionals should be educated to the normal secondary standard (or better), and should have received a specific training in the tasks they have to do: this is usually given by apprenticeship, or by in-house training courses, but there is a growing tendency for training courses aimed at these to be developed. There is a considerable need for organized training at this level in most countries, and for a corresponding career structure. Technical and specialist training has to be provided in specialist institutions.

During the 1980s there emerged an international movement towards the harmonization of professional training in the main branches of the information services. This movement failed to make much impact on the structures of existing training schools in the more developed countries, but the concept of harmonization has received a good deal of assent. Recently founded training schools, particularly in Africa, have assumed that the three information professions would be trained together.[37] Studies have been produced to show how outline requirements for common core courses in management studies, technology and user studies could be integrated, while retaining distinct specialist courses for the three branches.[38]

At the end of the 1990s, there is a growing tendency to promote career development opportunities and pathways for professional staff, as the need to maintain and update skills and expertise becomes more obvious. The professional associations necessarily play a large part in this aspect. Training in this way becomes diffused through the whole experience of professional life. One result of this is that staffing structures should become less hierarchical and more collegial. Colleagues in a team, each exercising particular skills, should be able also to discharge delegated responsibilities without an oppressively overt pattern of control by superiors. Controls are superseded by consultation, in a system that encourages frequent reporting on progress and discussion of common problems.

Within the service, it is necessary to delegate responsibilities explicitly. The model presented in Figure 2.2 suggests that this may best be done by dividing the processes between departments. This would certainly be the best way of delegating responsibility for technically different processes such as records management and conservation. However, when the management of archival materials within the service is considered, it may prove more efficient in the long run to divide responsibility by allocating the whole management of particular archive groups to specific archivists, rather than by allocating to them the supervision of particular processes.

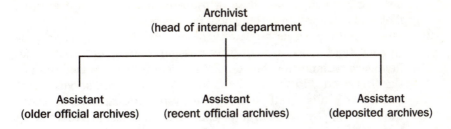

Figure 2.2   Distribution of responsibilities by archive groups

An arrangement like this would mean that each archivist would have a specialist interest broadly corresponding to a subject, and would acquire a stock of information on the field. Archivists need to have this kind of expertise, and the relationship with user groups which goes with it; in any case, it is a good approach to personnel management.

An archives service may have other specialists not mentioned in these models. It is quite common to have specialists in the exploitation of archival materials in school education. These members of staff may be qualified teachers, or qualified archivists who have experience in teaching. Other specialists may include people working on outreach, publication or copying projects. There is a standard for the legal status and constitution of archives services, their staffing and resourcing.[39]

There are some activities that are necessary components of most archives services. As in all areas of information work, it is possible to divide these activities for convenience into three fields: input, process and output.

INPUT

All archives services have to make arrangements for identifying the materials that fall within their field of operation, and for bringing them under control. So many different kinds of material are involved that the fieldwork and accessioning systems to be found are very diverse. Examples of some of the main types of archives service are as follows:

1.   A few archives services exist purely as databases of information about archives held entirely or mainly elsewhere. This would include, for example, the National Cataloguing Centre for the Archives of Contemporary Science at the University of Bath, and the British Political Records Project at the London School of Economics. In these projects, the main effort is to create (and

perhaps publish) a database of information on relevant archive materials that fall into the whole field selected.

2. Many archives services draw their material from a territorial or subject field, specified in the mission statement. Here, too, fieldwork is important but tends to be less fully organized than in the first group. Provision for fieldwork varies from services that employ specialist staff to carry out systematic surveys, to those that take no positive action to secure new material but are willing to accept appropriate material when it is offered by an owner or creating agency. Most archives services operate somewhere in the middle of this spectrum of activity, usually by allocating a proportion of the time of their regular staff to fieldwork. In these circumstances, it is unusual for the coverage of the field to be at all complete.

3. Other archives services may draw their material from a captive field, usually from the record systems of their employing authority. Most archives services of this type will run at least some elements of a records management programme. Here also there is a spectrum of activities. At one extreme there will be a full records management programme, which aims to control all the processes involved in the generation of records, the flow of records and information within the organization and the storage, retrieval and use of records and information. At the other end of the spectrum is an archives office that simply accepts consignments of records when the originating department decides to transfer them.

Systems that operate between these extremes are quite usual. A common situation is one where the records management programme exists but is limited to controlling the processes whereby records are retired from current systems and placed in intermediate or limbo records centres.

From a staffing point of view, archives services vary widely. A full records management programme demands full-time staff, whose job therefore would include carrying out the necessary fieldwork surveys and liaison with creating departments. A minimal or partial records management programme may depend on part-time activity by staff who have other duties as well. Where there is no records management, the archives service still has the responsibility for the fieldwork necessary to fulfil its agreed tasks.

There are also differences in the mechanics of accessioning new record material. A developed records management system will probably include an intermediate records store – usually called a records centre – which is an active repository for semi-current records that have long retention periods. Records held in the centre that pass appraisal tests may be transferred eventually to the archives. The important control point is that at which records pass out of currency and into the records centre.

Archive materials should not be received or accessioned unless they have passed an appraisal test. Records management systems incorporate appraisal in their processes: indeed it is a central principle of records management that ephemeral records should be disposed of as early as possible. The archives should contain only such material as has been judged worthy of retention. Appraisal therefore must inevitably be one of the main professional responsibilities of archive staff, and it is hard to imagine an archives service, however idiosyncratic, which does not carry out this function.

PROCESS

When received as new accessions, archive material is normally subjected to a series of processes grouped under the headings of arrangement, description and conservation.

Chronologically, the first processes are those of arrangement. In these, archivists seek, usually but not necessarily by physically sorting the material and investigating its background, to arrange the components of an archive accumulation into an order which reflects that of the system by which the documents were originally created and used. This involves arrangement rather than classification: the components of the archive are put into an order which depends on the relationship of one part to another, and not into an order which is a pre-established analysis of concepts or subjects. Archival order usually demands treatment at two or more different levels, which are determined by an analysis of the original system that created the archives, and which are treated differently in description.

Arrangement processes are completed by the physical storage of the material in containers on shelves in the repository, and by attaching retrieval labels to the containers.

Archival description is a better term than cataloguing because:

O   the great variety of archival formats make it difficult to establish a regular system of bibliographic descriptions that would resemble a library catalogue
O   differences of level mean that each archives accumulation must have a compound description.

The objective in archival description may be administrative control (the control of the material through the physical processes and in storage) or intellectual control (the ultimate exploitation of the information contained in the media).

Archival conservation includes environmental as well as remedial conservation. Storage conditions should include protection from environmental hazards, and should be secure enough to ensure the survival of the archives for the period of time for which they are planned to survive: in many cases in perpetuity. Fumigation may be needed before material can be brought into storage, and repair may be necessary where newly accessioned material has been subjected to bad conditions. In some cases repair involves highly skilled craft work, in others a more mechanical process. Standards exist for all these operations,[40] and for the buildings required for housing the materials and carrying on the processes.[41]

OUTPUT

The output from an archives service takes the form of usable data and the services that promote use of the materials. Activities generally cover a range, from provision of access facilities to incoming users (passive exploitation) to the conduct of active publication, educational or outreach programmes (active exploitation). In either case, the design and completion of a finding aid system based upon archival description is necessary. Finding aids are normally published, but the outreach activity may often involve a specific programme of publication.

Output to users must be regarded as the final end of archives services, which are therefore user orientated. This is a feature they have in common with other information services, but it is important to notice that there are two respects in which user orientation must be limited:

1. The input of new archival materials is determined mainly, if not entirely, by the nature of the materials generated by the target organizations. Archivists can only acquire materials that have actually been created by the organizations whose archives they are managing, even though in some cases these may be supplemented by materials collected from other sources.
2. Access to archives is regulated by statute or by some similar controls, and is based upon a considered access policy. This may be more or less liberal, but in principle there are few archives services which give totally unlimited access to their holdings.

These areas of professional activity are looked at in more detail in the chapters that follow.

◼ NOTES

1. Kitching, C. (1988), *The History of Record-keeping in the UK to 1939*, London: Phillimore for the National Council on Archives.
2. International Records Management Trust, Institute of Commonwealth Studies, London. The previous model is d'Olier, J.H. and Delmas, B. (1975), *Planning National Infrastructures for Documentation, Libraries and Archives*, Paris: Unesco.
3. Summarized in Evans, F.B. (1983), *Writings on Archives Published by and with the Assistance of Unesco: a RAMP Study*, Paris: Unesco.
4. A list of German archival websites is maintained by the Archivschule Marburg. See www.bundesarchiv.de.
5. (From 1998 termed the National Archives of Australia.) See McKemmish, S. and Piggott, M. (eds) (1994), *The Records Continuum: Ian Maclean and Australian Archives First Fifty Years*, Monash Occasional Papers in Librarianship, Recordkeeping and Bibliography, No. 5, Melbourne: Ancora Press with Australian Archives.
6. Ketelaar, E. (1985), *Archival and Records Management Legislation and Regulations: a RAMP Study with Guidelines*, Paris: Unesco.
7. Published in seven volumes of the ICA's journal *Archivum*, Munich, London etc.: K.G. Saur. Legislation up to 1970 are in vols 17, 19, 20 and 21. Legislation 1970–80 is in vol. 28. Legislation 1980–90 is in vols 40 and 41.
8. Public Records Act 1958, c.51. British legislation is summarized in *Archivum* (1995), **17**, 173–208; **28**, 387–407; **41** 234–9. Cantwell, J. (1991), *The Public Record Office 1838–1958*, London: HMSO.
9. *PRO Framework Document and Corporate Plan 1992/3–1996/7*, London: Public Record Office.
10. These are the archives of the former India Office, a department of the British government based in London. They are therefore not 'migrated' archives, and were never generated or kept in India. The India Office Library does, however, hold some deposited private archives that were originally generated in India.
11. Cited in Cook, M. (1977), *Archives Administration*, p. 13, Folkestone: Dawson.
12. Hefferty, S. and Refaussé, R. (1993), *Directory of Irish Archives*, 2nd edn, Dublin: Society of Archivists, Irish Region.
13. Wagner, A. (1970), 'The Policy of Access to Archives: from Restriction to Liberalisation', *Unesco Bulletin for Libraries*, **24**, 73–6.

14. These developments are summarized in the *World Information Review* (1997), Paris: Unesco.

15. *Archives in the European Union: Report of the Group of Experts on the Coordination of Archives* (1994), pp. 32–44, Luxemburg: European Commission Secretariat General.

16. Data Protection Act 1984, c.35. See also Bourn, C. and Benyon, J. (eds) (1983), *Data Protection: Perspectives on Information Privacy*, Leicester: University of Leicester, Continuing Education Unit, European Union Data Protection Directive 95/46/EC.

17. British Museum Act 1753, 26 Geo II, c.22.

18. Society of Archivists and Museums Association, *Code of Practice for Archives in Museums*.

19. Direction des Archives de France (1993), *La pratique archivistique française*, Paris: Archives Nationales.

20. Forbes, H. (1993), *Local Authority Archive Services 1992: a Survey Commissioned by the Royal Commission on Historical Manuscripts and National Council on Archives*, British Library R & D report 6090, London: HMSO.

21. *An Archives Policy for the United Kingdom: Statement of Principles and Policy Objectives*, prepared by the National Archives Policy Liaison Group, National Council on Archives, 1996.

22. Royal Commission on Historical Manuscripts (1997), *A Standard for Record Repositories on Constitution and Finance, Staff, Acquisition and Access*, 2nd edn, London: HMC. Smith, B.S. (1991), 'A Standard for Record Repositories', *Journal of the Society of Archivists*, **12**, 114–22.

23. The London Metropolitan Archives collects from the whole area of Greater London; several London boroughs maintain an archives service in connection with their libraries.

24. Mainly the Public Libraries and Museums Act 1964, c.75, and subsequent provisions.

25. The publications of the Specialist Repositories Group (SRG) of the Society of Archivists are intended to apply to the operation of similar bodies. The series began with *Methodologies in Specialised Archives*, papers read at an SRG seminar, April 1983, at Canterbury, SRG Occasional Papers No 1.

26. Information is disseminated through the Lis-Jisc-archives email list managed by mailbase@mailbase.ac.uk. The work of JISC is publicized through their website at http://www.kcl.ac.uk/srch/reports/. A report commissioned by the JISC-NFF Committee on British university archives and records services is at http://www.kcl.ac.uk/srch/reports/tfpl.html.

27. Society of Archivists and SCONUL (Standing Conference on National and University Libraries) (1989), *The Role and Resources of University Repositories: a Report and Discussion Document,* London, November.
28. Proceedings of Business Archives Council conferences are published annually from 1983. Also Business Archives Council (1992), *Directory of Corporate Archives*, 3rd edn, London: BAC.
29. Seton, R.E. (1984), *The Preservation and Administration of Private Archives*, Paris: Unesco. Raspin, A. (1998), *The Transfer of Private Papers to Repositories,* Society of Archivists Leaflet 5.
30. National Archives of the USA at http://www.nara.gov/nara/.
31. Maike, W. and Ansell, L.J. (1984), *The Small Archive: a Handbook for Church, Order and School Archivists and Historical Societies*, Toowoomba, Australia: Church Archivists Society. The annual journal of the Catholic Archives Society (UK) contains similar material, and publishes *Directory of Catholic Archives* (1994), 3rd edn: CAS.
32. Foster, J. and Sheppard, J. (1995), *British Archives: a Guide to Archival Sources in the United Kingdom*, 3rd edn, London: Macmillan.
33. Kitching, C. (1996), *Archives: the Very Essence of our Heritage,* London: Phillimore, for the National Council on Archives.
34. ARCHON is 'the principal gateway for UK archivists and users of manuscript sources for British history', at www.hmc.gov.uk/archon/.
35. d'Olier, J.H. and Delmas, B. (1975), *Planning National Infrastructures for Documentation, Libraries and Archives*, Paris: Unesco. There are many Unesco reports proposing models for particular countries: e.g. Cook, M. (1981), *Professional Training Needs for Archivists in the Caribbean Region*, p. 5, Paris: Unesco. Roper, M. (1996), 'Unit 6: Management and Staffing', in Society of Archivists (1996), *British Archival Practice: the Society's Archive Diploma Training Manual*, London: Society of Archivists.
36. Cook, M. (1982), *Guidelines for Curriculum Development in Records Management and the Administration of Modern Archives: a RAMP Study,* Paris: Unesco. This will be superseded by the training modules produced after 1997 by the International Records Management Trust.
37. General Information Programme, meeting of experts on the harmonization of archival training programmes, Paris, 26–30 November 1979; *Final Report* (1980), Paris: Unesco. International symposium on harmonization of education and training programmes in information science, librarianship and archival studies; *Final Report* (1984), Paris: Unesco.

38. Thurston, A. (1990), 'New Directions in Archival Training,' *Janus*, **1**, 48–52.
39. See note 22.
40. British Standards Institution, *Conservation of Documents*, BS 4971: 1973; *Recommendations for the Storage and Exhibition of Documents*, BS 5454: 1977; 2nd edn revd, 1989. A draft International Standard is in progress (1997).
41. Duchein, M. (1988), *Archive Buildings and Equipment*, ICA Handbooks Series No. 6, 2nd edn revd and enlarged, ed. P. Walne, Munich: K.G. Saur. Kitching, C. (1993), *Archive Buildings in the United Kingdom 1977–1992,* London: HMSO.

3

RECORDS MANAGEMENT

Not all archives services carry out a records management programme, though in principle most would have the possibility of introducing one to cover the records created by their governing authority. Where an archives service has the primary duty of serving an employing authority, institution or firm, the records management aspect is of major importance, and affects all the processes which come after it. Records management can also be considered as a function exercised independently of archival management, but the two logically go together and either may suffer from the absence of the other.

Records management (RM) is a field that has attracted increasing attention. The growing sophistication of administrative practices, and the increasing complexity of organizations, together with the enormous expansion of the quantity of records produced, has made it necessary to introduce conscious management into this area, and to develop it as a set of techniques or as a discipline.[1]

The national standards body of Australia has published a standard for RM which may lead to the adoption of similar standards in other countries, or may become an international standard.[2] This standard forms one of several that fall under the general heading of quality control. The foreword to the standard summarizes the scope and functions of RM in a way that highlights the main underlying principles:

> Records management is the discipline and organisational function of managing records to meet operational business needs, accountability requirements and community expectations.
>
> Records management plays many roles within an organisation and in the organisation's relationship with the world. Thus records management is concerned with the following:
> a) Managing the records continuum, from the design of a recordkeeping system to the end of the records' existence.
> b) Providing a service to meet the needs, and protect the interests, of the organisation and its clients.

    c) Capturing complete, accurate, reliable and usable documentation of organisational activity to meet legal, evidential and accountability requirements.

    d) Managing records as an asset and information resource, rather than as a liability.

    e) Promoting efficiency and economy, both in the management of records and in organisational activity as a whole, through sound recordkeeping practices.[3]

These clauses all enshrine important principles that operate throughout the programme. The 'records continuum' refers to changes of function that occur as records age. Traditionally, records managers treated records as passing through three stages during their period of existence: current, semi-current and non-current. In reality, records pass through stages that vary according to their type and function. Records management seeks to manage them to the best advantage throughout these stages, and in order to do so seeks to establish control over them at the start of the continuum that runs from their creation to their final disposal. This means that the scope of RM covers the design of recording systems as well as the disposition of the physical media.

Records management provides a service that should be apparent to and appreciated by all parts of the employing organization, and which will deliver quantifiable advantages. The interests and needs of the organization can be essential to its continuance. All organizations need to be able securely to meet the requirements of the law, to understand their exact position at any moment, and to discharge the general duty of being accountable to government and to society. This can only be done through records.

It has been customary only too often for organizations and individuals to regard the accumulated records as being a liability – either as one to be unwillingly maintained or, quite often, as a burden to be discarded by indiscriminate destruction. In reality, the records of an organization are an important – indeed a vital – resource that allows it to discharge its responsibilities and carry out its programmes. Properly handled this resource is a quantifiable asset. The benefits of good administration of this asset can be felt through all aspects of the organization's activity.

Historically, interest in records management has arisen from different points of origin. In some cases the initiative has come from archivists, whose main concern is the control of material passing out of current record systems into archival care. Records management in this tradition is concerned mainly with retirement of records from currency and their appraisal. In other cases the initiative has come from business efficiency or management advisory units, whose main concern has been the reduction of administrative costs. In yet other cases the records management system may have originated in central secretariat departments, whose main concern has been to regulate the flow of information and documentary media within the central offices. There may also be cases where records management has begun with legal advisers, whose concern has been to preserve and retrieve official documents. Finance and management accountancy departments have also had to develop systems to serve the needs of audit.

The historical point of origin impresses its character on the resulting programme, and it may determine where the main thrust of management effort is placed. The present study takes as its starting-point the view that records management is, like archives management, a branch of information management. The quality of the information it supplies is the main criterion for the evaluation of an RM programme, and this information supply is radically affected by its relationship with an archives service.

Records management is a field of management whose material is the data, media and systems used in the record-making and record-storing processes in any organization. Its aim is to achieve the best retrieval and exploitation of the data held in these media and systems, and incidentally to reduce the cost and improve the efficiency of record-making and keeping processes.[4]

The earliest textbooks of RM were written from the standpoint of a commercial firm, and the emphasis was on efficiency and economy. These qualities remain important to records managers, and it is a basic principle that a working RM programme should be capable of being rigorously costed, and should be able to demonstrate significant (and sometimes very great) savings when compared with systems in which recording systems are not controlled. However, the literature of this branch of information science has moved towards the management of records in the public sector. This has meant that the main stated aim of records management has now moved to a new emphasis: RM is now seen as primarily concerned with accountability. No government or public authority can convincingly demonstrate its accountability to its electorate without establishing good RM procedures.[5] No private firm can convincingly demonstrate its accountability to its auditors, shareholders and to the public without establishing good RM procedures.

The relationship between archives and records management can be illustrated by two models, given in Figures 3.1 and 3.2 overleaf.

Two current developments reinforce the validity of an information-centred approach to RM. One is the advent of office automation, which after a generally slow start is now spreading rapidly; the other is the increasing tendency of legislators to introduce or develop specific or unspecific legal requirements for record retention and access.

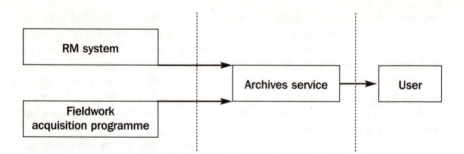

Figure 3.1   Records management as a front-end system

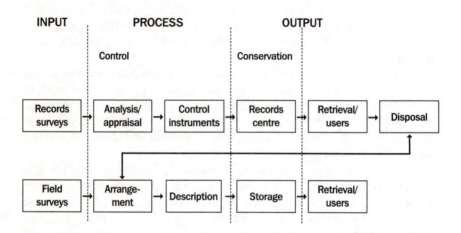

Figure 3.2   Records and archives management as parallel systems

■ OFFICE AUTOMATION

All administrative and recording processes are now subject to automation. An early study sponsored by the Records Management Group of the Society of Archivists in 1981 still provides an interesting baseline by which to judge the progress and effects of this.[6]

Adapting the categories adopted by this study, the automation of office processes can be considered under four headings:

O   word processing
O   (integrated) computing systems
O   imaging
O   communications.

WORD-PROCESSING

Word processors of various sorts have now replaced typewriters as the main means of creating text. They are inherently more efficient and flexible than earlier methods of writing, provided that a complex infrastructure of services can be maintained. Much laborious and time-consuming clerical work is avoided by using them, but at the same time much of the craft work involved in writing, and in transmitting texts, has been transferred from specialist workers to the authors of the text itself. This has begun an important change in the social structure of offices, and has initiated even more radical changes for the future. Despite the flexibility of word processors, they are not yet widely used for the storage of text after creation.

In the first stage of change, manually generated pieces of writing are translated into formal shapes by clerical staff typing them: this is traditional, but the work involved in checking and proofreading is so reduced that it tends to lose all prominence as a cost factor. In the second stage, administrators themselves write directly on to electronic keyboards, which are capable of transmitting their words to colleagues or addressees and also, if required, of storing them electronically. Thus a system originally thought of as means for formalizing text ends as one for communicating it. Much of the secondary work involved, including tasks such as filing, is reduced or lost. The distinction between clerical support work and management origination is also blurred, and new roles have to be found for secretarial staff. It will be noticed that writing, transmitting and storing messages has always constituted a large proportion of all administrative work.

COMPUTING SYSTEMS

Computing systems for administration followed quickly on the introduction of word-processing. Organizations generally pass through intermediate stages before they move to adopt an all-embracing management information system (MIS). An early stage commonly found is the adoption of computer-held databases and/or spreadsheets for holding and using the working data. From the archivist's point of view databases are of two kinds, the accumulated and the regenerative. Accumulated databases (or datasets) consist of collected data used as a whole or at one time. Regenerative databases are constantly, or at least periodically, updated with new information, so that there is never a moment when the information is in a definitive state. Most administrative systems are the second kind: they are commonly used to hold data on finance, legal holdings, personnel, stocks, property management, and operations. In the most advanced cases these are linked to become integrated systems, held together by a communications network that allows many people to access and update data from different parts of the organization with very little formality. Databases are therefore not only constantly in a state of flux, but are a shared facility. They are also often relational – that is, data entered in one part of the system automatically modifies data held in other related but distinct parts.

IMAGING

Imaging systems originated from a different starting-point, and sometimes are not fully integrated into central information systems. They depend on a recognition that management information depends primarily upon sets of documents, particularly documents that have identifiable importance in themselves as objects. Legal deeds, patents or licences, operational plans or drawings, or formal directives would be natural material for translating into image form. In this shape they would then become easily accessible to any department that had the necessary equipment, and could be transmitted or stored without trouble and cost. Microforms have long been used for some of the same purposes, and do continue in use in some cases. Electronic imaging in some ways solves the problems that microfilming had, but at the expense of creating new problems. Microfilm is expensive to create, unwieldy to use, but is a good medium for long-term storage and is convenient for transmission. Computer images are easy to create and to access and transmit, but present many difficulties of storage and retrieval if they are to be kept for more than a year or two.

The growth of imaging systems has stimulated the development of a discipline known as document management. This is clearly of central interest to records managers. A successful document management programme in an organization depends on the ability of a manager to set up (or recover) the disciplines involved in recognizing, processing, using and storing all information items that can be identified as 'documents'. It is necessary to have a well-organized office, in which all members of staff are aware of these disciplines and accustomed to observe them. This looks very like a rediscovery of the old idea of the registry, or formal shared filing system, that was a strong feature of organized administration in the nineteenth century, but which has suffered a long decline in the present one.

COMMUNICATIONS

Communications are the key to all administrative development. All the systems mentioned so far are apt for development as aspects of a communications network. Here, too, there have been stages of development, and many (perhaps most) organizations are still in a primitive condition. The use of fax (transmission of documentary images over telephone lines) is now general, but the integration of these into email and office computing systems is not yet common.

Electronic mail is the best known aspect of administrative communication. When fully adopted it has a radical effect on the shape and ethos of any organization, but there are many obstacles to it being rapidly and universally used. The chief obstacle is usually the reluctance and lack of expertise of senior management and executives. A second obstacle is the slow spread of compatible facilities among people who would be the natural correspondents of these managers: government agencies, branches and departments of the same organization, customers or users, information services. A study carried out by the German archive training school at Marburg has identified some of the radical implications of a general adoption of email as the normal and natural means of communication within an organization.[7]

Email can perhaps be seen as in some ways representing an opposing tradition from that of document management. It is essentially anarchic and hostile to hierarchy and discipline. Anyone with access to the network – and this can include people working from home – can simply and directly initiate or respond to messages, locally, nationally or internationally. This militates against older traditions in which messages and documents had to be approved by senior officials and formally recorded. Email messages can contain any sort of information. They may have the text of legally binding contracts, or convey essential decisions on policy; but equally they can be completely informal and ephemeral. The messages are transmitted quickly and by methods invisible to the user, and can be deleted or retained by the press of a button. This militates against systematic appraisal and retention policies. Messages retained are not necessarily filed appropriately, files are often automatically deleted after a time, and in any case their long-term retention is a technically difficult matter. The coming of email is a challenge to the records manager in many ways.

All four sectors of automated recording interrelate, and all are rapidly advancing. It is interesting to notice that all concern the management of information, and of the media that retains it. Whether or not we shall ever see the advent of a 'paperless office' – and so far this does not seem likely – it is clear that the advance of information technology has reinforced the importance of RM as central to management planning. An extreme view might be that in high-level administration only two kinds of manager are needed at the centre: the decision-makers, who rely on the data provided for them by the service; and the records managers, who devise and maintain it.

The design and retention of automated databases is subject to some statutory controls that have not been applicable, as yet, to similar records held in hard-copy form. Data protection restrictions are to be extended to cover personal databases held in manual systems from 1998.[8] Many governments, including the British, have appointed officials to register and supervise them, and have instituted legal codes to protect the individual. Data protection legislation is based to a great extent on international accords, and supplements the increasingly detailed requirements of law over other forms of record. Records managers must of course be equipped to observe the law in these respects, and to design their systems in accordance with relevant codes of practice.

All this shows that RM has an increasingly important role in an automated administration, and that the design of the records series to be generated, stored and accessed is a central concern of management. An example of how RM services could be integrated in an organization is shown in Figure 3.3.

LEGAL CONTROLS

The second modern development is that in all countries, but especially in North America and the European Union, the law is taking an increasing interest in specifying the retention of records and in allowing litigation to be based upon record evidence over longer periods of time.

There is no comprehensive summary of these legislative requirements, which would indeed be difficult to assemble from a wide variety of statutes, regulations and legal decisions. Newton's brief survey of the general law of civil and criminal evidence, and of contract, remains a useful starting-point.[9] More detailed studies of legally based retention requirements in the fields of social service and education show how this aspect of appraisal has to be rooted in the specifics of the topic dealt with.[10] The more specialized the area the more the subject becomes technical and difficult. Drugs control legislation has been particularly prolific with retention and access controls expressed in the small print of detailed instruments. Health and safety legislation has affected the retention of personnel records, and dictates the creation of records of accidents and hazards, with long periods of currency. Courts of law have increasingly tended to accept cases based on personal experiences over long periods, which therefore call for records over the same length of time. As mentioned before, databases containing personal information are specially regulated.

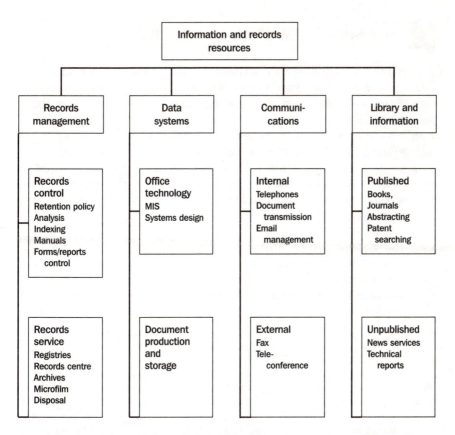

Source: Adapted from Newton S.C. (1981), *Office Automation and Record Management,* London: Society of Archivists.

Figure 3.3   Model showing how RM services could be integrated within an organization

We are all aware of the growth of personal rights litigation in all spheres of life: medical practice, equal opportunities, government service (for example, the effects of the early atomic bomb trials; the Gulf War Syndrome, etc.), industrial injuries. None the less, legal draftspersons continue to be imprecise in the rules they incorporate into draft laws that deal with records. For example, recent education legislation specifies that records shall be created on the attainment of children at stated ages in standard tests.[11] There is a general statutory right of access to such records, and there are signs of a growing tradition of parents litigating against schools on the basis of these test results. However, the Act does not specify in what manner or how long the records must be kept. This omission remains a general constant in new laws and regulations.

■ THE STRUCTURE OF AN RM SERVICE

Records are information media that have been generated by an administrative system. They may also hold data which originated outside the organization (for example, in incoming letters or forms) but are themselves essentially an internal information source. Most organizations need also to provide and manage information services that seek for and use information of wholly external origin: books and documents. No single source of information will by itself satisfy the total information requirement of any organization, so that the RM service depends for its success on building up a workable relationship with four other facets of the organization (see Figure 3.4):

○ the administration (financial, legal, general and specialist) in which the records originate
○ the special library service
○ the technical documentation centre
○ the archives.

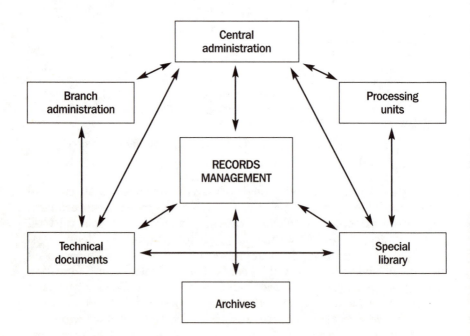

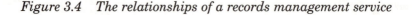

Figure 3.4   The relationships of a records management service

ADMINISTRATION

The administration generates records that carry the information it acquires and uses in the course of business. It arranges these records in systems which are the stock-in-trade of administrative departments. The RM unit must be able to build up a relationship with these administrative units which will allow the records manager a degree of responsibility for the design and maintenance of record systems, and for the disposition of particular series. The relationship should also allow the administrative departments to become accustomed to using the RM system and to call on it for information.

It is often difficult to define the concept of administration. Most organizations have a central office, the headquarters of management. It is common to find that there are also important administrative centres outside this. Some will be specialist or technical departments or units; others will be branches or sub-organizations, often situated away from the main administrative centre. Processing or manufacturing units also generate records, and may be administratively distinct. If it is to deal with all these, the RM programme has to be able to enter into relationships with all the different kinds of administrative entity.

An internationally accepted model for RM within government and business administrations proposes that it should be responsible for the design and maintenance of what have traditionally been the three main types of record created.[12] Under this model RM should include mail, reports and forms management. Mail management covers not only systems for receiving, distributing and storing incoming mail, matching it with mail sent out in reply, but also extends into the design of form letters and even into campaigns for improving the language used in official letters.

Mail management also involves the design of systems for filing. A filing system is essentially the practical application of a classification scheme covering the organization's area of interest; but it also has another dimension – the control of movement of documents round the office, plotting a lifecycle for each. Incoming documents are filed, the file placed before the manager who is to take action, and the resulting outgoing document takes its place next on the file. In this way a full and retrievable record is available on the whole transaction: but to set it out in this way involves a good deal of structural organization in the office.

Reports should, of course, be succinct and accurately expressed, should conform to established standards and be available to any proper user for reference. Forms must be well designed, must make the data they carry easily usable, and (as is often remarked today) should be understood by those who have to fill them in.

SPECIAL LIBRARY SERVICE

The special library service assembles books, journals and published materials, including non-book materials, on subjects relevant to the information needs of the organization and its staff, and runs a service based upon these.

TECHNICAL DOCUMENTATION CENTRE

The documentation centre assembles published and unpublished technical papers of relevance to the organization and its staff, obtaining these from sources outside the organization itself (probably mainly from electronic sources), and running a selective retrieval and information service based upon these materials. An automated documentation service provides the organization's access to international, local or specialized databases: as executives become more used to searching for international source material on the Internet, the shape and function of documentation centres is changing in this respect. Reports generated from within the organization should also be dealt with in a documentation system.

All these services may have a similar structure, consisting of input, store and user services. The arrangements for input differ between the different services, but it is easy to suggest that storage and output could be combined. In particular, finding aids, systems for disseminating information and the arrangements for communicating data have no theoretical need to be separate.

ARCHIVES

The archives service receives all or some of its material from the RM programme, as a result of the process of appraisal which is the interface between them. It shares with the RM programme a concern over the completeness of the documentation assembled by the system, because in the end this is what determines the value of the archive. Looked at from the other direction, the RM service uses the archives for the storage and use of its most valuable materials, over long periods.

In view of the closeness of the relationships suggested above, one could hardly suggest an RM system that does not incorporate them as an essential feature. Records management systems ought to function hand in hand with the other information services.

■ SURVEYS, AND THE REGISTER OF SERIES

The first important job of a records manager is to find out what records are being produced by the employing organization, and what systems are being used for their deployment.

Previous writing on RM has sometimes neglected the second half of this statement. Walk-through surveys are often recommended with or without complementary surveys by questionnaire. These surveys identify series of records, and note details of these on fieldwork sheets. This is a good way of doing a survey which notes the existence of particular records series, but it is not sufficient if the objective is to evaluate systems.

It is possible, therefore, that an RM survey should be carried out in two parts, one to establish what series of records are being produced, and the other to determine the production and retrieval processes used. The normal method in the first case would be for the survey team to use worksheets which can later be turned into a register of series. In the second case, the survey might use flowcharts, indicating the contributory flows of manpower which lead to the production and use of record series. Figure 3.5 overleaf refers to these methods.

Surveys of records have two main outcomes: an estimate of bulk, cost and distribution of records in the organization; and a register of series. It is necessary to be clear, at the outset, about what is meant by the term 'series'. The definition of this term was established, through international agreement, by archivists working on standards for archival arrangement and description.[13] Further discussion of the significance of this and related terms, together with formal definitions, is therefore to be found in Chapters 5, 6 and 7 of this book. Series are systems that hold integrated sets of records designed and used for a particular purpose. Components of series are called 'items'. Although specific information is held in record items, which are therefore mostly used for retrieval and reference, records management is mainly carried out at the level of the series: for example, retention periods are determined at series level. It is most important that records managers should be aware of this principle, and should apply it to all their work.

BULK AND COST

During the survey, an attempt can be made to estimate the relative size of series, considered as assemblies of material falling into the following categories:

RECORDS SURVEY WORKSHEET

Department	Division/unit	Location

Series		
Title/Description		
Format		

Storage accommodation

Equipment	Shelving (lin.m.)	Volume (cub.m.)
Floor space (sq.m.)	**Total office space (sq.m.)**	**Spare/unused space (equipment)**

Frequency of reference proportion %

Active	Semi-active	Dormant

Retention period proportion %

Short-term	Medium-term	Permanent

Accrual rate (lin.m. per annum)

Legal requirements	Staff commitment	Value of equipment

Figure 3.5   Records survey worksheet

1.   Retention categories
      a) permanent or long-term
      b) medium-term
      c) short-term.
2.   Frequency of reference
      a) fully current (active)
      b) semi-current
      c) non-current.

Each record series encountered could have an entry in each of these categories, specifying the accrual rate, the volume of space occupied in
cubic or linear measurement, the shelving or other equipment used and
the floor area occupied. This information will allow a plan for the
orderly disposal of items in each series and the optimum use of office
and off-site storage. It will also allow the RM staff to calculate the relative costs of maintaining each series, either in active office space or in
dedicated storage.

REGISTER OF SERIES

The second outcome of an RM survey will be the establishment of a register of record series. This is a basic management tool for the RM programme, and has a long-term value. The register should contain all the
information necessary to allow the RM staff to understand what series
exist, what they are used for and how they interrelate. The register may
also be used to produce schedules for controlling the retirement of semi-
or non-current records, and the disposition of the records in the series.
These two functions suggest that the register should usually be based
upon a description of the records at two levels at least; a description of
the series as such, and a finding aid which gives access to the individual
items forming part of it. Figures 3.6 and 3.7 on pp.60 and 61 give
examples of listing records as series and as items.

Where the RM system is automated, it may be convenient to give each
record series a registration code, which will uniquely identify it within
its department of origin. A reference code has several advantages, since
it can appear as a linking field in a database. On the other hand many
records managers prefer to use free language titles for their series.
Office staff are accustomed to use a particular name for the series they
create and service, and it may be better not to introduce unaccustomed
technicalities.

The register of series allows the records manager to maintain control
over the whereabouts and use of the various series in the organization.
By it any one series can be located, and it can be used to moderate

RECORDS TRANSFERRED TO RECORDS CENTRE	
Series information	Consignment:
Originating Office:	Date:
General description of series (Continue on separate sheets)	
Storage accommodation cleared: Filing cabinets: Transfer boxes: Shelving: Cubic metrage of records transferred:	
Recommendations for retention:	
Classified: Confidential/unrestricted	
Transferred by	

Figure 3.6   Part I of a records transfer list, giving a series-level description and consequential data on bulk, storage and format

TRANSFER LIST				
Originating Office:			Consignment: Page No:	
				Records Centre use
Ref No.	Title/description	Span dates	Action date	Location

Figure 3.7   Part II of a transfer list, giving an item list

periodic transfers out of the current records system into the records centre or into the archives, extract data when required and advise on system changes. The most important single function of the register, though, is to construct a retention schedule.

RETENTION SCHEDULES

A retention schedule is an analytical list of records series, arranged either under the functions carried out by the creating organization or under the structural headings of a departmental organization plan. The main purpose of the schedule is to record and implement the appraisal decisions which have been made, so that these decisions can be routinely put into effect. A secondary purpose may be to set out a list of the record series in a way which will illustrate the organization's record activity.[14]

Retention schedules usually list series by title, and note the periods during which they should be retained in the active department and in the records centre. These schedules are apt for inclusion in database management systems, and in automated systems the expiry dates can be automatically implemented.

Establishing and maintaining the retention schedule (see Figure 3.8) is one of the main tasks of an RM programme. In drawing it up, the records manager may take the opportunity to consult as many executives in the organization as possible, but the final responsibility for the eventual retention decisions, and especially for their implementation, should rest with the RM service. This important principle is illustrated by an examination of how appraisal decisions are made and implemented.

DRAFTING THE SCHEDULE

The register which results from RM surveys can be used to provide an alphabetical list of record series, arranged under the departments of origin. Each of these can be allocated a proposed retention category:

○ permanent or indefinite retention
○ destruction after the lapse of a given period
○ review after a given period, when a decision will be made.

Proposals made in this way for retention periods can then be circulated to all relevant staff in the organization; indeed a wide circulation and discussion is recommended. It should be made clear by what date or on what occasion replies or comments should be received. Comments by originating departments will normally be accepted and incorporated

Retention schedule		
Series title	Retain	
	in local store	in Records Centre

Figure 3.8   Part of a retention schedule

into the schedule, though if they seem perverse some further discussion should be initiated. For example, if it seems that a wholesale retention for long periods is being suggested, the records manager will be able to cost the effect of this course of action. Appraisal decisions should always be taken in the light of specific costings.

The retention schedule may also lay down the date at which items are withdrawn from current systems and transferred to local or intermediate storage, as well as to the records centre and final disposal.

After the lapse of the agreed discussion period the retention schedule is finalized and promulgated as an item of official policy. Since schedules can and should be regularly revised, policy can always be modified in the light of experience.

Retention schedules are formal directives. They should visibly have the endorsement of senior management and be widely distributed for use by departments. In automated RM systems the retention schedule can be held online and accessible (if necessary with restrictions to user departments) as formatted screens.

APPRAISAL IN RECORDS MANAGEMENT

The main professional activity of archivists and records managers is the evaluation of record series to determine their most appropriate retention period. It is an activity built into RM programmes, for planned retention and disposal is necessary to effective RM. Purely within a context of RM, the main concern of the records manager is to see that those records are retained which are specified by the law, or which are judged to be of clear administrative value to the organization; and to see that all other records are disposed of. Archivists have a broader viewpoint, and must also consider what potential research or long-term values can be identified in the records. Archivists are trained to perceive these values and, because they are participants in relevant research activities, should have acquired experience which will reinforce their ability to recognize these values. Because they involve important decisions which bear upon all aspects of the organization's work, appraisal judgements should be made after extensive consultation, but it is the business of archivists and the records managers to see that they have been made and that they are implemented.

It is a fundamental rule of records management that no record series should be permitted to continue in existence without an appraisal status, and above all that no record should enter the storage system without a specific, dated, disposal instruction. Similarly, it is a fundamental rule of archives management that no document or series should be admitted to the archives without having undergone an appraisal. In both cases, retrospective appraisal, or a periodic reassessment of retention criteria, may be valuable, or even necessary. The criteria for appraisal at the two stages, in RM and at transfer to archives, are somewhat different, and this difference has been recognized in the RM practices of central government in Britain.

The system used in this context is based upon the recommendations of the Grigg Report of 1954, and was evaluated in the Wilson Report of 1981.[15] The central principles of this system, as it has been developed over the years in the management of public records, are as follows:

1. As many series as possible should be dealt with under a retention schedule.
2. Series which must be reviewed are examined at two separate points in time. The first review, carried out within the first five years after closure, seeks primarily to determine whether there is a continuing administrative value. The second review, ideally at 25 years, asks whether there is also any research value.
3. Particular instance papers (series of records each of which documents a particular instance of a general policy or activity; e.g. case files) are registered separately, and should have a retention instruction incorporated into their initial design.

The Grigg system assumes that the main records to be appraised by review are subject files held in a central registry, and that appraisal is to be applied only when these files have ceased to be current (have been 'closed'). Neither of these assumptions is generally applicable outside the civil service.

As far as appraisal criteria are concerned, the Grigg system outlined above depends on the validity of one central principle, that there is a broad correspondence between research values and administrative values. It is unlikely that records which are not seen as being useful for business reference will turn out to contain data of long-term value; equally material of long-term value will tend to be contained in records which are felt to be of continuing reference use. There is a convincing practicality in this view, and it has not been seriously challenged in subsequent commentary, despite the many criticisms that this method has attracted.

The Grigg Report did, however, note that the first review should be carried out soon after the records' closure, or there would be a danger that inaccessibility would affect the administrative value judgement. It was also noted that where a record series arose from a function which had been discontinued, there would be no administrative value in the records (except possibly as a precedent), and therefore a judgement would have to be made on research grounds. One might also note that central government can make assumptions which are questionably relevant to the situation of other types of administration. One is that a considerable lapse of time is needed to determine research values, and that documents must be archived only when they are 30 years old. Another assumption, not universally valid, is that all records will be organized in orderly registry systems, and that appraisal is a function end-on to the registry.[16]

Finally, we have to note that administrative convenience can sometimes conflict with long-term research interests and perhaps also with the accountability principle. The most serious criticism of the Grigg system is that selection is made in the first place by those who have an interest in secrecy.

For organizations outside central government, the appraisal theory that has held sway since the 1950s was formulated by the American writer T.R. Schellenberg.[17] According to this theory, records should be examined with a view to determining whether, or to what degree, they possess either evidential or informational values. These two terms of art have passed into general currency in the archival community. Evidential values are those that deal with the origin, foundation, status and operation of the organization that produced the records. Documents that contain data on persons or subjects extraneous to the organization itself (as, for example, case files contain data on the cases dealt with) are said to have informational value.

These criteria present the archivist or records manager with two problems:

○   They assume that appraisal is only carried out by examining accu-mulations of semi- or non-current records: the procedure is therefore reactive.

○   No provision is made for a cost-benefit analysis. Most archivists in reality have to balance the cost of retaining records against the value that can be realized by their use.

In the 1980s some new approaches have been suggested, which have led to a re-examination of the ways in which archivists and records managers should approach appraisal procedures. These new approaches, generally described under the term 'documentation strategy', are more proactive, and demand a greater involvement in the daily work of the record-producing organization. Archivists or records managers working within this system start by analysing the essential aims and functions of their organization. Having established what these are, they can then draw up a plan under which each of the functions can be documented. It may therefore be necessary to look for records, and also other sources, that cover some of the functions. The more traditional methods of appraisal have naturally concen-trated attention on administration and internal housekeeping func-tions, simply because these have been the producers of records. Other functions, perhaps more fundamental, have often been neglected because record production has been peripheral to them.[18] Although these ideas have been debated in the archival community, clearly they offer valuable insights to records managers as well.

The procedure of analysing organizations in order to establish their essential aims and functions can also be applied to wider fields. Archivists in public service, for example, may choose to analyse their territorial areas and set up strategies to ensure documentation for each of the essential facets in the analysis. This practice has come to be termed 'macro-appraisal'.[19]

The Australian standard for RM, referred to at the beginning of this chapter, summarizes the scope of appraisal, which is a process that should determine:

○   what records are needed for each function
○   what are the risks involved in not creating or keeping these
○   that adequate records are, in fact, created and kept
○   that records that are needed for long-term purposes are migrated between recording systems as appropriate
○   which records are to be eliminated when they are no longer needed
○   that the transfer of custody or ownership of records between organizations, where appropriate, is documented.[20]

■ RECORDS CENTRES

Records in full current use must, of course, be kept where they are most convenient to their main users. It is one of the principal functions of the records manager to see that records which have passed out of full currency are regularly retired from these current systems, and that for the remainder of their agreed life they are managed in a suitable place. It is normal for an RM system to have such a place, known as the intermediate records store, or, more usually nowadays, the records centre.

Records centres have been in use in larger organizations for up to 50 years, and a good deal of experience has been accumulated on them. There are specific standards for their physical characteristics, and for the services which they should provide.[21]

Experience has shown that there are two main types of records centre, and that there are important record series which cannot be administered in records centres at all.[22]

IN-HOUSE RECORDS CENTRES

In-house records centres are generally connected with smaller organizations, with compact central administrations in confined quarters, or with RM systems confined to a few central departments. These records centres will tend to be in relatively high-cost accommodation and, so, will tend to be cramped for space. The space problem is usually so important in these circumstances that it is not unusual to have off-site supplementary records centres for less actively used material. (Duplication like this can be economically difficult to use.) Retrieval of records from in-house records centres will be rapid, with document delivery perhaps after only a few minutes, and the RM staff will have a relatively intimate acquaintance with the systems in use in the administration served, and will also tend to know the departmental office staff personally.

It is common for RM programmes to start out with in-house records centres, and use them to establish trusted services for senior management or central administrative departments. When these are well established, the RM programme can expand to include services to production departments, outlying subsidiaries or branch installations. This kind of expansion will have to be accompanied by expansion into off-site records centres.

OFF-SITE RECORDS CENTRES

Off-site records centres are needed by larger or scattered organizations, or where the parent organization is confined to high-cost premises in a city centre. The off-site records centre is a low-cost, high-density store, situated in an accessible but remote site. Retrieval of records from it will be relatively slow – perhaps a 24- or 48-hour delivery service, using public means of transmission or transport, might be envisaged. The selection of records for transfer to the records centre is obviously affected by the delivery delays, though the appearance of electronic document transmission systems is now an important planning factor.

Records management programmes generally have to deal with such a large bulk of records that some sort of off-site records centre will become necessary. All RM services should be costed. It will be found that central management of records, allowing early retirement of records from costly central storage, will always provide economies, sometimes very significant economies, as against systems that retain non-current records in prime sites. To maximize these economies the full benefit of cheap bulk storage should be used. Rapid retrieval is certainly an important consideration, but the cost of providing it in particular cases may be weighed against the certain and heavy cost of keeping a large bulk of records in high-cost areas.

RECORDS UNSUITABLE FOR RECORDS CENTRE TREATMENT

The concept of the records centre is that it should be the best environment for all records which have a retention value longer than that of immediate currency, and which do not have to be kept in prime office space. This definition covers the great majority of records other than those in full currency. There are, however, cases where an important record series with long retention value is still required to be kept near workstations. A typical example might be a central personnel record. If this is held in hard copy it has to be near the administration. A series like this should certainly be regarded as a vital record, and so the case would be strong for duplicating it, by using microforms, or for translating it into electronic form. In doing either of these, the archival aspect should be borne in mind.

Other cases of the same sort are series which receive a regular accrual at short intervals. If these are brought into the records centre, the records manager has a difficult choice: the successive accruals may either be given new locations, which means that it will be difficult to find any given record quickly; or they will have to be integrated into a single series within the records centre – but this is wasteful of space and labour. The solution may be to translate the series to microform, and keep the working copy near the point of use, or to automate it.

A third example can be taken from medical case records, where it may be necessary to provide virtually instantaneous access even to record items that have not been accessed for some years. Microforms may be unacceptable owing to the need to have a reading machine appropriately sited. A solution may be to retain a special series near to the point of access. Here, too, electronic methods would seem to offer an answer.

There are also cases where it may be efficient to exclude certain branches or departments from the records centre service – for instance, where retrieval would be exceptionally costly in their case. Situations like this are unfortunate, since they expose defects (perhaps necessary in the circumstances) in the design of the RM system. The danger is that defects like this may be so serious that they lead to *ad hoc* or rival RM practices growing up in separatist departments. To avoid this danger records managers need to build in compensating features, and take special measures to maintain control over the records systems held in outlying departments.

These cases where certain series of record appear to be unsuitable for management in a records centre illustrate the dispersed responsibility of a records manager, who must understand the needs of the user and be able to design or deal with records series which do not conform to standard procedures.

In general, however, the records centre is a tool which allows records managers to establish physical control over most records which are to be retained beyond currency, and to organize them to provide the best possible reference service.[23]

INFLOW OF RECORD MATERIALS

No record should enter the records centre unless:

○   there is a retrieval instrument controlling it; and
○   a disposal instruction has been set up to provide for its appraisal and ultimate removal.

Failure to observe either of these rules will lead to important failures in the system.

The usual control instrument in records centres is known as a transfer list, for which there are established models.[24] Examples are illustrated in Figures 3.6 and 3.7 on pp. 60 and 61.

It is a curious fact that RM systems usually depend on these lists being made out by the originating department.[25] This custom, which emulates central government practice, has the advantage that it reduces the costs of the RM programme itself, by shifting a significant burden on to the originating departments. It is anomalous in that it is the RM staff who have the expertise to list and index records, and that if others are to do this work there must be close supervision. On the other hand, the staff of the originating departments have the best knowledge of the content and use of the series they are describing. It would be foolish to suggest that such a deeply ingrained tradition should now be changed. However, there are serious defects in the make-up of traditional transfer lists, considered as instruments for intellectual control of the materials.

The main need is for a description of each record at the appropriate levels. This means that in most cases, if not in all, there will have to be two different descriptions at two different levels: the series and the item. Ensuring that this is done will certainly involve the RM staff in some descriptive activity. Secondly (this is already well recognized), the description given to each set of transferred records must correspond both with the title normally given to them by the originating office and with their actual content and nature: thus, it should be possible to retrieve these records either by their customary name or as the result of a subject enquiry. Thirdly, the retrieval system must have some means of entry into the accumulated file of transfer lists. These three points will be dealt with in turn.

1. *Multi-level description.* This point has already been mentioned in connection with the register of series and retention schedules. To ensure control of the information within materials entering the records centre, descriptions should be designed to provide as much detail as possible at both series and item levels. Series descriptions may be based on what appears in the register of series. Figures 3.6 and 3.7 show a specimen transfer list using both a series description, consisting of a free-text abstract and five dedicated fields, and item descriptions within it.

2. *Customary titles.* The use of customary titles is very ancient. Documents such as the Black Book are quite familiar to students of the Middle Ages. Since the term 'Black Book' is valuable for retrieval only if the external physical appearance of the document is the main characteristic sought for, some further description is usually necessary. In this example, this has been provided by a published edition.[26] The original customary name is still necessary, though, not only because it is called by this in the originating department (until it becomes an ancient relic) but because it has probably been cited under this name in published research work. Records management staff have the continuing and necessary

duty of ensuring that document descriptions always identify and match the contents of the documents.

3. *Means of entry into the finding aids.* Large RM systems customarily limit their problems of document retrieval by referring these problems back to originating departments. These departments are given a copy of the transfer list at the time of the records' transfer. If they wish to consult their records, they must scan their file of transfer lists and specify the document they need, together with its location code. The RM staff are then only responsible for identifying the document and issuing it: their responsibility is only of an administrative kind, and therefore they only need finding aids which give administrative control. Originating departments, of course, may construct indexes if they wish.

The practicality of confining the RM service's responsibility in the way indicated should be carefully examined. The system has the additional advantage (from the point of view of the RM staff), that it reinforces the security of the records. Since they can only be retrieved by way of a request from the originating department, that department is clearly solely responsible for controlling access to it.

However, the narrowness of the principle operating here becomes obvious as soon as the overall interests of the employing organization are considered. This organization presumably runs an RM programme so that it can exploit the information held in internally generated media. The RM programme employs staff trained in information management; the originating departments employ staff trained in the product or function of those departments. To force departments to be totally responsible for record retrieval (both in the original listing and in the identification of documents to be searched) could be regarded as an abdication of responsibility on the part of the RM specialists.

This critique becomes more powerful when the finding aid itself (the transfer list) is examined. Though it gives reasonable administrative control, it is not well designed for intellectual control. Therefore, if the RM service is to be regarded as managing information rather than physical documents, some better finding aids will have to be designed. It will also be necessary to define the extent of the service's responsibility for the provision of information, as opposed to the provision of specified documents.

Improving the transfer lists may involve increasing the depth (or fullness) of information provided there. This may apply where series of correspondence files are concerned, or where technical reports are embedded in other records. In other cases, increased depth of description may not be possible. This must be a matter for specialist RM staff to judge. In any case, some form of index to the transfer lists will certainly be necessary. This may well involve the records centre staff in the necessary infrastructural work of making vocabularies or thesauri, corresponding to the work of the organization. Computerizing the transfer lists naturally allows online searching, and is probably destined to become the norm.

PROCESSING RECORD MATERIALS

It is important to maintain a physical distinction between the records centre and the archives. Cost limitation is always a very high priority in RM, and storage conditions must reflect the fact that the RM service's responsibilities are confined to storing the records for a limited (but possibly long) period of time. On the other hand, the records in the centre contain some which are particularly sensitive, and they should be kept securely. This suggests that the building should be adequate, but not lavish. A clean, orderly warehouse is the best model.

It is traditional in RM that physically the records in the records centre are arranged in random access order. Boxes are given random shelf locations which are keyed to the finding aids. This method is obviously convenient and saves space, and adds to the security of the records. Boxes are anonymous in appearance, and have nothing written on the outside except the brief location or reference code. On the other hand, records stored in this way do not display any of the relationships created by their original system or arrangement. They cannot be accessed by browsing, and it is not possible to concentrate any particular department's records in one area. Random access storage can only be operated – in full, at least – where the RM service has full operational control over the storage area. It is incompatible with any strong concept of departmental ownership of the records.

All the procedures necessary to manage a records centre have been set out in operational manuals, which can usually be used to set up systems specific to any organization.[27]

OUTPUT: EXPLOITATION AND DISPOSAL

Records centres have two forms of output: the retrieval and exploitation of information, and the outflow of records under the terms of the retention schedule. These are of unequal value, but both present technical difficulties.

The question of responsibility for the retrieval of information, and its influence on the design of finding aids, has already been discussed. There remains the question of provision of access facilities. Experience shows that while it is normal for retrieved records to be returned to the originating department, provision should still often be made for some degree of access on site. Originating departments may need to sift through or consult large amounts of their records, and it may then be better for them to send staff to the records centre rather than to arrange for mass movement of materials. The RM staff must also always be alert to the possibility that research access by external authorized persons may be required, and even that such access ought to be stimulated in some cases. Either way, searchroom facilities, backed by copying facilities, will be needed, including searchroom supervision.

Close liaison between the records centre and the documentation centre may suggest that an active programme for circulating information may be feasible. If so, record descriptions in the transfer list should be good enough to work as abstracts, and should contain the necessary keywords for profile matching.

Records series which are to be reviewed should be brought up at the appropriate date. The records manager needs to set up a system for reviewing, and for implementing the findings of the review. Ideally, reviewing should be done by RM staff, who should forward their recommendations on retention or disposal to the senior management of the originating department. This can be done on a review report form, such as is shown in Figure 3.9 overleaf.

This method of review minimizes the movement of records, and avoids the difficulties and delays involved whenever this responsibility is dispersed. It may not be feasible in very large organizations in which specialist knowledge of particular functions is needed. In these cases, the situation to be avoided is one where the most influential advice on retention is given by people who are remote from the responsibilities and costs involved in records retention. Relative cost is always an element in appraisal, and so too is relative frequency of reference. On both these points the RM staff are likely to be the most aware of the facts.

Transfer of records to the archives should occur where records are specified as being for permanent retention. In the archives they can have a more carefully controlled environment, and entry there will provide the opportunity for a more refined retrieval system. Because of these factors, there is often a case for the transfer to occur at a relatively early date. In central government the statutory principle is that transfer should occur when the selected records are 30 years old, at which period they become available for public access. In other situations, for instance in business firms, the whole concept of public access at a particular date may be questioned. Early transfer to the archives may then allow for access by specially authorized users at any date, and will provide better for conservation as well as retrieval. In any case, the

RECORDS CENTRE
(Address details)

To .... (Department of origin)

Disposal of records

The records listed below have now been reviewed in accordance with the official retention schedule. Items from this series have been issued on request .... times since transfer. It is recommended that:

a) they should be transferred to the Archives and kept permanently;
b) they should be retained for a further period and reviewed again after .... years;
c) they should now be destroyed.
    (Strike out as appropriate.)

If you agree with these recommendations, you need take no action. If we do not receive any comment by the end of the month following the date of this letter, the action proposed will be carried out routinely.

Date: Signature
                                         Records Manager

Ref. no.	Description	Dates	Location

Figure 3.9   Review report form

retention schedule and the reviewing procedures should provide a date at which the transfer operations should happen.

It sometimes happens that there is no physically separate archives repository, and the records centre has to perform both functions. This doubling up may have some advantages. For instance, it may be useful to keep some important series, that are scheduled for archival retention, in a single centrally available place. In other ways the different functions of the records centre can only be reconciled with those of the archives with some loss. Typically, this will be a loss of environmental and conservational conditions.

It is established in Britain and in most advanced countries that records which have been appraised as appropriate for archival treatment can be deposited in a publicly financed archive repository, and administered free of charge. There are no universally applicable conditions, even as to eventual freedom of access, but there is a tendency today for restrictions to be introduced on the right of owners to withdraw deposited records after a period during which they have been maintained at public expense.

Some records series have to be retained in the records centre for long or indefinite periods, but are not scheduled for eventual transfer to archives. These may include personnel records (which must be retained in some form up to and well beyond the period of service of the persons concerned – say up to 60 years), and case files (which may have an indefinite closure date dependent on some external event not notified to the RM staff). The existence of these may affect the standard of storage conditions given in the records centre, and will certainly affect the calculations involved in predicting the amount of record storage needed in the planning period ahead.

AUTOMATION IN RECORDS MANAGEMENT

Where RM is run as a service distinct in itself, successful automation so far has concentrated on providing a streamlined version of manual administrative control. System-generated information provides a better guide to bulk, location, issue control and measurement of use than is common in manual systems. The databases used in RM – register of series, retention schedule and transfer lists – are well suited in themselves to be computerized. Doing so would solve many problems of retrieval. Difficulties may arise when there is a need for linking the RM systems to the user departments. In some modern models this is done by using the local network or email system.[28] This kind of linkage is also helpful in automating the process of issuing and returning records required for reference.

As organizations move to automate and integrate their central administrative systems, by introducing a planned MIS, it is necessary for the appropriate RM functions to be built in. Each database in the MIS therefore needs to be assessed from the point of view of essential records, disaster control planning and disposal/retention. Where series are identified as having a long-term retention value, the system should include a procedure for making archive copies, which should be automatically upgraded whenever a change of system occurs.

The coming of large-scale computerized management information systems brings out an important point that many practical and long-established RM systems have obscured. This is that, fundamentally, the responsibility of records managers is not to collect and conserve the records physically, but to manage the ways in which information is stored and provided for use. When the information is mainly held on paper or other hard-copy media, the best way often is to collect these materials centrally and provide services based on the collection. When the information is held in a dispersed, multi-accessible system, policies based on physical collection are not so likely to work. Here, the work of the records managers will be concentrated on seeing that the right information is held and made available to the right people: it can be clearly seen as a branch of the broader discipline of information management.

NOTES

1. The principal textbook of (archivally oriented) RM in a government context is Schellenberg, T.R. (1956), *Modern Archives, Principles and Techniques*, Chicago: University of Chicago Press, with subsequent reprints. Outside government, the foundation text is Benedon, W. (1969), *Records Management*, Berkeley: The Trident Shop, California State University. The textbook currently authoritative is Penn, I.A., Pennix, G.B. and Coulson, J. (1994), *Records Management Handbook*, 2nd edn, Aldershot: Gower. Also see Emmerson, P. (1989), *How to Manage your Records,* Cambridge: ICSA; and Cook, M. (1993), *Information Management and Archival Data*, London: Library Association Publishing.

2. Australian Standard AS4390-1996, *Records Management*, Canberra: Standards Australia. Stephens, D.O. and Roberts, R. (1996), 'From Australia: the World's First National Standards for RM', *Records Management Quarterly*, **30**, 3–7.

3. AS4390.1-1996.
4. Durance, C.J. (1990), *Management of Recorded Information: Converging Disciplines*, Munich: K.G. Saur.
5. Public Sector Records Management Project, International Records Management Trust, London.
6. Newton, S.C. (ed.) (1981), *Office Automation and Records Management*, London: Society of Archivists.
7. Menne-Haritz, A. (ed.) (1993), *Information Handling in Offices and Archives*, Munich: K.G. Saur.
8. Data Protection Directive 95/46/EC. Also *Privacy in the European Union*, Conference of EU Data Protection Commissioners, Manchester, April 1996.
9. Newton, S.C. (1977), 'Selection and Disposal: Legal Requirements', *Records Management 1*, London: Society of Archivists, RMG.
10. Whittick, M.H. (1988), *The Records of Social Services Departments: Their Retention and Management*, 2nd edn, London: Society of Archivists, RMG. Bloomfield, P. (1987), *The Records of Education Departments: Their Retention and Management*, London: Society of Archivists, RMG.
11. Education Reform Act 1988, S.22; Statutory Instrument 1992/1385.
12. Cook, M. (1982), *Guidelines for Curriculum Development in Records Management and the Administration of Modern Archives: a RAMP Study,* Paris: Unesco, chs 6–7.
13. Feather, J. and Sturges, P. (eds) (1997), *International Encyclopedia of Information and Library Science*, London and New York: Routledge. The new edition of the International Council on Archives *Dictionary of Archival Terminology*, Munich, London etc.: K.G. Saur, is not available at the time of writing, but is advertised for 1998.
14. Cook, M. (1972), 'Surveying Current Records', *Journal of the Society of Archivists*, **4**, 413–22.
15. The Grigg Report (1954), *Report of the Committee on Departmental Records*, Cmd 9163, London: HMSO. The Wilson Report (1981), *Modern Public Records, Selection and Access*, Cmd 8204, London: HMSO.
16. A commentary on the Grigg recommendations and the resulting system is in Cook, M. (1977), *Archives Administration*, pp. 63–6, Folkestone: Dawson.
17. Schellenberg (1956).
18. There is a considerable literature on the development of documentation strategies. A good summary is Cox, R.J. (1992), *Managing Institutional Archives: Foundational Principles and*

Practices, New York: Greenwood Press. A good case study is Samuels, H.W. (1992), *Varsity Letters: Documenting Modern Colleges and Universities*, Metuchen, NJ and London: Society of American Archivists and Scarecrow Press.

19. Cook, T. (1992), 'Mind over Matter: Towards a New Theory of Archival Appraisal', in B.L. Craig (ed.), *The Archival Imagination: Essays in Honour of Hugh A. Taylor*, pp. 38–70, Ottawa: Association of Canadian Archivists.

20. AS4390.5-1996.

21. Mabbs, A.W. and Duboscq, G. (1974), *The Organization of Intermediate Records Storage*, Paris: Unesco. Standards are in Gondos, V. (ed.), (1970), *Reader for Archives and Records Centre Buildings*, London: Society of American Archivists.

22. Cook, M. (1982), 'The Case against Records Centres', *Journal of the Society of Archivists*, **7**, 32–5.

23. Hampson, J. (1978), 'Running a Records Centre', *Records Management 2*, pp. 40–59, London: Society of Archivists, RMG.

24. Hardcastle, S. (1989), 'Providing Storage Facilities', in P. Emmerson (ed.), *How to Manage your Records*, p. 84, ICSA, Cambridge: ISCA.

25. Public Record Office, Records Administration Division (1983), *Manual of Records Administration*, London: PRO, or subsequent editions.

26. Twiss, T. Twiss (ed.) (1871–76), *Black Book of the Admiralty*, London: HMSO.

27. International Records Management Trust, Public Sector Records Project (1997), *Module 9: Records Centre Operations*, London: IRMT.

28. University of Liverpool archives department, 1996.

CHAPTER

ACQUISITION AND ARCHIVAL APPRAISAL

Up to this point, appraisal has been treated in the context of RM, in which the main considerations are administrative value and legal requirements. However, international guidelines for a training curriculum in archives and records management place the subject of appraisal clearly within the area of archival management and not in that of RM.[1] This (to some, eccentric) determination suggests that there is more to be said about the acquisition of archival materials, the assessment of the information within them and the principles behind an archival appraisal programme.

One of the most fundamental activities of an archives service is the delimitation of its field of activity. One naturally assumes that this question might ordinarily be settled at the time when the service was first established, and its aims decided upon. It is a historical curiosity, though, that frequently the question was not considered at an early stage. Many archives services would find it useful to bring the matter into discussion again at suitable intervals, perhaps at the time of their annual report. Things change; new needs are perceived, new absences are spotted in the network of coverage nationally.

It is useful to think of the service's field of activity not only in terms of materials but also in terms of subject, or information, coverage. These two approaches are interlinked. An archives service exercises its interest in subject information by obtaining delegated powers and duties over the records of certain organizations, or by running an RM programme within certain organizations. There are, therefore, two distinct ways in which the assessment of materials for input to the service can take place: by collection and deposit, or by management. In both cases, appraisal must be a part of the acquisition procedure.

Figure 3.1 in the last chapter (p.48) shows the function of RM as a front end to the archives service. The remainder of this chapter explains how RM procedures are used to determine what records are being created and kept, and how they are appraised to determine retention periods.

■ AIMS OF RECORD MANAGEMENT AND ARCHIVES ADMINISTRATION

There is an important difference between the aims of RM and archives administration. RM sets out to control and exploit the information that happens to be contained in the record materials and systems produced by the employing organization. Its value as an information service must always be limited by the boundaries of that information, or by the nature of those materials. Any deficiencies in the information stock that result may perhaps be made up by liaison with special libraries or documentation centres (Figure 3.4, p.54). But in the end, if the organization excludes from its recording work the media which carry a significant area of information, then the RM programme will not be able to provide access to that area of information.

In the case of archives, however, there is a much wider freedom to establish information-directed goals. This is true even in the case of archives services which are closely connected with specific employing organizations, or which are responsible for RM programmes. For example, in the British context, the Public Record Office, ordinarily regarded as limited to the management of narrowly defined public records, is still occasionally prepared to accept important groups of archives from outside central government, if those groups are judged to be closely related to the stock of central government archives. In other countries, the national archives may have the objective of assembling an archive of materials dealing with any important aspect of the national life, or at least of publicly organized aspects of it. Consequently it is common for national archives services to accept and even to seek non-official archive accumulations, if they are judged to have relevant research values. It can perhaps be concluded that there can be such a thing as a national archives policy, which aims to compile, in one institution or in several, a database composed of archival materials, giving subject coverage of national affairs as complete as possible.

Local and specialized archives services, and libraries and museums, naturally play a part in the overall national archives policy. The specific programmes and objectives of archives services, in the field of acquisition, are therefore information directed. They seek to build up banks of information which will cover their chosen field of operation and, ideally, that field will have some sort of link with a national or regional plan.

Choosing its field of operation may be the first serious difficulty encountered by an archives service. Despite talk of a national archives policy, there is a tradition of freedom of action which at times resembles a free-for-all. The positive side to this is that where many institutions compete to provide a service, one result is that there is a multiplication of new resources. This is good because, in fact, the total job is too big for any one institution. The negative side, of course, is that excessive and uncontrolled competition leads to wasteful duplication, and perhaps to the scattering of materials which should be kept together. There ought to be a framework of co-ordination which maximizes the usefulness of the entire bank of resources, but minimizes unproductive competition. Such a framework could aptly be provided by a central agency, for example as a national register of archives, armed with executive powers but working with the trust and co-operation of archivists within the country. As things are, in Britain the NRA lacks statutory powers, and the resources to do much active co-ordination in the face of a tradition of the autonomy of archives services. There have been efforts to establish a broad agreement by informal means, but these have had limited effect.[2]

Informal co-operation between archives services, aided by the professional associations, has indeed improved over the last couple of decades. Cases of virtual piracy which once occurred when important or striking archive accumulations became available have largely disappeared, and only tend to recur where new archives services are generated by institutions which are outside the tradition of debate and consultation developed by the archives profession. A wider knowledge of the issues would be desirable.

The aim of any archives service, within its own agreed field of operation, should be to build up holdings which contain a balanced documentation of the chosen subject area. To achieve a final adequacy these holdings may have to be supplemented by information derived from the holdings of other services, including library and documentation services: this may be achieved by the transfer of materials, but more commonly by producing joint finding aids and co-ordinating access facilities.

The most successful subject-oriented archives services have always been those which have employed full-time staff to do the fieldwork. The task of these archivists would be to identify all possible sources of relevant accumulations, track down their whereabouts and get access to them for the purpose of inspection and (if appropriate) transfer. It is not usually feasible to ask archivists who are fully engaged on other, internal, tasks to take on this aspect of the work as well. Consequently, where there are no full-time fieldwork staff, acquisition of materials from a defined external field tends to be haphazard.

Many archival field projects are aimed at discovering and listing materials arising from a defined set of sources, but not at acquiring them. Such surveys can build up a data bank of information about the materials they find, and can perhaps do something to encourage their deposit in appropriate repositories. The main purpose of these projects remains distinct from questions of custody and access.

Whatever decision may be made as to the field in which archival acquisitions are to be looked for, a survey is the most likely initial tool to start with. Its findings will allow a programme of activities to be drawn up. The survey results will serve as the basis for a file of (actual or potential) creator agencies or persons that fall within the terms of reference. This file can be used to store information concerning the provenance and context of any archival materials that come to hand as a result of the acquisition programme. There is an international standard that can be used to structure the file of creator agencies: this is the International Standard Archival Authority Record for Corporate Bodies, Persons and Families (ISAAR(CPF)). This standard is explained further at the end of the chapter.

Initial surveys and agreements lead to the establishment of an acquisitions policy for the archives service. This might usefully follow the structure of the acquisitions policy adopted by the PRO in 1998.[3] At the head is the strategic objective, which sets out an intention to record a particular area of information, and so to provide a research resource 'for our generation and for future generations', or for a defined user group. Then follows a set of collection themes, which allow the main functions of thematic areas of influence of the creating body to be specified. In the case of central government these include the formulation of policy and control of public resources, the actions undertaken by the executive in the pursuit of agreed policies; certain specific policy areas (foreign relations, social policies, justice) are highlighted; and a general clause, 'the documentation of the social and economic condition of the UK (to include personal data)' is a reminder that archivists should seek to document the environment and exterior effects of their employing organization as well as its internal doings. The acquisitions policy then concludes by listing specific collection policies, summarized as follows:

O   Collection policies are implemented in consultation with research communities and interested parties.
O   Documenting administrative contexts is undertaken in order to make the record of public activity understandable.
O   Costs must be taken into account.
O   Records that are to be kept but are mainly interesting to other bodies may be sent to other places of deposit.

O   Contact will be maintained with creating departments.
O   Exceptions to the main policy are noted.
O   The acquisitions policy is to be reviewed at regular intervals.

ARCHIVAL APPRAISAL

TRADITIONAL APPROACHES

It was recognized in Chapter 3 that there had to be some awareness of research values in those carrying out appraisal for the purposes of an RM system. These values could best be provided for in the system of reviews which are part of most RM programmes.

The Grigg Report of 1954 (rather long ago), concerned only with the records (mainly subject files) of central government departments, led to the setting up of a system of regular reviews for them. Under this, the working principle of the reviewing bodies was to be that there is a close relationship between current administrative values and continuing, or future, research values but that the processes for determining these two kinds of value can be clearly distinguished. In selecting for preservation series which have clear administrative (including legal or financial) values, the records managers were probably also selecting the majority of records which would eventually turn out to be wanted for the archives. The objective of the writers of the Grigg Report, and of the system which was ultimately set up in the public records Acts, was to find a way of shifting the administrative burden of appraisal from the archivists to the administrators.[4]

The main reason for the adoption of this principle was doubtless pragmatic. The size of the archives staff, and its logistic support is never large enough to achieve the full task. Archives services are seldom perceived by Treasury officials as being central to the continuance of government service. The decision was taken to shift the main burden of archival work, appraisal and listing to the originating departments, while encouraging these to adopt RM programmes. The departments were not directly recommended to appoint archivists, but the Inspecting Officers appointed by the PRO were intended to allow an archival viewpoint to be expressed at times when review decisions were made.[5]

A contrary course is always a theoretical possibility, and it has been adopted in countries where RM is carried out as a major service within the Civil Service structure. Here, the task of managing records over all the agencies of government may be undertaken by staff directly employed in the RM administration. Where this is done, the programme naturally has to employ a larger staff than does the PRO. The size of this staff is justified by the fact that they provide services of direct value to the economic and efficient conduct of business.[6]

It might be thought that this approach was in principle a better one than the British example, since it allows professional judgements to be made by professionally qualified people. Experience has shown, however, that this model also has its defects. When recession occurs, arguments of economy and efficiency tend to be discounted either on the grounds that ultimately the archives are a cultural and not an administrative service; or on the grounds that it would be more efficient for the managers of current records to be employed by the record-creating agencies themselves. There is truth in both these arguments, but resulting changes have tended to be to the disadvantage of archives services. On the one hand, they have had to suffer the severance of staff with current RM responsibilities and, on the other, they have tended still to be institutionally subordinated to the demands and structures of current administrative oversight.[7]

The record of the British government in the area of reviewing and appraisal was the subject of an evaluation in the Wilson Report in 1981.[8] The tone of this report was determined by the view taken by the committee that no proposal which involved new expenditure was likely to be successful; the committee also ignored pressures to improve public access to government-generated information. The resulting report found defects in the selection process, but has been criticized as being subservient in tone. The PRO, acting through its small staff of Inspecting Officers, has had great difficulty in making appraisal at all uniform, and in making it operative in all the main departments of government; in fact, there is a general impression that government departments are able to hide the truth in awkward cases, and also sometimes allow uncontrolled destruction of records.

The Grigg rule that appraisal should be delegated to the originating departments derives from a point of high principle which is peculiarly English, and was enunciated in the writings of Sir Hilary Jenkinson. This influential author considered that neither archivists nor researchers should be involved in the appraisal process. This should be done solely by administrators, who would take into account only their own administrative needs. Appraisal should be impartial: the historical record should reflect the biases and idiosyncrasies of the administration of the day, and not those of the academic researchers of that time or of a later time. Of course Jenkinson was right in this, and the phrase in which he recorded his judgement has a fine ring about it:

for an Administrative body to destroy what it no longer needs is a matter entirely within its competence and an action which future ages (even though they may find reason to deplore it) cannot possibly criticise as illegitimate or as affecting the status of the remaining Archives; provided always that the administration proceeds only upon those grounds upon which alone it is competent to make a decision – the needs of its own practical business; provided, that is, that it can refrain from thinking of itself as a body producing historical evidences.[9]

Archival appraisal certainly should be done with impartiality; but as Jenkinson tacitly admitted in the parenthetic qualification, it should be done with expert knowledge. The knowledge required is that of someone who can represent the interests of research to the world of administration; and who can represent the needs of administration to the world of research. This is a definition of an archivist. In any case, it is clear that archivists are themselves administrators. Many commentators would also say that government agencies ought to see themselves as producing evidences, if only to ensure that they themselves can be held to account.

The principles behind the American approach were laid down by T.R. Schellenberg.[10] This analysis, like Jenkinson's, perceives that there are primary and secondary values in records. Primary values are the ones which the administrators had in mind when they created the record; secondary values are those other values, such as research values, which might eventually become apparent. This looks very like the Grigg distinction between administrative and 'historical' values, and though Schellenberg's perception of administrative practice was not close to that of Jenkinson's, most archivists may accept this correspondence in practice, as a useful rule of thumb.

Archival appraisal centres upon the secondary values. In Schellenberg's model, these are now subdivided into 'evidential' and 'informational' values. These two terms of art, although now fairly widely accepted and used outside the National Archives of the USA, still remain rather opaque to most readers. This terminological difficulty may suggest that the words do not strictly correspond with real concepts, though there is now a considerable weight of experience behind them.

Certainly there is something suspicious about the first of the two terms. Evidential values attach to records which give evidence as to the origin, development and conduct of the organization itself: therefore, the records of evidential value are the ones which spring to prominence when the history of the organization itself is being studied. They cover subjects which are useful for writing administrative histories and structural descriptions, traditionally the stock-in-trade of archivists. Descriptions like this depend on the archivist's ability to establish and write down the information required to record the provenance of the archives of the organization he or she is working on. The training of an archivist, in most countries, also depends considerably on learning national administrative, institutional or legal history. From this we can see that evidential values correspond very closely to one of the archivist's main professional preoccupations. Is it possible to conclude that an archivist's tendency to preserve, first of all and perhaps mainly, the materials for the institutional history of an organization, is based upon a delusion, and that they should be concentrating instead on identifying and preserving records which give useful information on subjects external to the creating organization's history? These would be documents which belong to the alternative category, those that have informational values. Such a view might be reinforced by the fact that, unlike the 'evidential' concept, this one is easier to understand and remember.

If records contain information about subjects external to the direct work of the creating agency, they have informational values. These values should be substantial: they should belong to records 'contributing substantially to research and scholarship in any field of knowledge'.[11]

The registers of a company's shareholders may be evidence of that company's financing and control (an evidential value); but they may also be a source of information on the financial activities of certain individuals (an informational value). Many (but not all) records of informational value are case papers of some kind. Among the records of a social service department, the evidential values will reside in the records of policy-making, and the statistical effect of the service. The informational values may well prove to be in the case files which document the individuals affected by the service. These are likely to be voluminous, and difficult to manage.[12]

Informational values have had unfavourable comment from archival writers. The Grigg Report accepted the principle that no record should be preserved simply because it might be valuable either for historical or for genealogical research.[13] This view follows naturally from the report's decision to put the main emphasis on administrative (primary) values. There is a corollary, however. If an ephemeral record is destroyed after appraisal, the judgement of the appraiser is not necessarily to be called into question if, thereafter, someone happens to call for that record. All records carry some information, and if it is granted that most records (in terms of bulk) must be destroyed, and only a small proportion of the most valuable preserved, then we must reconcile ourselves to losing items which some people would have liked to keep. Nevertheless, it would be perverse to carry the principle further, and say that because there is likely to be public interest in a record, that is a contra-indication to adjudging it worthy of retention. The public pays, ultimately, and so has a basic right to have access, and to have its wishes respected in appraisal.

If it is accepted that an important reason for keeping archives is that they can be used to call their creating organizations to account, then that accountability may as well reside in documents kept for their informational values. In Britain the declared policy of the archival profession is that accountability is one of the main reasons for keeping archives. Its 1996 declaration included as its first principle the following: 'A civilised society, concerned to uphold the rights of the citizen, to encourage efficient administration and to ensure that the true facts of its history are accessible to all, should make provision for its archives to be preserved and made available for consultation.'[14]

Both Jenkinson and Schellenberg based their appraisal analyses on an examination of the actual documentary material upon which a decision had to be made. This approach can therefore be fairly called reactive: no one is called upon for a decision until the records have been long produced and have passed out of full currency. Modern RM, even where electronic records are not concerned, demands a more proactive approach, and at least preliminary appraisal should be applied to records at the time of their creation, or during their period of currency. Moreover, by appraising records which are no longer current there may be a danger that some activities of the creating organization are not being documented.

MACRO-APPRAISAL AND DOCUMENTATION STRATEGIES

Recent discussions of the principles involved in archival appraisal have therefore emphasized the need to look first at what information should be held in the record. To do this demands that the appraiser's first act should be to analyse the functions that are or ought to be discharged in the body under examination. Appraisal continues by seeking out documents or sources that would record those functions. This approach is variously termed the 'documentation strategy' or (especially if applied to government agencies) 'macro-appraisal'.[15]

Documentation strategy has turned out to be of major importance both as a reassessment of archival appraisal and in the subjects taught in archival training. The functional analysis of creating organizations is not perhaps fundamentally different from the historical study of them that has always been the business of archivists, but does point them towards the functions and activities that are going on today in preference to those of previous times. The approach, though, is fruitful in all kinds of contexts. Samuels's study of university records is a useful guide to applying the technique to other kinds of institution.[16] She herself applied it to documenting the activities carried out by a group of firms in a science park.[17] Cox has gone on to develop the approach in relation to institutions and also to territorial areas, so we may see that it is valid for collecting bodies as much as for institutional archives services.[18] Recent developments in archival training show that teachers on archival courses are increasingly ready to shift the emphasis from administrative history to functional analysis of institutions.

THE CONCEPT OF PERMANENCE

Traditionally, archival appraisal is intended to be a process that will select those few records that should be kept permanently from those many that should at some point be destroyed. Until recently the concept of permanence has been taken with the utmost seriousness.

There are some archives which are national or international treasures and which we must seriously strive to keep for ever.[19] There are not many of these: each reader will doubtless have his or her own list. Since archives are inherently bulky, some of these treasures will occupy a great deal of space. One person might accept the great series of medieval rolls held in the PRO as being in this category; but another might include only the Domesday Book and the Magna Carta. There are two characteristics of archives in this category of permanence, which serve to define it: they are 'worth a visit' (in the words of the guide-books) by the public; and they have been or are the subject of intensive study and publication by scholars. For these, the best form of descriptive finding aid is a full transcript, probably with a facsimile. To preserve them for ever (setting aside doubts about the overweening nature of human pride and self-absorption) requires costly and elaborate preparations: in fact, logically it would require precautions which not many countries have been prepared to undertake, such as bomb-proof storage dug into mountainsides.

Archives, nevertheless, are voluminous. Every year the PRO takes in records which will fill an additional 1.5 kilometres of shelving, and this after rigorous selection. It might seem that there should be two main retention categories, which might be labelled as follows:

1. 'These I am going to try to keep for ever.'
2. 'These I am going to keep as long as they last, with reasonable care.'

The second category might be termed, in more official language, as destined for indefinite retention. The length of time meant by indefinite may sometimes be extended by using microfilm or other copying systems. Good quality storage, a controlled environment and careful access management are still required; but there is a notional acceptance of the view (probably not explicitly stated anywhere) that there is a limit to the resources which are to be committed to the conservation of these materials.[20]

A good way to calculate where this limit may be is by working out the financial implications. In most circumstances it should be possible to establish what is the cost of keeping a given quantity of archives over a given period of time. Capital expenditure amortised, plus recurrent costs (including staffing), can be divided by the number of linear metres of shelving in use. This will provide the cost per year of each linear metre. In the case of the most valuable materials, the usefulness of this information is limited since, if the archival material has unquestionably passed the tests of permanent retention, then it is not justifiable to introduce economies which would have the effect of directly reducing its life expectancy. In all other cases it is a piece of information that should be known and published. Cost is one of the two specific and measurable criteria to be taken into account in the course of appraisal. The second measurable criterion is, of course, the actual rate of reference access to the series over its period of existence. It is hard to see how any sort of systematic appraisal can be carried out without these two pieces of information. With them, a cost-value ratio can be established, which will be important, though perhaps not always decisive, in the retention decision.

Cost-value calculations are not the whole answer to appraisal problems, but they are a necessary part of the data on which appraisal decisions may be based. A document's value to research, and the value of the research itself, are both matters of opinion; although of course it should be an informed opinion held by someone with experience of research. The judgement eventually reached should be one which has a term of years in mind. Thus records which have successfully passed the archival appraisal test, will have done so as 'to be archived and kept 100 years' or 'indefinitely' (i.e. in category 2 above); very rarely, or perhaps even never (nowadays) 'to be kept for ever'. We live in a world of relative values, and one in which values have to be quantified.

Appraisal periods for archives should be long by any current standard. Access controls for many documents that hold personal information (and these are often very much in demand) frequently continue for 100 years, and this type of restriction appears likely to be extended rather than reduced in data protection legislation.

SAMPLING

Sampling remains a possibility when considering the acquisition of long series. An important RAMP study by Felix Hull has clarified issues which had long been doubtful.[21] This report comments that the appraisal process itself, being concerned with the selection of some material and the rejection of others, is a form of sampling. In this sense the debate and use of archival sampling may continue indefinitely into the future. Apart from this, the Hull report may have come almost too late. We have already begun to think about using computers to interpret archival data, and about the special problems of appraising databases held in machine-readable form. These two developments may mean that the experience painfully learned about how to sample hard-copy records may not continue to be useful long into the future.

Hull's report makes it clear that there are several preconditions before sampling can validly be used as a solution to appraisal problems. These are specified in the guidelines for sampling procedures which it contains. In particular the technique can only be applied where there is a series of uniform or homogeneous records which cannot be retained in the original or in a microform copy.

Five alternative methods of sampling are discussed:

1. *Keeping typical examples*. This traditional method of indicating the presence and general nature of a series which has been destroyed is still sometimes useful. Finding aids should indicate what has been kept and why. The technique is perhaps particularly apt in a museum context, since the items retained are mainly useful for illustration or display.

2. *Purposive sampling*. This, too, has been a traditional method used by archivists dealing with large series, especially where these have not been fully homogeneous. The principle is to keep those items which relate to a selected subject (for example, all records relating to riot), or to defined individuals (for example, all records mentioning persons included in *Who's Who*).

3. *Systematic sampling*. In this method a rule is adopted for the selection of certain items. Topographical examples may be taken where there are topographical items within the series. An alphabetical criterion can be used if the items are alphabetically coded or titled. Numerical or serial sampling can be used if they are numbered; and chronological sampling if the records are kept by date. The selection rule will specify which are to be kept: one from each topographical point, all representatives of the letters H-P, every twenty-fifth numerical entry; records for every year ending in '5'. These examples do not suggest the best possibilities which this method has. A systematic sample could be devised to record and illustrate specially characteristic items of information, and may be based upon significant patterns or periodicities in the records.

4. *Random sampling*. This is the only method which allows a scientifically satisfactory evaluation of the quantitative meaning of the whole series, calculated from the surviving sample. In a true random sample, each item has in principle an exactly equal chance of being chosen to represent the series. There must be a numerical method of identifying items, and a random number table, or its equivalent, must be used. The size of the sample taken is also significant; the larger the better.

5. *Mixed systems*. The discussion of the problem in the Hull report and elsewhere suggests that in an archival context no single one of these sampling methods is likely to be entirely satisfactory. A mixture of methods is possible, provided that they are applied in an order which does not interfere with the operation of the system. Thus it is possible to combine random and purposive samples, but the random sample must be applied first, and any resulting empty spaces in the second sample would have to be supplied with cross-references.

PREDICTION OF RESEARCH VALUES

The most difficult part of archival appraisal is the prediction of future research value. It is notorious that currently popular research themes, and the sources for them, were neglected in the past, and that new lines of research come about as a result of the initiatives or discoveries of gifted individuals. Yet, at the same time, appraisal is necessarily based upon the prediction of likely lines of development in research.

Prediction can never be wholly successful. Nevertheless, systematic attempts to marshal the existing evidence both on the nature of the sources and the research which has been done on them will lead the appraiser a good way towards success. The popularity, or practicability, of any topic is profoundly affected by the accessibility of its sources, so it is also possible to stimulate new research by publicizing these. These two activities were undertaken in a series of major conferences organized by the National Archives of the USA in the early 1970s, the results of which were published by the Ohio University Press,[22] but there are many other examples where research topics have been stimulated by thoughtful publicity.

Another way in which the course of research can be predicted to some extent is by encouraging archivists to maintain an active role in research fields. The archives service may set itself the goal of being an active research institute, and many do so. It is doubtless easier for a specialist archives service to achieve this position than a generalist one. The Glasgow University Archives, which has an important special interest in business archives, is known as a centre of information for that subject and several publications have been the result.[23] On the other hand, a county record office, which contains multifarious archives from all sorts of sources but whose area of specialization is territorial, may find that, though it has successfully become a centre of local studies, its best chance of achieving prominence as a research institute is by developing a specific interest proper to the area. The former Clwyd Record Office, for instance, has developed an expertise in the history of mining.[24] Archivists must remain active participants in subjects of research on which their office has significant holdings or else they will not be able to represent research interests in administrative settings.[25]

APPRAISAL AS PROCESS

The discussion so far has suggested that appraisal is something which may occur once and for all at a given moment. Although this does happen, it is not the only or, perhaps, the best way.

First, there may be retrospective appraisal. Most recent commentators have accepted that appraisal decisions made too loosely in the past should be reconsidered.[26] Of course, this only applies to affirmative appraisal decisions, for the sad fact is that records which are turned down at first appraisal are usually destroyed. Should we go back over our archival holdings, test them against the frequency of research reference or against our mission statement, or even against our budget commitments, and reappraise? Most archivists would agree that there are cases where this might be beneficial, but also perhaps that the dangers outweigh the possible benefits. Academic fashions exist just as much as clothing fashions. If the passing of one fashion and the coming of another were to lead to the wholesale destruction of archives, we would ultimately be sorry.

Secondly, appraisal is a process rather than an event. Maynard Brichford set this out well in an earlier training manual:

> Records appraisal is best considered as a process that requires extensive staff preparation, a thorough analysis of the origin and characteristics of record series, a knowledge of techniques for the segregation and selection of records, an awareness of the development of research methodologies and needs, and a sequential consideration of administrative, research and archival values.[27]

DELEGATION

Even where the conservational aims are redefined narrowly, archives management and storage is expensive. It may be necessary to call in help, particularly where a large accumulation of archives, bearing on some definable subject area, is concerned. Storage and access costs could often be borne by an appropriate research institution, at the cost of taking that material away from the archives repository which in strict custom should have looked after them. Institutional pride may be hurt, but it is the overall increase of resources which is the end benefit to society. Thus the PRO's decision to allow the University of Newfoundland to retain and manage on its behalf the residue of the Crew Lists may be applauded because it brought into play new repository space and new staffing resources.[28]

Many appraisal decisions may be aided by introducing the possibility of delegation to a specialist agency. In many countries it has been established that any sort of archival materials may be deposited in publicly financed repositories, without cost to the owner and without loss of ownership. Of course, in this case, the burden of appraisal decisions is shifted to the repository's staff, who will approach the problem in the light of their own stated aims.

■ THE PROCESS OF ACCESSIONING

Since provenance and custodial history remain important in interpreting archival sources, it is essential that consignments of archives should be registered on arrival, and that the register of accessions remains as a permanent record. This requirement is one of the many points of difference between libraries and archives services. Contextual and provenance information is part of the metadata that must be retained with any acquisition of archival materials. The register of accessions may be derived from the file of (actual or potential) creator agencies or persons that may have been compiled at the time of the initial survey. Consequently, it will best be structured in conformity with the relevant international standard, ISAAR(CPF).[29]

The decision to use the formats laid down in ISAAR(CPF) may involve a decision to place all contextual or provenance metadata in this file and to exclude it from the main descriptions, which will follow the format of another international standard, ISAD(G).[30] If this is done, there must be provision for cross-referencing. Archival descriptions always consist of both contextual and content information, but it is perfectly acceptable for these two categories to be held in separate but cross-linked files. This question is dealt with in Chapter 6.

> There are a number of reasons why separate capture and maintenance of contextual information may be useful. Such a practice enables the linking

of this information to descriptions of archival documents from the same creator(s) that may be held by more than one repository, or separately held archival documents and library materials that have the same creator(s), or records that remain in the custody of their creator. Such links can facilitate historical research and improve records management practices.[31]

As its name suggests, the standard is also intended to allow for the authority control of names of creating bodies and persons. The question of authority control in archives work is discussed in Chapter 7. The purpose of it is to ensure uniform usage, so that files containing these names can eventually be exchanged and joined into a single finding aid. The main principle is that the names entered as headings in the file should be controlled. They must first be composed in accordance with appropriate rules, and then submitted for inclusion in an authority file. No further entries should then be permitted to the file unless the proposed new entry either:

○   appears already as an entry, or
○   follows the rules and is authorized.

THE STRUCTURE OF AN ISAAR(CPF) FILE

The ISAAR(CPF) contains three areas, each divided into dedicated fields, as follows:

1.   Authority control area: provides for the creation of the authorized entry in the file.
   1.1   Identity code. Identifies both the organization creating the authority record, and the material being described, uniquely. International country codes and national codes may be used
   1.2   Type of archival authority record. Indicates whether this record relates to a corporate body, person or family.
   1.3   Authority entry. Creates a standardized access point filed under the name of the creator agency.
   1.4   Parallel entry/entries. Indicates any standardized alternative access points. In practice this field is only used in situations where more than one official language is used.
   1.5   Non-preferred terms. Creates a 'see' record, providing an access point to a form of the name that may be encountered by users but which is not the form adopted under the authority rules.
   1.6   Related authority entry/entries. Creates a 'see also' record, linking to related material held under a different creator's name.

2. Information area: allows for any contextual data to be added to the authorized entry.
   2.1 Corporate bodies. Allows for the insertion of relevant data, such as names, places, dates etc.
   2.2 Persons. As with corporate bodies.
   2.3 Families. As with corporate bodies.
3. Note area: provides information on how and when the authority record was established.
   3.1 Archivist's note. How it was established and by whom.
   3.2 Rules or conventions. Names the specific rules or conventions which were followed.
   3.3 Date. When the authority record was created.

See Figure 4.1 for an example of an entry structured according to ISAAR(CPF).

GBR HCRO/LA/NP

Newton Parsival Rural Sanitary Authority

see also Harperton, Humberland, Sponton

Newton Parsival Rural (named Newton under Forest 1872–79) Sanitary Authority was set up under the Public Health Act 1872. The Rural District Council of Harperton, established under the Local Government Act 1894, inherited the functions of the former Rural Sanitary Authority in 1895 when the Act came into operation. Harperton Rural District Council was abolished on 1 April 1937 and the area split up among the neighbouring local authorities, namely Sponton Urban District Council (UDC), and Humberland UDC.

From 1872 to 1894 the office of Clerk was discharged by a local firm of solicitors, Messrs Smith and Jones [address]. Subsequently the clerkship was discharged by officers of the UDC.

Archives deposited at the Hertbury County Record Office in 1937.

Entry established by WB at HCRO.

In-house rules

23 Mar 1984

Figure 4.1   An example of an entry structured according to ISAAR(CPF)

As with all such standards, it is not obligatory to enter data into any field or area, except of course (if the standard is used at all) into the authority entry itself. Fields not immediately relevant should be left empty. The completeness of the data entered should be determined by the archives service that is using it, under house rules aimed at quality control. The rules and forms adopted should, where possible, follow those in force or used customarily in the country, region or house. There is therefore a need for these to be developed where they do not already exist.

One of the reasons for adopting ISAAR(CPF) as a structure for an authority file of creating agencies is that this file can be a powerful tool for many purposes in the service. Most obviously, the entries in it are a list of sources that fall within the collecting remit. They can be used as a checklist of organizations that have and have not yet been contacted. It is in this context that combined authority files can be used jointly by groups of specialized repositories, by regional archives services or to concern activity nationally.

An authority file of creating agencies can be linked with the accessions register, in order to provide the contextual metadata for any particular acquisition. It is most important that an accessions register should be kept. The register may be used for two purposes other than simply recording the acquisition's arrival and origin:

1.   To provide some sort of acknowledgement to the originator or former custodian of the archive.
2.   To control the various processes in the archives service.

Therefore, it has been suggested that the best form of accessions register might be a loose-leaf one, in which each accession is described on a triplicated form. The top copy, which should be treated as permanent, would contain details of the archive, its origin, provenance and custodial history, including the date of transfer. The second copy might carry a printed letter of acknowledgement, with the archives service's address, which could be sent to the transferor of the archive. The third copy, to be kept perhaps in the central workroom, might contain columns for completion when the various stages were complete: sorting, boxing, shelving, listing, indexing, repair.[32] Of course, all these manual processes can be effected in a single operation if the accessions register is held as a computer database.

Since central registration of archival transfers is a national interest, a note might be appropriate for sending to the NRA. This might be done by means of a fourth copy, or incorporated into the computer system.

Registration of new accessions begins the administrative control of the material, as it passes through the processing stage towards final exploitation.

NOTES

1. Cook, M. (1982), *Guidelines for Curriculum Development in Records Management and the Administration of Modern Archives: a RAMP Study*, Paris: Unesco.
2. Such as that established by the Merseyside Archives Liaison Group. Information from Liverpool City Archives.
3. PRO draft proposal 20 January 1998.
4. Grigg Report: see discussion in Cook, M. (1977), *Archives Administration*, pp. 63 ff., Folkestone, Dawson.
5. Public Record Office, Records Administration Division (1982 and later), *Manual of Records Administration*, Part II, London: PRO.
6. Following the model proposed by the International Records Management Trust. At the time of writing the best example of this model in practice was the National Records Administration set up by the Government of Ghana (1997).
7. This paragraph was written in the light of the experience of the National Records and Archives Administration in the USA over the post-war decades: see also the Wilson Report (1981), *Modern Public Records, Selection and Access*, Cmd 8204, London: HMSO; and *Modern Public Records* (1982), Cmd 8531, London: HMSO.
8. Wilson Report (1981).
9. Jenkinson, C.H. (1922), *A Manual of Archive Administration*, original edn; 2nd edn revd (1965), pp. 149–50, London: Lund Humphries.
10. Schellenberg, T.R. (1956), *Modern Archives, Principles and Techniques*, Chicago: University of Chicago Press.
11. Rieger, M.(1979), 'Modern Records Retirement and Appraisal Practice', *Unesco Journal of Information Science, Librarianship and Archives Administration*, **1**, 200–209.
12. Whittick, M.H. (1988), *The Records of Social Services Departments: Their Retention and Management*, 2nd edn, London: Society of Archivists, RMG.
13. The Grigg Report (1954), *Report of the Committee on Departmental Records*, Cmd 9163, sections 105 and 108, London: HMSO.
14. National Archives Policy Liaison Group (1996) *An Archives Policy for the United Kingdom: Statement of Principles and Policy Objectives*, London: National Council on Archives.
15. The term 'macro-appraisal' was coined by Terry Cook in the context of Canadian federal government appraisal: Cook, T. (1992), 'Mind over Matter: Towards a New Theory of Archival Appraisal', in B.L. Craig (ed.), *The Archival Imagination: Essays*

in Honour of Hugh A. Taylor, Ottawa: Association of Canadian Archivists. See also Cox, R.J. (1995), 'Archival Documentation Strategy, a Brief Intellectual History', *Janus*, **2**, 76–93; Cox, R.J. (1992), *Managing Institutional Archives: Foundational Principles and Practices*, New York: Greenwood Press.

16. Samuels, H.W. (1992), *Varsity Letters: Documenting Modern Colleges and Universities,* Metuchen, NJ and London: Society of American Archivists and Scarecrow Press.

17. Samuels, H.W. and Simmons, B.T. (1985), *Appraising the Records of Modern Science and Technology: a Guide*, Chicago: Society of American Archivists; Samuels, H.W. (1995), 'Appraising Records of Modern Science and Technology', *Janus*, **2**, 8–19.

18. Cox, R.J. (1996), *Documenting Localities: a Practical Model for American Archivists and Manuscript Curators*, Lanham, MD and London: Society of American Archivists and Scarecrow Press.

19. Unesco's Memory of the World project is aimed at the identification of these.

20. The concept is not explicit in Kitching, C. (1996), *Archives: the Very Essence of our Heritage*, London: Phillimore, for the National Council on Archives, although this presents the argument for preserving materials and the work of the National Manuscripts Conservation Trust.

21. Hull, F. (1981), *The Use of Sampling Techniques in the Retention of Records: a RAMP Study*, Paris: Unesco.

22. Fishbein, M. (1973), *The National Archives and Statistical Research*, Columbus, OH: Ohio University Press.

23. Moss, M. and Hume, J.R. (1977), *The Workshop of the British Empire: Engineering and Shipbuilding in the West of Scotland*, London: Heinemann.

24. Now the Flintshire Record Office. Chaloner, W.H. and Richardson, R.C. (1976), *British Economic and Social History: a Bibliographic Guide*, Manchester: Manchester University Press.

25. Brichford, M.J. (1977), *Archives and Manuscripts: Appraisal and Accessioning*, Chicago: Society of American Archivists Basic Manuals series. This manual has been replaced by Ham, F.G. (1993), *Selecting and Appraising Archives and Manuscripts*, Archival Fundamentals Series, Chicago: Society of American Archivists. However the latter is more sceptical about the process.

26. Rapport, L. (1981), 'No Grandfather Clause: Reappraising Accessioned Records', *The American Archivist*, **44**, 143–50. This has given rise to extensive debate ever since.

27. Brichford (1977), p. 2. A good summary is in Reed, B. (1993), 'Appraisal and Disposal', in J. Ellis (ed.), *Keeping Archives*, Sydney: Thorpe, in association with the Australian Society of Archivists.

28. Cook (1977), pp. 73–5.
29. International Council on Archives (ICA) (1996), *ISAAR(CPF): International Standard Archival Authority Record for Corporate Bodies, Persons and Families*, Ottawa: Secretariat of the ICA Ad Hoc Commission on Descriptive Standards. These ICA documents are available at http://www.archives.ca/ica/dds/.
30. International Council on Archives (1993), *ISAD(G): General International Standard Archival Description*, Ottawa: Secretariat of the ICA Ad Hoc Commission on Descriptive Standards.
31. ICA (1996), 1.3.
32. Cook (1977), pp. 100–103.

ARCHIVAL ARRANGEMENT

The arrangement of archives is an essential operation in the process of managing the information contained in them. Arrangement is also an important step in the conservation of the materials, governing their disposition and housing in the repository. For the same reason, it is a process necessary to their administrative control. But, in addition, arrangement is an essential part of the eventual exploitation of the archive in reference and research: it is an aspect of intellectual as well as administrative control. The arrangement of an archive is an essential part of the process which will lead to the creation of a representation file, the basis of a system of finding aids, which will provide the user (including staff users) with both a conceptual and an administrative overview of the material. Most importantly, however, the arrangement of an assembly of archives perpetuates and demonstrates relationships between its components, explaining and authenticating the significance of the information in them. The activities which support this have traditionally been known as the moral defence of archives, and are central to the professional ethic of archivists.[1]

 THE MORAL DEFENCE OF ARCHIVES

T.R. Schellenberg observed that arrangement:

> is largely a process of grouping individual documents into meaningful units and of grouping such units in a meaningful relation to one another. An archivist, continually and instinctively, must bring order and relation to unrelated things by sorting and categorising – to the end of revealing the content and significance of the records with which he works.[2]

Initially, the main purpose of archival arrangement is to reduce disorder and restore (or introduce) order into the mass of materials which makes up an archival group or collection. This is a management exercise, not merely a physical process: it involves research and planning, and it ought to be carried out at a level which will provide overall control over what are usually large quantities of material. The aim is to organize these quantities into manageable divisions and subdivisions, but also to protect and demonstrate the meaning, authority and significance of the information content. Moral defence is concerned with managing information, even though it may depend on an examination and ordering of physical materials to do so.

The purpose of moral defence is to establish the evidential significance of the archives. Why should this be necessary? In a library or documentation centre, any particular bibliographic item should be able to explain itself. Its title identifies it, and its content can be adequately delineated by an abstract. By contrast, an archival accumulation has to have additional information (the general term for which is 'metadata') which can explain to the user the basic facts about the system and organization that originally created the material. Single documents or sets of documents taken from an archive are usually not fully self-explanatory. They are most often identified by a reference code rather than by a title, and neither the meaning nor the authenticity of such fragments can be taken without investigation.

The work of an archivist in arrangement therefore begins with the study of the context or provenance of the material being processed, and of the system which was employed to bring it into existence, and to store and use it during its period of currency; it is also often necessary to understand the custodial history of the material since that initial period. By placing the archives in an order which is the same as, or which corresponds to or reflects, that of the original system, an archivist is providing a statement on meaning and authenticity: this statement is the main strong point of the moral defence of the archives, for it ensures that the evidential meaning of the archives will be understood for ever afterwards. To do this work, archivists must spend time in research, investigating and analysing the provenance of their material, the administrative systems which, historically, have produced the archive, and the story of its adventures since.

T.R. Schellenberg said:

> Basic to practically all activities of the archivist is his analysis of records. This analysis involves him in studies of the organisational and functional origins of records to obtain information on their provenance – subject, content and interrelations ... Analytical activities are the essence of an archivist's work; the other activities that are based on them are largely of a physical nature.[3]

The term 'evidential' is used because (as has often been pointed out) archives have the special characteristic that, since they actually formed part of the administrative or business process which their information relates to, what they say carries a particular weight as primary evidence for statements made, or conclusions drawn, about that process.

Therefore, archival arrangement cannot generally use universal classifications, since the material cannot be sorted into predetermined categories. The categories (subgroups) which can be used are discovered by carrying out an analysis of the origins and functions of the archive-creating agency, and then by a study of the relationships between physically or organizationally associated sets (classes or series).

Since an important objective is the administrative control of the material, groups, subgroups and series of archives must in the end be of manageable size and shape. Archival management should take account of this need. Nevertheless, the principal purpose of archival arrangement is the moral defence of the archive, and its outcome should in general be the sorting of the materials into an order, and into groupings, which demonstrate their original meaning.

The chief source of information used by archivists in their research into the provenance, archival order and custodial history of the group is the materials themselves. By noting their physical shape, reference codes or other control information in them, the names and status of officials or important personalities mentioned, and the functions of each as reflected in the documents, the analyst can establish the outlines of an administrative history for the group. Additional sources of information will frequently have to be found, in reference books, secondary works, or sometimes in the recollections of people associated with the creating organization.

Some groups or collections do not have a clearly perceived provenance, or an easily outlined administrative or custodial history. These may have to be treated in ways which seem (at least) to set aside the rule of restoring original order. The arrangement of materials in this special case is discussed separately.

LEVELS OF ARRANGEMENT

Following these principles of moral defence, the archivist's first action in taking over a newly acquired mass of archival material is to decide how to break it down into a structured series of levels and groupings. Since they are based upon an analysis of the originating system, these breakdowns both assist a logical understanding of the make-up of the archive accumulation, but also perpetuate and reinforce the original relationships of parts of the archive to each other.[4]

The number and nature of the levels used to control a group depend not only on its original structure but on the management needs of the archives service itself. It is important that the archivist should be quite clear how many levels are to be used, which level is being treated at any particular moment and how the different levels relate to each other. The relationship of levels within groups should be understood not only within the group being treated but also between the groups in the repository's holdings and (since there is an international standard for this) across those in the holdings of other repositories. Finding aids might include a statement on the levels used, and this could appear at the beginning, or in the introduction.

The most commonly used levels of arrangement are groups (fonds), subgroups, series and items. For the sake of clarity, these are the terms that should be used. But if there are more than four levels (in a more complex arrangement), it is probably better to use numbers, rather than terms such as sub-subgroup. This is illustrated in Figure 5.1, which explains the numeration used.

The division of an archive into levels is always a most important part of its arrangement. There will always be at least two, and probably at least four, levels in any particular accumulation of archives. Each level needs to be dealt with in an appropriate way. The higher levels, in which larger groupings are dealt with more or less in bulk, can be considered as 'macro' levels; the lower ones, where documents or other units can be taken item by item, and in detail, are 'micro' levels. The concepts of macro and micro levels relate principally to archival description, but since arrangement and description are closely interlinked activities in archival management, a full definition of the levels normally applicable can be given here.

This analysis of levels in archival arrangement, and the names they should be given, is based on recent writing, mainly American, but there has been discussion for many years and in many countries both on the nature of levels of arrangement and on the terminology suitable for them.

Sir Hilary Jenkinson established the definition of an Archive Group in his *Manual* first published in 1922.[5] He naturally based his thought upon the practice and terminology of the PRO, which at that time used the stable and historic ministries or government departments as the basis of its principal divisions of material. The archives emanating from each of these was known as an Archive Group. Within these the PRO used the class as its only subdivision and main control point. Within classes, individual items ('pieces' in PRO terminology) were listed serially.

0.	Repository level	
1.	Management group	Management levels
1.n	Subgroup	
1.nn	Possible sub-subgroups	
2.	Group/collection: *fonds*	Macro description levels
2.n	Subgroup	
2.nn	Possible sub-subgroups	
3.	Series (class): *series*	Main control level
3.n	Possible subseries	
4.	Item: *file*	Micro description levels
5.	Piece (document)	

Source: MAD2, ISAD(G)

Figure 5.1   Levels of arrangement and description

In current discussion, it has been assumed that the PRO term 'archive group' can be used as a synonym for the international 'fonds'; 'class' may be used for the international term 'series', although it should be recognized that, in the past, practice at the PRO has not always been consistent. A careful study of PRO descriptions shows that levels intermediate to the group and class were at times admitted, but usually were not reflected in the reference codes. Both then and now reference codes in the PRO consist simply of a letter-number sequence which suggests only three levels: for example, FO 84/2030 refers to file no. 2030 within class 84 of the Foreign Office archive group. In citation, a fourth level often appears when individual papers upon the file are quoted. The example would then be FO84/2030, no. 140, which is a letter from Lord Salisbury to Sir Edward Malet written in May 1890.

North American practice, both in public archives services and in manuscript libraries, was based upon a variation of the same principle.

The American 'record group' could either be the same as the British archive group (i.e. the archives emanating from a particular autonomous administrative unit), or it could be a portmanteau within which were assembled, for administrative convenience, the archives of a number of originating units. These units might be linked in this way because they had some common characteristic, but also might be brought together arbitrarily.

There was no development of theory from this point in Britain, but by the early 1960s, O.W. Holmes, in a staff instruction paper for the National Archives of the USA, proposed a standard five-level system.[6] Simultaneously, faced with growing administrative instability at archive group level, P.J. Scott, writing from his Australian experience, suggested in 1966 the possibility of abandoning the archive group as the main administrative control, and adopting the series (class) as an alternative.[7] However, it was not until the publication of the work of two American analysts, R.H. Lytle and R. Berner, that the distinctions underlying the principle of archival levels became fully clear.[8] What are now universally recognized levels of archival arrangement and description are now expressed in the relevant international standards.[9]

Lack of precision in the meaning of the terms by which levels of arrangement are known had certainly fogged the issues to a considerable extent up till then. In particular, there had been widespread confusion as to the distinction between subgroups and series; this can have serious consequences as series are today often designated as the principal level of control in archives services.

The publication of MAD2 in 1990 made possible a generally agreed definition of the levels of archival arrangement, with a terminology assimilated to British practice. In Figure 5.1, a model showing a system of ten levels of archival arrangement is shown, using level numbers according to the system used in MAD2. The international standard archival description, ISAD(G), agreed at the International Congress on Archives in Montreal in 1992 also uses the same model for the levels, but does not set out to establish numbers for them.

LEVEL 0: THE REPOSITORY

This level is apparent only where multi-repository sets of archives are concerned. It is clear that archives are distributed among repositories, and therefore this must logically be regarded as the upper level of arrangement. The level is numbered zero, since it will not be used in arrangements of material within the repository. It will be important, though, when a national or regional catalogue is published.[10]

The reference code of an archive cited in a research document must carry as its first element an identification of the repository where it is kept. In international exchanges, this element should also include a code to indicate the country in which the repository is situated.[11]

LEVEL 1: MANAGEMENT GROUP

The term 'management group' is used in MAD2 to indicate groupings of actual or potential creator bodies that are above the level of the *fonds*, or (archive) group. There is no international term for this level of arrangement and description, since ISAD(G) deals only with levels at or below the group, but during discussions in the international congress there were calls for a definition of what some colleagues then termed 'super-fonds'. The need for levels of arrangement and description of this kind is underlined by the growing acceptance, internationally, of the Australian practice of managing archival holdings at series level, and maintaining separate files to hold descriptions of creating bodies, potential creators, and bodies that had or might have had some contextual relationship with the archives. An example of a management group description is shown in Figure 5.2.

The practice of conceptually gathering the holdings of a repository into large categories with some common characteristic related to provenance is widespread. When used in this way (like an American record group), this level of arrangement is operative only in the organization of the repository and in its published finding aids, and not in any physical arrangement of the material. Repositories can certainly be found where components of the main management groups are stored

---

SMALL BOROUGHS AND TOWN TRUSTS

Many small towns and large villages had anciently acquired some of the attributes of borough status but were not accepted as boroughs under the Municipal Corporations Act 1835. Other settlements had bodies of feoffees who acted for the freeholders as owners of common property, as at Upton, where the freeholders had purchased the manor in the sixteenth century.

The archives usually include minutes, accounts and title deeds, and often papers concerning schools and charities.

Figure 5.2   Example of management group description

together in dedicated strongrooms, but it will be broadly recognized that there is a strong element of administrative convenience in this system of allocating space.

The original purpose of arrangements at level 1, therefore, was to help with the orderly administration of the repository, to apply legal provisions governing certain types of archive, and sometimes to help with the production of co-operative finding aids. A logical analysis of the holdings of a repository, in which the material is divided into management groups, is also a help to users. The division of the holdings into management groups may also help to allocate responsibilities to members of staff.

The concept of the management group is familiar in the practice of the PRO, and can be seen demonstrated in their published *Current Guide*.[12] Descriptions of ministries that were responsible for the creation of series, including composite ministries, are held in a separate section of the guide, with linking references to the classes they produced or influenced.

In local archives services, the use of management groups is widespread. They are usually based on broad areas of provenance. The minimum number of management groups is usually three: official, ecclesiastical and private. Increasingly, a larger number of management groups is being established. A typical list is given in the discussion on classification. (Figure 5.3 on p.116 illustrates a case where ten are in use.) Management groups may also be distinguished between accumulations of archives which are, and which are not, subject to the public records Acts.

In specialist repositories there is no established practice, but there is a tendency to introduce management groups to distinguish between materials of internal and external provenance, where this is relevant.

As with other levels, it is possible to use any number of subordinate levels, so that distinct categories of the group can be identified. It would be natural to term these 'management subgroups'.

These are all genuinely levels of description as well as of arrangement (or administrative convenience), since it is possible to set up descriptions of entities featured in the management levels, and use these as contextual or provenance information. Descriptions of these entities are not necessarily restricted to those bodies that actually created archival materials, and they may follow or be influenced by the international standard ISAAR(CPF). This practice is discussed in Chapter 4.

LEVEL 2: GROUP (FONDS)

The group is the largest unit of management related to physical control. Since a group usually (though not always) comprises a relatively large amount of material, it should be defined in a way which will bring together the whole of a major fonds, or single complex source of archival material. What is intended is a 'natural' division, something which arises from the nature of the archive-creating agency whose products are being administered.

The ICA commission that was charged with designing ISAD(G) decided that the term it would use to designate the total archive resulting from the activities of a distinct organization or, in the case of private papers, a person, would be 'fonds'. Although this term is generally understood, archivists often feel doubtful about relying on a French word to describe one of their main working concepts. In Britain, outside the PRO, the normal term for the fonds is, in actual practice, 'collection'. Originating in librarianship, this term has come to be used loosely for any set of archival materials which arises from a common source, as well as for accumulations which have been assembled artificially. It would be preferable if 'group' (or 'archive group') could be used instead where the materials are a natural archival accumulation. Whether or not this custom is adopted, where collections consist of materials wholly or partly unrelated archivally, brought together by a collector, these may also, at least in many cases, be treated as groups.

For the sake of clarity, it should be recalled that a group as defined here resembles what Jenkinson called an archive group. His classic definition, still valid in the PRO, may be repeated: 'all the Archives resulting from the work of an Administration which was an organic whole, complete in itself, capable of dealing independently, without any added or external authority, with every side of any business which could normally be presented to it'.[13]

This definition applies naturally, not only to the archives of government departments (for which it was originally devised) but also to such entities as business firms, the papers of eminent individuals, landed estates, churches, university departments, and to most organizations which are structured into more than one sub-unit. However, there are notorious difficulties in arriving at consistent and clear guidelines by which archivists can determine whether or not an entity should be treated as the creator of a fonds or not.

In general, archivists are advised to choose to have many smaller fonds rather than few larger ones. Jenkinson's definition can be used as the basic test, and links of dependence or subordination may be ignored. For example, a local rehabilitation unit may depend financially and for direction on the social services department of its district council, but nevertheless is seen by everyone as being distinct: it has its own building, staff, clients, programme, and is called by a distinctive name. If its archives are treated as those of a group, then the links of dependence can be explained in the contextual section of the finding aids. On the other hand, the purchasing department of a manufacturing firm should not be regarded as originating a group because, even though it might be based in a separate building, its work cannot be understood except in the context of the production processes it serves to supply.[14]

LEVEL 2.NN: SUBGROUPS

Groups may be (and usually are) subdivided naturally. Subgroups may be formed which correspond either to:

○   administrative subdivisions in the originating organization, or
○   functional groupings in the material itself.

The first is the easier to deal with. If a group consists of the archives of a business firm, for example, then the subgroups will consist of those which derive from each of the firm's departments – company secretary, legal adviser, public relations office, etc. These will be 'natural' divisions, distinguishable by the original markings on the archives themselves, or by an analysis of the company's departmental structure.

The second case may be more difficult, but may be necessary in cases where the originating agency had no clear structural divisions. The success of this approach depends on the archivist's ability to analyse the functions distinguishable in the material. The papers of a private individual, for example, often cannot be arranged according to the organizational structures of that individual's original system, for he or she probably did not have one. In this case, functional subgroups (if they are needed) may be established by grouping together the papers arising from an appointment to a particular post, membership of a particular movement, participation in a particular project or campaign, dealing with a particular activity or corresponding with a particular individual. These are arbitrary divisions, though they may correspond with an embryonic classification which may have been in the mind of the originator, but not formally expressed.

Like all these levels of arrangement and description, the subgroup level may be omitted if it is not relevant or useful for the job in hand. Moderately sized groups that have no obvious internal structure should probably be treated as undivided units. However, in more complicated cases it is useful to distinguish more than one level of subgroup. An example shows this:

Level 2   Registrar's Department
Level 2.2   Academic Secretary's Office
Level 2.4   Statistical Section

The level numbers here conform to MAD2 usage. Decimal figures allow as many intermediate levels of subgroup as may be necessary, while retaining the leading level number '2', to indicate that groups and their components are being described.

It is important to distinguish subgroups from series. Subgroups represent organizational or structural divisions of the originating agency of the group. The distinction is not based upon any physical likeness or relationship the records may have: this is the province of the series. It is quite common to find a confusion between subgroups and series in archival finding aids. This confusion does not necessarily impair the usefulness of the finding aid, but archivists would produce a better result if they were clear about what they were doing; and a confusion at this level may hinder data exchange or co-ordination projects later.

LEVEL 3: SERIES OR CLASS

'Class' is a British term for what is known internationally as 'series'. A series is the basic unit of administrative control of archives, and hence of arrangement. It is a division based primarily upon physical characteristics in the records, but these arise from the administrative systems of the originating organization.

A standard definition is that used by the Australian Archives: 'A series is a group [sic] of records that are recorded by the same agency (or agencies) and that are in the same numerical, alphabetical, chronological or other identifiable sequence; or result from the same accumulation or filing process and are of similar function, format or informational content.'[15]

This definition, like all others of the same subject, seems rather abstract. This is because it has to cover an enormous variety of different cases. In actual practice, it is usually fairly easy to recognize a series of records because of its unitary character. A simple alternative definition might concentrate on this, and emphasize that a series is an organized assembly of archives or records which belong together in a system and which have a common name.

Series, like any of the other levels of arrangement, may be of any size. Some are very large: the central filing unit in an administrative department, for example. This may contain many thousands of items, papers or folders. It may occupy a large number of filing cabinets or vertical file units, it may spread over several rooms. There may be a heavy turnover of papers coming in and going out of it. There may be an extension to it in the intermediate store. If the mass belongs together, is run as a common system, has broadly a common physical appearance, and is called by a common name ('the central filing system') then it is a series, and can be used as a unit of management.

Alternatively, series can be small. A register of particular occurrences, for instance, could be a series, and might consist of only one item – say a bound volume containing the registration details. Accruals of new data may be either rare or constant – frequency of reference is not important in the definition.

If series are to be the unit of management, it makes sense to treat them as units when archives are being arranged. As they are distinguished essentially by physical characteristics, it should be natural to store them together. Allowance may have to be made for the accrual of new material to an existing series.

LEVEL 3.NN: SUBSERIES

Series may have to be subdivided where there was an original subordinate or dependent system. For example, a set of files within a filing system may have been divided out and given a subset of reference numbers. The new subordinate system may subsequently be the basis of a separate series, or may have been reabsorbed into the original one. Either way, it may best be treated as a subseries. However, there is a general perception that subseries are not seen every day.

LEVELS 4 AND 5: ITEMS AND PIECES

Items, too, are physical units but they are also units of management. An item is the lowest physically convenient unit of archival material: a folder, volume, bundle or box. It is a physical entity, but not necessarily an indivisible one. It should be possible to give items unique reference codes or titles by which they can be recognized; and it should be possible to pick the item up as a unit. Items are the units of handling: they are what is handed to readers in the reading room.

The corresponding term in ISAD(G) is 'file'. This term has been avoided in MAD2 and in the present work because, although intelligible in terms of government archives, in other archive work items can be all sorts of things different from files. For example, items can be volumes, bundles or boxes, sets of index cards, microfiche, etc.

Items should be arranged in relation to each other. The final order should be one which reflects the original system by which they were created. Physically, items may be conserved by any convenient means, by boxing them in tens for instance; but a record of the original provenance should be kept, and should be expressed in the archival reference codes written on the outside of the box, and in structural descriptions.

Any item may contain a number of pieces – letters in a file of correspondence, for instance, or pages in a volume. MAD2 gives these the level number 5, so as to allow independent descriptions of important documents that happen to belong within larger units. Since these are not units of management, it should not usually be necessary to arrange these lower units. Where component pieces are in confusion, and had an original arrangement, this can be restored. Otherwise they could be sorted chronologically or alphabetically within the folder. Many archives services would avoid putting too much effort into arrangement at this level. The essential thing is to arrange the items within their series, and control the series as units of management.

CLASSIFICATION

Levels of arrangement can be expressed logically by means of a classification scheme. The PRO does not have such a scheme, and since it officially uses only three levels, has not found one necessary as an explanation of its system of arrangement. In other archives services, the attraction of classifications has always been felt, and a great deal of effort has been put into devising them, in many cases under the influence of library practice.

Experiment in some library-based archives services has shown that, generally, universal subject classifications are not suitable for determining the arrangement of archives. More useful schemes are based upon an analysis of functions and/or of record types. Clearly, the guiding principles of an archival classification scheme should be the same as those for archival arrangement. The scheme may, however, incorporate some additional elements, such as provision for some degree of subject retrieval.

Historically, classification schemes for local record offices began where a particular kind of archive accumulation was commonly held by more than one repository. County record offices usually hold the ancient archives of their county, the archives of the Courts of Quarter Sessions. Archivists working in these offices found themselves faced with the problem of arranging these at an early stage in the development of the service. In one sense, these archives are unique in each case: the personnel who created them in each county were different individuals, they dealt with different cases, and frequently the system they devised to discharge their responsibilities had some unique feature. However, at the same time, the various courts of quarter sessions were generically similar, subject to the same ruling statutes and government intervention, and produced similar types of archive. Consequently the county record offices which first began to arrange and describe their quarter sessions archives established an arrangement which could be copied in other counties. As a result, the Essex/Bedford scheme for quarter sessions has become a system used (with some local modifications) by all other counties. It is a flexible scheme, based upon a combination of function and form.[16]

Similar circumstances led to the wide adoption of a small number of classification schemes in the case of other sets of archives. The main ones deal with the archives of parishes, Poor Law authorities, modern county councils, churches and educational administration.

Some archives services have also developed general classification schemes which govern their entire holdings. These have not been copied or become in any sense standard, except in the sense that the procedure is familiar. Outside the PRO, archivists have tacitly agreed that library examples were to be followed as far as possible. As will be seen from the example given below, the principle on which schemes are constructed is similar to that of the quarter sessions scheme: function modified by form.

One of the advantages of a classification scheme is that it can provide a system of reference codes which reflect the relationships between the components of an archive. Although there has been no uniformity of practice, in what follows an attempt has been made to identify some conventions. One of these is that levels 1–2 should be represented by alphabetic codes, level 3 and below by numerical ones. This convention, which is fairly widely observed, and which is recommended in MAD2, has proved useful in structuring archival descriptions in finding aid systems, and generally users have grown accustomed to it.

The function of a classification scheme is to formalize the archival order established during the process of arrangement, and relate it to administrative control instruments (such as location indexes) and to the finding aids generally. It can also help to introduce a degree of compatibility between the finding aids of different archives services, where these services hold groups of similar general character. A survey of some common classification schemes in use in British archives services may help to illustrate these points.

An example of an overall classification is the scheme for Cheshire Record Office (amended for the purposes of this discussion), which uses five levels is shown in Figure 5.3 on p.116. In this scheme, the top level is represented by a single letter code. In the context of this record office, these divisions represent the management groups. In this case, there are ten. The next level is marked by the addition of a second alphabetical character. Most of these are groups but some are management subgroups (only a selection is given as examples). After this, level 3 is provided for particular cases. Most of these are management sub-subgroups but some are groups. The next level is represented by a numerical character, and refers to series. Note that in the two examples level 3 is left empty. Subseries are possible. Note that an entry at the first two levels is obligatory, but below this fields may be left empty, or levels unused.

It is generally agreed that changes in the structure of local government as a consequence of the Local Government Acts from 1972 onwards should be reflected in the archival classification. Even where there was no substantial boundary change, the council that assumed power in 1974, and again in or after 1996 was a new foundation, and not a modified continuation of the one set up in 1888. Even apart from this, there have usually been radical changes of departmental and committee structures which would have necessitated new features in the classification. A model is therefore needed for 'new' councils. Although several record offices produced suitable schemes for their own use, there has been no observable tendency for any of them to be adopted elsewhere. An example is the scheme upon which the Kent Archives Office based its guide in 1974.[17] A model for authorities which were set up entirely new in that year and in the 1990s with no historical predecessors is also needed, as is one for specialized bodies.

This discussion illustrates the value of the concept of management levels. In the actual practice of local government, the administrative functions continue through any series of organizational changes: therefore the archives generated by these functions continue to be generated and are best treated as continuous series, irrespective of changes in the governing fonds. A separate set of descriptions of the changing superior hierarchies, with pointers to and from the series descriptions, is a good way of dealing with this problem.

Since parish archives exist in great numbers, several attempts have been made to establish a scheme for these. A family likeness can be seen in many of them, and Figure 5.4 (p.117) attempts to give a fairly typical version, with modifications.[18]

All local government record offices and many other archives services solicit and accept deposits of archives of external origin. Many have classification schemes which cover private, family and estate papers, and some have attempted classification work in other areas, such as the archives of industrial and business firms, and political bodies.

Archives of private origin are often regarded as one of the main management groups. Since by tradition these are mostly deposited archives, it is common (although not universal) to designate them with the symbol 'D', and each group or collection with this designation will have additional characters to identify it as a second-level entity. In the past these characters have often been adopted on a mnemonic basis, for example:

Level 1 (Management groups)

C – County council

D – Deposited archives (from private sources)

E – Ecclesiastical archives

L – Local and statutory authorities within the county

M – Lieutenancy (militia)

N – Public records of local provenance

P – Parishes

Q – Quarter sessions

S – Schools

W – Probate archives (wills)

Level 2 (Management subgroups)

EB – Ecclesiastical: Baptist churches

LB – Local authorities: borough councils

NH – Public Records: hospitals.

But note level 2 entries that are actually groups:

CE – County council: education department

Level 3 (Management sub-subgroups)

NPR – Public Records: public utilities: railways

But note level 3 entries that are actually groups:

EDC – Ecclesiastical: Diocese of Chester: consistory court

LBA – Local authorities: borough councils: Altrincham

Level 4 (Series)

CF 1 – County council: fire brigade: research reports.

Level 5 (Subseries)

CH 111 – County council: highways dept: traffic regulation orders: speed limits.

Note: these level numbers are not those set out in MAD2. They are simply intended to show the relationship of one category to another.

Source: Cheshire Record Office.

Figure 5.3   Example of a classification scheme with five levels

```
Group: the individual parish
Subgroups:
    Incumbent                                   Ecclesiastical
    Churchwardens
    Vestry
    Parochial Church Council

    Constables                                  Civil officials
    Overseers of the Poor
    Surveyors of the Highways

    Parish Council or Meeting                   Civil assemblies
    Burial Board
    Special committees

    Charities                                   Other functions
    Schools
    Statutory deposits (tithe)

Sub-subgroups:
    Incumbent:      registration
                    glebe
                    tithe
    Churchwardens:  rating
                    accounting
                    fabric/property administration, etc.
Series:
    Overseers: settlement: indemnity   bonds and certificates
                                       removal orders
                                       examinations, etc.
```

Figure 5.4   Scheme for the arrangement of parish archives

DBC Archives of Messrs Birch, Cullimore and Co. DDX Miscellaneous small deposits.[19]

As the number of such deposits has grown, mnemonic characters have tended to run out. Their value in any case is limited. Probably it is best nowadays to adopt arbitrary alphabetic symbols from the start, as DAA, DAB, etc. In this way the distinction between subgroups (whose reference code is alphabetic) and series (numerical codes) can be maintained. If this convention is disregarded, then groups can be given serial numbers for identification purposes: D103, etc., and this would have the advantage that group reference codes could be made the same as the accession reference.

The portmanteau group represented in the example by DDX, is widely agreed to be a useful catch-all for deposits which consist of single documents or small numbers of unrelated individual items. It demonstrates, at a lower level, the administrative convenience of the American record group.

There is as yet no classification based upon the archives of manufacturing or business firms. L. McDonald has carried out the basic analytical work but has not yet published a scheme.[20] It is clear that the general outline will follow an analysis of the company's structure and functions, in the usual way (see Figure 5.5).

It will be noticed that in the absence of an existing classification which has been made up by an examination of actual archive accumulations, a structure can be devised by analysing either the actual organization and functions of a specific company or, less satisfactorily, doing the analysis in the abstract, from first principles and a knowledge of how companies are structured.

The theoretical analysis of a company given in Figure 5.5 is a functional and not a subject classification. The terms in the left-hand column, which are based upon a theoretical analysis of a company's make-up, do not correspond to the headings (some of them broadly

Source of authority	Archive-creating structure
Governing body	Shareholders' meetings
Membership	Registers, transfers
Legal instrument	Charter, etc.
Controlling body	Board of directors
Committees	Executive, finance, etc.
Officials, departments	Chairman, managing director departmental heads
Finance	Accounting departments etc.
Legal	Statutory, patents, etc.
Process	Manufacturing controls

Figure 5.5   Scheme for the arrangement of business archives

similar) which could appear in a subject classification. One record office uses a broad division of business archives into three subgroups (Administration, Finance, Operational); but this is based upon a simple subject classification and is in many cases operable only by allocating particular archive entities to one of the categories, irrespective of its actual place in an archival context. A financial record, for instance a ledger, may be produced and kept by a production department in a manufacturing firm: in an archival analysis these volumes ought to be placed with the records of the appropriate department, not transferred to those of the finance office. Adopting a subject classification always means that some materials must be allocated to a category out of context; whereas a functional classification will provide a correct archival category for each component.

The West Sussex Record Office has devised a classification scheme for political archives which is based upon a simple matrix (see Figure 5.6).[21]

To incorporate the double classification at the second level, archival entities must be given a double reference code, e.g. LA + CH. Logically, however, the constituency entries are on a level below that of the party entries, and so must appear second in the code. Subordinate entities within the parties (constituency, area, ward, etc.) can then be numbered or coded as Level 3 (subgroups), but, since they are subdivisions of the parties (and not of the constituencies) the code for these must appear before the constituency code: e.g. LA + 3CH – Labour Party, constituency party, Midhurst.

Level 1: Political records

Level 2:

Party	*Constituency*
LA Labour	AR Arundel
CO Conservative	CH Chichester
LI Liberal	CR Crawley
SD Social Democrat	HO Horsham
CM Communist	MS Mid-Sussex
NF National Front	SH Shoreham
EC Ecology	WO Worthing
	EU European constituency

Source: West Sussex Record Office.

Figure 5.6   Scheme for the arrangement of political party archives

STANDARD SERIES

Several schemes recognize that series often exist within subgroups on a regularly repeating pattern. Thus a subgroup which contains a committee will normally have series for agenda papers, minutes, reports and submissions, and correspondence. In some cases it is possible to establish a standard pattern in which regularly repeating series are given the same numerical code; when a series abnormally is not represented, the field represented by the code would then be left empty. The Modern Records Centre at Warwick University has such a scheme, operated as far as possible over the entire field of its holdings (see Figure 5.7).[22]

Item and subseries references are given after the regularly repeating series references, e.g.:

> MSS.5/1/4
>> Collection reference (accession no. 5)
>>> Series reference (minutes)
>>> Item reference (vol. 4)

The purpose of this repeating pattern is to help users identify relevant material across a number of rather similar small deposits. Provision has to be made for the arrangement and referencing of collections which do not fit the pattern.

/1 Minutes, agendas, reports
/2 Financial records
/3 Correspondence files
/4 Publications of the creating organization
/5 Other publications
/6 Subseries (e.g. personal papers of an individual official kept together)
/7 Miscellaneous
/8 Diaries
/9 Agreements
/10 Press cuttings
/11 Reports
/12 Photographs
/13 Statistics

Source: Modern Records Centre, Warwick University.

Figure 5.7   Scheme for the arrangement of standard series

In spite of all repeating patterns and superficial similarities, archives always remain unique. The recording systems and the actual documents produced by any organization in the end always carry unique information in forms that are not exactly paralleled elsewhere. Archivists therefore always have to respond to this uniqueness by using it, but in doing so they may look around at what others are doing, and follow any useful pathways.

ALTERNATIVE METHODS OF ARRANGEMENT

The methods of arrangement discussed so far might all be termed natural rather than artificial. They are based on the principle of provenance and of original order. The archivist establishes a logical structure based upon the original system. This is equally true with arrangement and classification at macro or at micro levels, at management group, group or series, or item level.

Cases where there was no original system or where analysis of the original system does not give useful results are not common, but they do exist. Where they are encountered, archivists may have to apply an artificial method. There are four possible principles of operation, listed in order of theoretical preference: function, form, alphabetical-chronological, and subject.

Analysis by function is often little different from an analysis of actual functional structures in the originating organization, and so has already been discussed. Equally, it was noted that form (the physical character or format of the archival material) has often been used as a modifying element in archival classifications. Form is usually more suitable for identifying series, and may not be successful if used as the principle for subgroups.

An arrangement of papers by alphabetical order of document title, applicable person, etc., or a chronological arrangement, or a combination of these, is sometimes the best way of dealing with a sequence of loose papers, especially a collection of correspondence. In fact, letters are such a common component of personal archives that there is probably a case for suggesting a standard method of procedure for them. Letters usually have six possible fields by any of which they might be sorted in particular circumstances (see Figure 5.8 overleaf).

If the group is archival, the archivist will seek to discover how the accumulation was built up. The correspondence file of a business might be based on a system of subject filing, in which letters to the organization and copies of letters written by the organization would be kept

---

1. Writer
2. Writer's address
3. Recipient
4. Recipient's address
5. Date
6. Subjects mentioned in the text

Figure 5.8   Scheme for the data structure of descriptions of letters

together where they dealt with a particular theme. On the other hand, the correspondence file of a private person, though containing the same components, might always have been stored in order of the names of writers/recipients, or in order of date sent/received, without regard to subject. A pure subject sorting would be difficult to achieve in the absence of an original filing system, since individual letters can contain references to any number of subjects at the same time. An alphabetical or alpha-chronological order (in so far as it can be established) would seem to be the best way to deal with this situation, especially if the finding aids can include an index. There is no rule which can override a common-sense solution.

REFERENCE CODING

All the classification schemes illustrated use a notation which serves to link one heading to another, and to preserve the hierarchical order of levels. These notations are customarily also used as part of the reference codes which identify actual archival materials. Because of this, the allocation of a suitable reference code is an important part of archival arrangement and description. It solidifies and establishes the arrangement which has been done, and hence the moral defence of the archives. If the reference code is derived from a classification scheme, it will permanently relate the archive to its context. If there is no classification, then the reference code can still reflect the methods of arrangement used within the repository.

Archival reference codes can have a number of objectives:

1.   *Identification of the document for retrieval.* A document is under control as soon as it (or its container) bears a code which is keyed to the finding aid system.

2. *Identification of the document in citation.* This is an important feature. The more archival documents are used in research the more they are referred to in published and other secondary documents. The citations must be accurate and intelligible. Since citations can occur over many years and in many different places, it is also important that archival reference codes, once allocated, should be permanent. It is perhaps worth noting that since archival materials often have no titles, and usually no author in the bibliographic sense, the reference code is often used in place of these items of bibliographical information. Identification requires that a full citation reference should include a code for the repository as well as for the document.

3. *Recording the archival context of the document.* The code may in favourable circumstances be used to demonstrate the way in which the materials quoted fit into the whole group, subgroup or series. This is particularly so when it has proved possible to incorporate some indication of level.

4. *Security.* A document bearing a repository's reference code is more difficult either to misplace or to steal.

It is not easy to combine all these objectives satisfactorily, especially in repositories which have large or complex holdings. There is an order of priority, and clearly the first of the quoted objectives must be the most fundamental. This makes it possible for some repositories to abandon objective 3 as unattainable, and simply allocate serial numbers. Most archives services, however, give at least the group or collection code in addition to a finding number, and thus take a step towards achieving this objective.

Archival reference codes often use mnemonic alphabetical symbols. This is a useful method as long as the supply of intelligible alphabetical codes holds out. After this, a mnemonic system becomes rather odd. Perhaps it is sound advice to avoid it from the beginning, where there is a choice. The PRO's semi-mnemonic system (group codes only) has been partially abandoned because of the large number of archive groups now in the system.

Temporary reference codes are also common, especially where a newly acquired group has been given an accession number. If accession numbers are retained in use for any length of time, there is a risk that they will prevent the attainment of objective 2 in the list above. It is probably better, in most cases, if the permanent reference code could be allocated at an early stage. The problem about this is that if the code is to reflect the considered arrangement of the materials, then it cannot be allocated until this work has been done. If this is a management problem in the repository, then consideration should be given to the possibility of using the accession number as the permanent identification. Systems which use a serial number identification avoid this problem. Reference codes that are inconsistent over time may cause problems when a new computer system seeks to use the code as a sortable field.

Ideally, a final reference code should be permanently but unobtrusively written on each document, in order to achieve objective 4. In practice, this is rarely possible. The best that can usually be done is to write the code on the containers at item level. If any part of the accumulation is taken out of the repository, for use elsewhere, exhibition or repair, the opportunity could be taken of writing on the codes.

PHYSICAL ARRANGEMENT

So far the discussion has centred upon the theory of archival arrangement. The practical process, however, is known as sorting. It is customary to point out that the physical resources of an archives service should include suitable secure space for carrying it out. A workroom with benches and shelves is usually suggested as the right environment. This area should if possible be close to the conservation unit, so that damaged pieces can be repaired, and so that steps can be taken to prevent moulds or pests getting into the repository. It should also be conveniently placed for moving the materials into storage.

The physical process of sorting has priority over any other part of the activity of arrangement. It is only by sorting that the information necessary to proper arrangement can be found, and management decisions taken, concerning the treatment of the group. No other method of procedure ever turns out satisfactorily. This point is insisted on because there is a tendency for inexperienced workers to try to list and store parts of the group piecemeal and to avoid preliminary sorting. This method nearly always means that the earlier sections of the work have to be done again, and that there is no effective overall management of the operation.

Archives once arranged should be boxed and stored, so that the storage location may be keyed to the reference codes, and a shelf list prepared.

Traditional practice is to store the components of an archive entity together, in structural order. This method has the great advantage that the actual physical layout of the archive preserves and demonstrates its archival relationships: storage becomes part of the moral defence of the archive. However, this method may have serious disadvantages from the management viewpoint. It may demand storing big things next to small ones, and so wasting shelf space; and special materials may need special storage conditions. On the other hand, it may also have management advantages. It may help when the archivists have to provide for a user who is working through a group systematically, since then the sequence of containers to be brought up corresponds to the sequence on the shelf.

It is also possible to store archives in random access order, provided of course that there is a finding aid which will indicate to the staff the address of each container. If this method is used (it is common in RM), then the moral defence of the archives must still be provided for, in the shape of a structural description of the archive. The original order is preserved on paper by this means. Random access storage may have considerable management benefits, in efficient use of shelf space and in the possibility of storing awkwardly shaped or frequently used items in handy places.[23]

A compromise between these two extremes is possible, and indeed is usual. This involves storing the bulk of a group together in structural order, but removing especially large, awkwardly shaped (such as maps) or specialized items (such as photographs) for storage in dedicated spaces. A finding aid, perhaps backed by a shelf dummy, can be used to bring these items under control. Some materials, such as film, audio recordings, magnetic tapes, etc., need carefully controlled separate storage conditions. The context from which they come should always be recorded.

Economical and efficient use of the high-quality storage space in the repository has a powerful effect on appraisal, and on the success or failure of the service as a whole.

◼ NOTES

1. The term was coined by Jenkinson, C.H. (1965), *A Manual of Archive Administration,* 2nd edn revd, p. 83 ff. London: Lund Humphries. See also Cook, M. (1977), pp. 103–8. *Archives Administration*, Folkestone: Dawson.
2. Schellenberg, T.R. (1965), *The Management of Archives*, p. 81, Columbia University, quoted by Gracey, D.B. (1977), *Archives and Manuscripts: Arrangement and Description*, p. 4, Chicago: Society of American Archivists Basic Manual series.
3. Schellenberg (1965), p. 118, cited by Cook (1977), p. 4.
4. This section is based closely on Part II of MAD2: Cook, M. and Procter, M. (1989), *Manual of Archival Description*, 2nd edn, Aldershot: Gower, and International Council on Archives (1993)

ISAD(G): International Council on Archives, Ottawa: ICA. http://www.archives.ca/ica. However, because of its original terms of reference, MAD2 treats questions of level as being aspects of description, and not of arrangement.

5. Jenkinson (1965), p. 101.
6. Holmes. O.W. (1964), 'Archival Arrangement: Five Different Operations at Five Different Levels', *American Archivist*, **27**, 21–41.
7. Scott, P.J. (1966), 'The Record Group Concept: a Case for Abandonment', *American Archivist*, **29**, 493–504.
8. Lytle, R.H. (1980), 'Intellectual Access to Archives: Provenance and Content Indexing Methods of Subject Retrieval', *American Archivist*, **43**, 64–75, and Lytle, R.H. (1981), pp. 191–207. Berner, R.C. (1983), *Archival Theory and Practice in the United States: a Historical Analysis*, Seattle: University of Washington.
9. ISAD(G): see Chapter 6, and ISAAR(CPF): see Chapter 4.
10. National Council on Archives, *Rules for the Construction of Personal, Place and Corporate Names* and *National Names Authority File:* both at http://www.hmc.gov.uk/nca/.
11. International Standards Organization, *ISO 3166: Codes for the Representation of Names of Countries*, Geneva: ISO.
12. Public Record Office, *Current Guide*, new edn, London: HMSO (microcard 364).
13. Jenkinson (1965), Part II, sect. 6, p. 101.
14. There has been considerable debate on the nature of the fonds. See for example Cook, T. (1993), 'The Concept of the Archival Fonds in the Post-Custodial Era: Theory, Problems and Solutions', *Archivaria*, **35**, 24 ff.
15. Wagland, M. and Kelly, R. (1994), 'The Series System: a Revolution in Archival Control', in S. McKemmish and M. Piggott (eds), *The Records Continuum: Ian Maclean and Australian Archives First Fifty Years*, pp. 131–49, Sydney: Ancora Press in association with Australian Archives. The quotation is from note 1, p. 147. The source document is Scott, P.J. (1966), 'The Record Group Concept: a Case for Abandonment', *American Archivist*, **29**, 502.
16. Godber, J. (1949), 'The County Record Office at Bedford', *Archives*, 1, 10–20. Emmison, F.G. (1949), 'The Essex Record Office', *Archives*, **1**, 8–16. Emmison, F.G. (ed.) (1969), *Guide to the Essex Record Office*, Chelmsford: Essex County Council.
17. Hull, F. (ed.) (1958), *Guide to the Kent County Archives Office*, Maidstone: Kent County Council; 1st supplement (1971).
18. Based on schemes used in several local archives services, including West Sussex, Gwent, Lancashire, Hertfordshire, Durham, Leicestershire Record Offices.

19. Based on scheme used in the Cheshire Record Office.
20. Information from L. McDonald, an unpublished paper for the Society of Archivists.
21. West Sussex Record Office, classification of political archives.
22. Warwick University, Modern Records Centre, *Notes for Researchers*, Coventry: University of Warwick.
23. Maclean, I. (1962), 'An Analysis of Jenkinson's Manual in the Light of Australian Experience', in A.E.J. Hollaender (ed.), *Essays in Memory of Sir H. Jenkinson*, London: Society of Archivists.

CHAPTER
6

ARCHIVAL DESCRIPTION: GENERAL PRINCIPLES

Archival description is the first area of professional activity in archives to be covered by published general sets of standards and authorities. In this chapter the relevant standards are those set out in MAD2, ISAD(G) and ISAAR(CPF).[1] A summary of other standards that are relevant or useful in certain contexts is given at the end of the chapter.

Physical control over the material is established by the arrangement of archives. To quite a considerable extent, arrangement also provides for intellectual control. Arranging the material has meant analysing it, and putting it together in a way which conserves the information so gained. Placing the materials on the shelves involves recording and demonstrating the original relationships between the components of an archival accumulation. Users who understand the original purpose of the creating organization, and some of the most important ways in which it operated, would be able to find their way around the archives, using only its physical arrangement.

Of course, this form of access assumes that users are able to examine the material physically, and also that it has been stored in something approximating to strict accordance with a structural arrangement. Neither of these requirements is easily met in practice. Documents have been boxed, and so are not easily visible; and it is not easy to write intelligible codes on the outside of the box until there has been a final listing. Awkwardly shaped items have probably been taken out of sequence and put on larger shelves. Then, there is the general question of control of access and who is to be allowed to browse among the materials in the storage area. Something more must be done to bring about a fuller intellectual control over the information recorded in the material.

To solve these problems of access, retrieval and exploitation it is necessary to write descriptions which can act as representations of the original material. These representations can then be structured and filed in different ways to make finding aids. If there are an indefinite number of representations, there can be an indefinite number of finding aids, and an indefinite number of different types of finding aid. Limitations would only be imposed by the difficulties inherent in designing representations – and by the resources needed to write them. It is clear that here, as in other sectors of information management, good initial planning is essential.

A common response to difficulties of resourcing is to introduce a system of two-stage listing: a quick brief list first, and return to do a fuller description later. This approach is quite common, and has been adopted, sometimes on an *ad hoc* basis, as a policy by many archives services. However, there are many disadvantages in the two-stage approach. It is almost certain that the initial brief description will not produce a usable representation file for many purposes, and it is equally likely that the opportunity to return and make a fuller description will be a long time coming.

Many archivists feel that in principle it is better to adopt a policy of once-and-for-all processing, and to aim at a system in which each archival entity is given its final treatment as early as possible. Initial administrative controls can be established by means of an accessions registration: this gives some flexibility in the time-scale and allows priorities to be set. It is true, though, that there are dangers in this approach. Final archival arrangement demands research, and once it is established and reference codes attached to the documents, it is difficult to make any changes: a definitive description must be treated as final.

ONE REPRESENTATION FILE OR MANY?

In library practice it is usual for either one or two representation files to be used. The principal one is generally the author/title catalogue, which is often backed up by an additional catalogue arranged under the subject headings of a general classification scheme. Since for most purposes a representation of a book is a standard bibliographic description, catalogues can usually be compiled by duplicating these descriptions on cards and filing the cards under different headings. In this way copies of a single representation can be used to provide entries in a number of different representation files, and it is the varying order in which the bibliographic descriptions are arranged which makes the difference. There are only two initial requirements, which are that each description must be accurate (that is, it can genuinely serve as a representation of the original document) and that the data contained in it must be structured into fields which are appropriate as labels for sorting. These two requirements are equally necessary in archival description.

It is also usual in library practice for one of the representation files to be arranged in approximately the same order as that of the books – generally this will be a classified (i.e. a subject) arrangement. The subject catalogue is not an exact duplication of the shelf order because it will contain extra entries representing books which have more than one relevant subject heading. Representations of these should appear in more than one place in the classified file. Consequently the representation file may be a better control point than the bookshelf, even where browsing is the main retrieval strategy. This principle is also applicable to archival description.

From these observations we can deduce that there ought to be a main representation file which broadly reproduces the arrangement of the original materials, but which has added entries. This main finding aid should be a structural representation file, in which the individual descriptions are put into an order which demonstrates the original system and provenance of the material, and which is based upon the structural divisions of the originating organization. The added entries in this case will mainly be cross-references and explanatory material. However, this is radically unlike the main representation file in a library system, for such a structural finding aid cannot easily be used by non-expert readers unless they have learned at least something about the basic administrative history of the originating organization.

This is why structural descriptions at group or subgroup (macro) level must normally contain at least the outline of an administrative history; and at series or item (micro) levels there must be an equivalent in the shape of an explanatory headnote. However, it must be a rule that normally the main representation file in an archives service should be of a structural kind, even though it has this defect, because without it the archival material will not be intelligible to users, and its contents will lose their authority as primary sources.

If the main representation file is not a good initial control point for non-expert users, then it must be backed up by additional representation files which can give different forms of access to the information. These files can correspond in number and in character to all the different purposes which an archives service can have in requiring control of or access to its holdings. Some of these purposes are connected with internal management, the administrative control of the processes which have to be carried out on the material. Some are connected with exploitation, the intellectual control of the information held in the material.

The structure of data elements (covered in the next chapter) sets out the data which may aptly appear in each of these categories. The data elements are listed in two parts (sectors), one part dealing with archival description and one with management control. The archival description sector contains the elements which are needed for intellectual control of the material, but embedded in these are the elements needed to write basic representations for the main file. The management information sector holds data elements which, when added to the main representation, give what is needed for administrative control.

The main and additional representation files do not necessarily consist of standard descriptions arranged in different orders: another important difference between archival and library practice. Not only is there a generic difference between descriptions at different levels but also a difference between the format of the data elements chosen for any particular file. Although the same data elements may appear in the central database, their presentation in the finding aid must be planned in relation to the use that the finding aid is to be put to.

Finding aids in archives systems therefore consist of a main (structural) representation file, additional (subject-based) representation files, specialized files for administrative control, together with secondary information retrieval instruments, such as indexes and user guides, which bind the whole complex together.

FINDING-AID SYSTEMS

The way in which the separate descriptions are put together constitutes the finding-aid system of an archives service. It is best if the result is truly a system, in which the components are planned, and the linkages between them designed from the beginning. In real life, most collections of finding aids have accumulated in response to particular needs in the past, and have not developed integrated linkages or common entry points.

There is an appropriate form of description for archival entities at each level of arrangement. These descriptions can be combined in various ways. One main finding aid consists in their being put together in structural order, level by level. They may also be linked horizontally or vertically, and they may be linked by common or cross-referenced supporting retrieval instruments. Figure 6.1 shows these combinations. There are essentially two kinds, which may be termed horizontal and vertical, as the figure shows.

A horizontally constructed finding aid is produced when an assembly of descriptions at the same range of levels is brought together. Putting

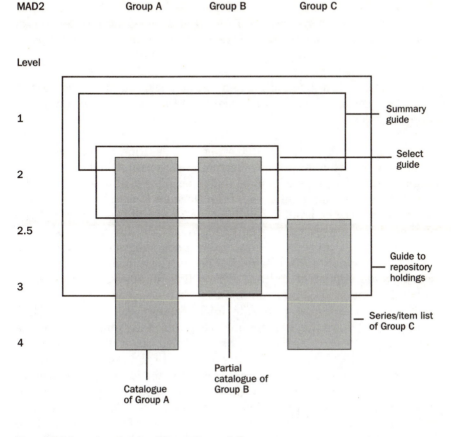

MAD2   Group A   Group B   Group C

Level

1   Summary
                                                       guide

                                                       Select
                                                       guide
2

2.5

                                                       Guide to
                                                       repository
3   holdings

                                                       Series/item list
                                                       of Group C
4

                              Partial
                              catalogue of
                              Group B
              Catalogue
              of Group A

Note: MAD2 numbers levels of description as follows:
2   Archive group/fonds/collection
2.5   Subgroup (other decimals allow further subgroup levels)
3   Series
4   Item

Figure 6.1   Horizontal and vertical finding aids

together the group/collection or group and series descriptions relating
to all the holdings of a repository results in a guide. The Public Record
Office's *Current Guide* is an assembly of macro descriptions of this kind.
This consists of descriptions of government agencies, past and present,
that were at some time responsible for the creation of groups, or for the
supervision and control of archive-creating bodies: that is, descriptions
within the levels numbered 1 (and sublevels 1.nn) and 2 (and sublevels
2.nn). Each group description (containing subgroups in the text) is

followed by all the class (series) descriptions in that group, in logical or structural order. This results in a typical horizontal collection of descriptions, at all macro levels. Integration between the different parts is provided by:

O   a general introduction explaining the background and context of the accumulation, and the make-up of the holdings in general, and
O   an index.

A vertical finding aid is created when the descriptions at each level relating to a particular group/collection are assembled and produced as a single unit. This type of finding aid is usually called a catalogue. The Londonderry papers, published by the Durham Record Office is a good example, at least of a published version.[2] The catalogue consists of the group/collection description, then subgroups (and further divisions of the kind) in logical or structural order. Each subgroup description is used as a headnote for an item-level description which is given with a considerable degree of fullness. The whole is bound together by a general introduction, and by an index.

These two examples illustrate fairly common types of published finding aid. Where the descriptions are not formally published there is likely to be less integration. There is also scope for many more published aids of both horizontal and vertical kinds, for instance inter-repository guides, co-ordinated or combined indexes. Horizontal finding aids can include material selected on a subject basis (provided the level of description remains constant) or, less commonly, material selected on the basis of its diplomatic character or format. An example of the former is the PRO Handbooks series, *Records of Interest to Social Scientists*,[3] and of the latter, collections of enclosure awards.[4] The Hampshire Archivists Group publications, on school and Poor Law records, are perhaps intermediate between the two but illustrate the some of the many possibilities of inter-repository finding aids.[5]

THE STRUCTURE OF ARCHIVAL DESCRIPTIONS

It is a general principle that archival finding aids do not consist of uncontrolled or free text, but are built up from descriptions which are essentially structured. They tend to contain two different kinds of component fields, those with free-text or narrative entries, and those which are dedicated to specific data. It seems to be true of descriptions at all levels that there are fields of these two kinds present. At the upper levels of description, narrative text constitutes the main substance of the entry, and may be very long. Dedicated fields may seem relatively peripheral, and be confined to short entries such as the title and reference code. At the lower levels, item lists often have one free-text field (the item title) which allows some freedom of description to the writer, but this field is usually embedded in a pattern of dedicated fields for reference code, dates, etc. At series level there is more of a balance. The main narrative description (called, in MAD2, the abstract) is supported by several dedicated fields for reference code, title, dates, bulk, condition, and so forth.

Since any archival entity, however small, ought generally to be described at two or more levels, there must be some way to link the two (or more) levels together vertically. Some archives services use the device of adding a title-page to the description of each entity. The title-pages could then be collected as a guide (this would be a horizontal finding aid), and they can also be used as an introduction to the lists that follow (this would be a vertical finding aid).

The concept of the title-page, however, does not allow for all the situations in which there must be an explanatory macro description to introduce and govern a micro description. A more appropriate concept is that of the headnote. A headnote is any introductory entry which explains and controls a finding aid which appears below (or after) it, holds common information, and gives overall reference codes. In many cases the headnote is the related vertical macro description: thus a series description can serve as the headnote to an item list, or a group description to a series list. This can be done with any combination of levels. In other cases the headnote can be something written specially.

Sometimes the headnote appears clearly for what it is, standing at the head of the text of the micro description. At other times the function of the headnote is being discharged tacitly by an introduction or by a macro description, and in these cases the headnote may be separated from its dependent list. There must, of course, be some linking device to indicate the connection. Headnotes are a pervasive element in archival finding aid systems, and can take many forms.

There are some customary rules about the content of headnotes, but not about their format. They should always contain a statement which links the following material to its larger archival context, if any. They should contain a broad description of all material or information which is common to items in the governed assembly of material, so that it is not necessary to repeat information constantly in the list. (Unnecessary repetition is a common fault in archival micro descriptions.) They should contain cross-references to related materials held elsewhere.[6]

Like all other archival descriptions, headnotes may consist of a free text field (the narrative information about what follows) accompanied by dedicated fields (reference code and title).

THE SEPARATION OF CONTEXT AND CONTENT INFORMATION

The ISAD(G), adopted as an international standard in 1992, sets out the principle that contextual (provenance) information should be clearly separated from content information in archival finding aids. MAD2 also applies this principle, at least implicitly, by providing different areas for the data elements concerned. There are important advantages for archival management in observing this separation.

These advantages are most clearly seen in the management of the archives of governments and large public bodies. These organizations often change their administrative structures and redistribute the responsibility for the discharge of particular duties and functions. Changes like this pose difficult problems for archivists, because the archival materials that document functions tend to continue to accrue, notwithstanding administrative changes at higher echelons. If new accruals in a continuing series come in after an administrative change, to which group are they to be ascribed – the original (but now superseded) authority, or the currently responsible one? There may be further changes to come, which will increase the complexity. Either way, both users and archival managers are likely to be misled.

Figure 5.2 in the previous chapter (p.107) gives an example of a brief contextual description. In this case, it is of a management level entity, but contextual data can relate to any level of description.

The eminent Australian archivist Peter Scott, studying this problem in the early 1960s, initiated an important new technique, now often called the 'Australian system' because it has been formally adopted by the Australian Archives.[7] In this system, administrative and intellectual control is concentrated on the series rather than on the group. The principal finding aid is therefore a set of series descriptions acting as macro descriptions to govern the appropriate item lists, and approached by indexes referring to government functions. Administrative histories of all actually and/or potentially connected superior agencies are then maintained in a separate file, with appropriate links. By following these linking pointers, users can easily see how a particular series of archives is related at different times to different controlling agencies.

Although at the time of writing the Australian system has not been formally adopted by any other important archives service, there have been significant developments of it. In particular, Canadian archivists have observed that keeping separate files of creator agencies can give archivists useful extra advantages. Administrative histories can be compiled of all the actual or possible creators of archives, and the resulting file can act as a guide to the completeness of the documentation achieved by the archives programme: it is therefore a tool in the field of acquisition and appraisal as well as in records management. Administrative histories can also be included, both of agencies that did not actually create archives but which had some related effects; and of sets or types of agencies. These descriptions can be filed under appropriate headings (primary access points, subject to authority control).[8]

For example, a British local archives service could include in a single creator file histories of superseded or amalgamated departments, and could also provide historical descriptions of sets or kinds of agencies that existed at one time. Grammar schools, municipal boroughs, Methodist circuits or public inquiries are possible examples. All of these can be described in terms of founding legislation, functions, date ranges, geographical coverage, and so forth, and the resulting descriptions will give necessary information to users who need to understand the contextual or provenance information relating to archival series on which they are working. These administrative histories can then be linked to descriptions of actual archives held, by means of cross-references. MAD2 recognizes these contextual entities by giving them the name 'management levels', and assigning the level number 1 (with possible subnumbers as 1.nn).

To assist archivists in realizing the benefits of keeping separate creator files, and looking forward to the time when such files may be exchanged internationally, the ICA has established a standard for them: ISAAR(CPF). This standard is discussed in Chapter 4.

QUALITY CONTROL

By far the most fundamental problem in archival description is ensuring that descriptions tell the truth: that they give the most appropriate and relevant information for the purpose of the description, and enough of it. MAD2 refers to this as depth, or fullness, of description. It is clear that in most or even in all cases a representation does not contain all the information that is held in the original. If it did, it would be a facsimile: of course, there is a role for facsimiles but it is not as part of the system of finding aids. A set of representations which, while not being so full as actually to be facsimiles, but containing so much of the content of the originals that it can serve to replace them for virtually all purposes, is called, in the British tradition, a calendar. This is a case where the representation file becomes a surrogate file.

Many years ago, the main effort of archivists (in the field of description) was directed at making surrogate files. At first this was done by publishing full-text transcripts. In the early years of the nineteenth century, before the foundation of the PRO, the publication of texts, as nearly as possible as facsimiles, was thought of as the main task. This work was taken so seriously that print conventions (record type) were introduced to improve the similarity between printed text and the originals of medieval manuscripts.[9] As time passed, economies were made by reducing the near-facsimiles to calendars, but these were still designed so that researchers could have direct access to the complete original text in virtually all cases where it was perceived as important. Overseas users can still quote the words of English Civil War generals, by consulting the *Calendar of State Papers Domestic* for the period.[10] Many of the finding aids produced since 1869 by the Royal Commission on Historical Manuscripts were produced on the same lines.[11]

At the end of the twentieth century, the Internet is presenting new opportunities for publication of this type, by way of imaging technology, and it is possible that it may even become commonplace.[12] The distinction between full-text (or virtually full-text) presentation of documents and 'bibliographic' databases remains valid, and archivists will continue to choose between them. But when constructing finding aids for the practical working of their services, archivists have come to think that the publication of full texts should probably not have a high priority. Much more effort is put into the construction of more limited representation files, whose immediate objective is internal control. The best that can usually be offered to remote users is an indication of the likelihood or otherwise that there would be relevant items in a group.

One reason for this change is certainly that there are fewer resources in the face of growing commitments, but it is not clear to what extent we have abandoned or displaced the concept of the surrogate file available to remote users. Possibly the coming of different and more bulky types of archive has reduced the feasibility of full surrogation in any case. Even so, the continued publication of series such as *India: the Transfer of Power* show that the appeal of full-text transcription has continued unabated in some quarters, and the willingness of governments and public bodies to pay for it still continues as well.[13] (The same applies to large-scale publication of original images in microform.) Even so, it is worth noting that this impressive series of full-text publication is carried out by a specialist team, and is not regarded as part of the normal work of the archivists on the staff of the archives service concerned. The construction of finding aids continues as an activity not directly linked to the publication of surrogate texts.

If full-text transcriptions and calendars can no longer be regarded as part of the main descriptive work of archivists, the question of the depth of description to be used in the finding aids which are produced remains a pressing one. A general principle might be that finding aids should be constructed at a depth of description which is the maximum possible in the circumstances. Finding aids should include rather than exclude data, and reductions in the depth of description should be justified by reference to planning decisions taken in the light of the service's priorities. They should also be governed by the systems established to ensure quality control of outputs.

There are four kinds of constraint which operate to restrict the depth of description. The first of these is the nature of the materials being described. Many archives do not lend themselves to varying depths of description. There is, for example, very little that can be added to an item description like the following:

(Head-note:) *Schools Advisory Committee*
AB1/1   Minute book 1964 Dec 5–1965 Jan 10

unless this is regarded as a case for the creation either of a surrogate, say by publishing the full text, or an image; or of an index to contents. In most cases, however, there is some intermediate possibility between these extremes. The archivist's responsibility must be to decide how much to put in, and therefore what must be left out.

Secondly, there are the aims and objectives of the archives service and of the archivist. The immediate purpose is to construct a finding aid which is to do a certain job, in administrative or intellectual control. The shape of the finding aid is determined by the nature of this purpose.

Thirdly, and most obviously nowadays, there are constraints of staff time, skill and motivation. Most of the time spent in the arrangement and description of archives is spent in some form of research or analysis. Research is need to establish the provenance and original arrangement of the archives, to translate this into suitable levels of arrangement for management purposes, and then to identify subjects and persons important in the content of the material. This kind of analysis and research is the central professional expertise of archivists and, consequently, it is the activity which gives most return in job satisfaction. To get it done demands not only that there should be time to do it, but also that there should be appropriately trained and talented staff members, and that they should want to do it. Motivation is affected by subject specialization, and the desirability of allowing staff members to follow their preferred specialisms within the service. This is an important constraint.

Finally, there is the question of user needs and demands. If one defines the term 'user' broadly, this could be an overriding factor.

Archival materials should, after all, be managed in such a way as to provide useful information where it is most needed. This may sometimes justify the construction of finding aids which are not much used at present, if it is expected that eventually they will be used, but in general one must imagine that an assessment of user needs will be made at the point where the finding aid system is being designed, or at least before embarking on a major listing exercise.[14]

Some of these constraints are more significant than others. In principle, lack of resources is the least important of them, since descriptions and control instruments should be made good enough to do the job they are intended to do. In the light of this, the most important thing to understand is the immediate objective of the listing exercise in the context of user needs. After this, the nature of the archive to be listed is the next most formative thing. Limitations of time and skill are the last consideration. However, life seldom follows theoretical analyses of principle, and in practice what resources are available (within the framework of office priorities) may be a dominant consideration. The newly popular term 'quality control', which applies (among other things) to this area of archives work, does suggest one useful practice: that the treatment of descriptions should be worked out and established as a service policy, and there should be a regular method for monitoring the consistency and appropriateness of descriptions operating over time.

The next difficulty in establishing depth arises from the levels to be treated. Each level has an appropriate form of description and, of course, each of these can be treated at different depths. Group descriptions are mainly narrative administrative histories: a bit of time devoted to research here is likely to produce quite lengthy essays on the development and significance of the organization. R.B. Pugh's administrative history and analysis of the diplomatic of Colonial Office records is almost as long as the list to which it is an introduction. This may be regarded as a rather extreme example, even though this introduction is an important contribution to the academic study of modern diplomatic.[15] It would normally be possible to produce analytical introductions, and administrative histories, which contain less detail and yet continue to be useful for their essential purposes.

Administrative histories of creator agencies are an important part of archivists' contribution to the intelligibility of archival materials. They may be handled separately from content descriptions, and held in separate files. Although MAD2 provides a structured set of data elements that can be used for them (the administrative and custodial histories area[16]), there is also a special international standard format for these descriptions.[17] This topic is discussed later in this chapter.

Series descriptions also centre round a free-text entry which can be of any length and must follow the material to be described. The data element structure suggests that sometimes it may be possible to set up an analysis of contents which could serve as a guide to the minimum data to be entered and to provide a set of access points. Unfortunately there are not many such guides available, and most series do not suit them.

The original analysis for setting up the data structure on this point was done in the archives section of the British Antarctic Survey in Cambridge. These archives contain, as one of their most important components, a series of technical reports on expeditions. They are fairly standard in character, and it is not too difficult to set up a grid which allocates fields to data items such as geographical co-ordinates, name of expedition leader, purpose of research, etc. This works well in the BAS reports, but in other archives services, series are usually too various to allow any sort of standard analysis of content. It does, of course, remain necessary to insist that free-text abstracts should contain the keywords needed for indexing or search. The main function of a pre-set content analysis would be to ensure (if possible) that all relevant keywords were entered in it.

No structure of keyword analysis can be valid for all cases. It must remain a matter of choice (within the guidelines laid down by office policy) of the individual archivist as to how fully the original material is to be represented by free-text descriptions.

At item level much the same choice is likely to exist. Where the items are strongly uniform (as in a series of minute books or financial records) as much common information as possible goes into the headnote, and the remainder of the list can consist simply of volume numbers and covering dates. Even here there is a policy choice to be made, as the following example shows.

(a) (Headnote:) *Advisory committee minute books,*
          indexed.
          AB1/1   1964 Dec 5–1965 Jan 10
          12   1965 Jan 11–1966 Mar 25 etc.
(b) (Headnote:) *Advisory committee minute books,*
          13 vols, indexed.
          AB1/1–13 1964–1972

For many purposes (b) would be a perfectly adequate finding aid. Users would be able to retrieve the volume they wanted by checking the dates of the minute books physically: brevity in the finding aid has to be made up by a secondary search on the shelves, but in cases like this, the secondary search would be justified. However, it is possible to imagine circumstances in which a more precise retrieval from the list is required, for instance if ordering by remote users is envisaged or if the material listed is more complex.

In a list of file (dossier) titles, much more discretion is possible. If a dossier has a title, this should be checked for accuracy and fullness, for it is notorious that original file titles can be very misleading. Indexes are drawn from the free-text fields of item lists also, and therefore the main need is that the right keywords should be there.

A good deal of difficulty is experienced in shortening the descriptions given to collections of title deeds. Traditionally it was common to give deeds a full, or almost full, calendar, which included a mention of the three main variables used in research reference:

○   the date and nature of the transaction recorded
○   the names and designations of parties
○   topographical details.

The advent of short descriptions meant that calendaring of individual deeds tended to give way to bulk descriptions of whole bundles:

DBT3/4–23 19 deeds relating to Ambridge. 1560–1900

This example of bulk listing is almost certainly too brief for most users. The secondary search that would be required to identify relevant documents or information is disproportionate to the time saved in the original listing. Some compromise is needed.

The solution would doubtless be to approach the description of a bundle of deeds in the same spirit of management in which a filing system would be approached in RM. The aim would be to give an overall control of the materials by mastering the main facts about the composition and content of the series. This involves reading the documents, at least rapidly, and making a summary of the sequence of events, main parties (including their connection with each other) and a locally identifiable note of the properties involved. A description of this kind exercises traditional archival skills, involves some research, and produces a result usable in further research. It takes resources of time and skill, but less time than a full calendar would have done. The result will be a two-level description which includes something like an administrative history at the macro level, and a brief list at the micro level.

There should be enough detail in descriptions to give some assurance that a user would be able to make a correct assessment of the character and likely content of the entity being described, and to be sure that all applicable keywords have appeared in the index. Large areas of omission (whether arising from policy or not) should be indicated somewhere, in order to avoid introducing a bias.

There is a broad inverse ratio between levels of arrangement and depth of description (see Figure 6.2). This is natural, considering that

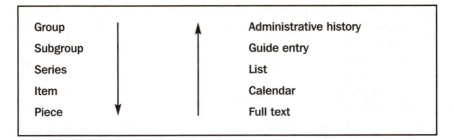

Group	Administrative history
Subgroup	Guide entry
Series	List
Item	Calendar
Piece	Full text

Figure 6.2   Depth and level: relationships

the higher the level of arrangement and description, the larger is the number of archive entities being covered in the one description. Equally, the larger the proportion of the description that is permitted in free text, the less will be the fullness of detail.

There may well be considerable variety of depth in a single finding aid. A common example is that of the archives of a landed estate. This may contain medieval deeds of title, which it has been customary to calendar (when prior to 1300 in very full detail); modern title deeds which receive a less full treatment but still one which mentions type of transaction, names of parties and details of the property conveyed; estate rentals or surveys that cannot be summarized; correspondence; a variety of legal, financial and administrative notes. The date range of a single series can be from, say 1500 to, say, 1900. In these circumstances it is normal to describe items at varying depths. In other circumstances, uniformity of depth at least within the same group would be an important objective.

SPECIAL PROBLEMS IN DESCRIPTION

ACCRUALS

The problem of accruals is more awkward in the area of description than it is in the area of management. A series which receives many new accruals need not be stored together as a physical unit, but must have a description which will allow it to be understood and accessed as a whole. The case of a series which receives annual new consignments is an example. If the new annual addition is listed separately, users must either know exactly the year they wish to search, or they must consult several year-lists. Related items may well recur through the lists for several years. Yet to integrate the lists without integrating the materials physically also leads to trouble, for constant renumbering, both in the lists and on the shelves and containers, or on the documents themselves, would be difficult. The same problem occurs in a records management context.

It is not possible to suggest a complete solution. H.A. Taylor hints that there is such a thing as a 'natural' size to a series, by which is meant, perhaps, that archival divisions should correspond to manageable units as well as to organizational or functional distinctions in the material.[18] Those in charge of the management of new accruals may take advantage of any change in the administrative status of the originating office to close the old series and open a new one – but this cannot be done too often, for the advantages of continuity in a series usually outweigh those of keeping the size of series down.[19]

Where the problems of accrual, and corresponding problems of administrative instability in the creating departments are particularly pressing (as they may be in government organizations), the practice of separating context and content descriptions, following the ISAAR(CPF) standard, is recommended.

BIAS

It is safe to assert that most archival finding aids are honestly meant, and are not intended to deceive. It is not so certain that their honest purpose is always achieved. Since the effectiveness of any representation file depends on the suitability of the representation to its purpose, it will hardly be surprising if there are cases of poor representation or inadequate notation of important features. This leads to bias in the finding aids.

Normally the danger of bias arises from of the omission of data which should be there, rather than from the inclusion of redundant data, but cases of both could certainly be found. If data is omitted from the finding aids, it cannot be found by any ordinary user technique and, of course, could not feature in the indexes. On the other hand, if a lot of irrelevant data is included in the finding aids, users are discouraged from systematic scanning, and indexes may be choked.

The distortion of a representation through the omission of data is easy to illustrate. The brief description of a bundle of deeds given above can be used. A closer examination of this bundle may show that the majority of deeds refers more to the marriage and investment policy of the Archer family than to the transfer of lands in Ambridge. If this is so, then the description is misleading as well as unhelpfully brief.

Bias may also arise from confusion between levels of description in a single finding aid. If, for example, series and item descriptions are brought together in a list, one result may be that a user may lose his or her way:

ART16/24 Student withdrawals   1964–1978
FIN83/20 Medical Research Council grant 17992, 1978–9
FIN83/21 Science Research Council grant 0661   1980

In this example of part of an RM transfer list, the first record refers to a series (or perhaps to an accrual to a series), while the second two describe items. The distinction will be clear only to those familiar with the system, or to those who access the material and find that the first entry produces several boxes of material, but each of the others only one slim dossier. The first entry could have an extension at another level:

ART16/24 Student withdrawals 1964–1978
          Box 1 Students A–H
          Box 2 Students J–Z

Another important cause of bias could be the lack of uniformity in depth of description, but this has already been discussed. Finding aids produced over many years commonly vary in this way. The early ones may be excessively detailed, the later ones too brief. There may have been variations in depth at different times, because of staff shortages or periods of crisis. These variations can have important consequences for the success of searches and the confidence of users in the finding aid system. If users put too much trust in the system, they may lose information just as much as when they do not trust it enough. A periodical monitoring of the continuities of the system may often be justified.

The essential rule is that a representation should be accurate for the purposes of the specific finding aid it is used in. An inaccurate reference code, for instance, might not be very important in a group description, where it could be checked against codes relating to other components of the group. An inaccuracy in the reference code in an RM transfer list, however, could well result in the effective loss of the document. No doubt it would be desirable if information were always accurate, but there is a scale of relative values. Some inaccuracies are more destructive than others.

SPECIAL FORMATS

Archives in special formats generally need different kinds of data in their descriptions. MAD2 has rules for describing several of them, and in fact devotes more than half the book, in terms of bulk, to their requirements. It is important to remember, though, that archival descriptions are generic, and that the main (structural) representation file should be a general and not a special one. It is important, as with all archives, to preserve the record of provenance and hierarchical structures. Special formats should preserve these, and specialized finding aids should normally be linked closely with the main descriptions.

For example, it may be felt that an index of photographs would be a desirable addition to the finding aids system, and that it should include many fields specific to the subjects dealt with in the images. The main finding aid should still show where the photographs in question belong, in terms of their provenance, and give a general description of them at the appropriate level. The specialized index of photographs may refer users to the individual items in which suitable topics are shown, but should also refer them to the place where contextual information is kept. Levels of arrangement should be indicated.

DATA EXCHANGE

The possibility of a system of inter-repository finding aids, amounting eventually to a national network, has become increasingly attractive, especially in view of the progress achieved in the USA. The National Union Catalog of Manuscript Collections (NUCMC) of the USA has never been exactly paralleled in Britain.[20] Since 1947 the NRA has nominally sought to establish a central collection of finding aids, backed by sectional publications covering segments of the collection. Despite periodical attempts to set up authority controls, it was not until the advent of online reference facilities in the 1990s that progress was made on making a general index to these finding aids available widely.[21] The index is backed by the commercial publication of a broad inventory of documentary sources in microform.[22] A large number of archival descriptions, mainly from repositories in North America, now appear in the widely used online bibliographical databases, Research Libraries Information Network (RLIN) and Online Computer Library Center (OCLC), but at the time of writing it does not appear likely that these bibliographical services will become widely used by archivists in Europe. Similarly, at the time of writing, only a small (but probably growing) number of archives services were using, or appeared to intend to use, the online public-access catalogues of major libraries.

In contradistinction to this, the appearance of the easily used World Wide Web has stimulated a large and growing number of archivists to put some version of their finding aids into this medium and so make them available remotely to a world-wide audience.[23] Training is now easily available for archivists who wish to join this movement, and a group of activists has produced a guide for the style and layout of archival descriptions on the Internet.[24]

Archivists have been stimulated by these developments and have ambitious aims that may be achieved by the end of the century. The NRA's ARCHON database now includes a directory of all the archives services recognized by them, and is linked to the indexes of their collection of finding aids. The PRO hosts a project for mapping the coverage of archives services over the country. The universities' funding bodies support projects to complete the body of standards and agreed formats that would underpin a widely used habit of exchanging data, and there are attempts to design and fund a dedicated national network to carry archival information.[25]

The problems inherent in constructing multi-repository finding aids are now well known. They centre upon two areas: the compatibility of the finding aids as between repositories, and the need to introduce new retrieval instruments to support the new multi-repository finding aids.

Compatibility within and between repositories would demand, for example, that levels of description should be correctly analysed, and suitable models taken for both depth and level. It is fairly certain that in most cases these have not been consistent in the past, even where they are so in the case of newly constructed finding aids.

Putting descriptive materials together in composite forms highlights the need to create access points to them. Traditionally this meant new indexes which would need structured and controlled vocabularies. When online databases are in question, provision must be made for searching facilities. Work is now actively in progress to establish the necessary authority controls, beginning with an authority list for personal and place names issued under the authority of the National Council on Archives.[26]

Compatibility demands that there should be a generally observed authority system: that is, entries in finding aids should be managed as to their form. This particularly applies to access points, the index or keyword headings under which representations are filed. A successful authority system demands:

○   rules for the construction and presentation of entries
○   an authority file, listing all existing entries
○   a procedure for making new entries.

The role and character of authorities is not identical with those in use in libraries, but archivists should take advantage of the existing structure of bibliographical authorities wherever possible.[27]

■ NATIONAL AND INTERNATIONAL BIBLIOGRAPHIC SYSTEMS

It should be possible to agree that archivists need to use both bibliographic and full-text databases. In this context, the term 'bibliographic' must mean that the database contains descriptions (representations) that serve to tell users what materials exist and where they may consult them. 'Full text' must mean that the records in the database contain material that represents the contents of the originals, and that therefore allow users to extract information directly from the database, at least in some cases.

Libraries have long been accustomed to using bibliographic databases. In recent decades we have seen developments of three kinds:

O Libraries have automated their online public access catalogues (OPACs).

O Libraries have made their OPACs available online in sufficient numbers to allow the claim that there is now a national, or even international, joint catalogue covering major libraries.

O Some large academic libraries have participated in the development of specialized online databases.

Archivists may consider to what extent they can benefit by these developments, but before doing so they must tackle the questions of compatibility and authority control.

Within the nation, and within library and documentation systems, there is a fair degree of acceptance that bibliographic standards have been established by the Anglo-American Cataloguing Rules (AACR2), which includes chapters both on manuscripts and on non-book materials.[28] Much book cataloguing is now organized on an inter-repository basis, and progress has been made with computerized bibliographical descriptions. Standards for this have been established by Machine-Readable Catalogue (MARC), which again includes specialized formats for manuscripts and non-book materials (NBM).

There has been a considerable degree of international linkage in the bibliographical field, especially where electronic databases and formats are concerned. There are international standards of compatibility, such as the International Standard Book Description (ISBD) (which controls the shape of bibliographic data entries), the various versions of MARC (which provide a format for data to be included in bibliographic systems) and Common Communications Format (CCF).[29] Specific standards for various types of material, particularly technical documentation, have been established, and the MARC formats, although split into national types as between the USA, Canada and Britain, do operate as an international standard.

In the USA, progress has been made in developing comparable standards applicable to archival description. Finding both the AACR2 standard and the MARC format unworkable, groups of archivists have rewritten both. The Society of American Archivists developed and promoted a revision of AACR2, known as *Archives, Private Papers and Manuscripts* (APPM), which is now effectively the only fully operational set of cataloguing rules for archives in use anywhere.[30] Online bibliographic databases that employ MARC as their format require users to employ recognized cataloguing rules. The APPM is available for this purpose, and has a reliable track record.[31] Canadian archivists are engaged in devising their Rules for Archival Description (RAD), but this task is not yet completed at the time of writing. British archivists at present have only MAD2, backed by the NCA's rules for name authorities, though some of the larger archives services have in-house manuals that approach this degree of complexity. Work is in progress on further standards.

Most archivists, at work within their own repositories, have not been actively conscious of the progress of this kind of co-operative work, but changing aims within the service and the rapid growth of technology are making it essential that technical standards and formats are known and applied at the workface.

The question is, how far have the archival standards and formats been successful? Certainly there have been successful ventures in the co-operative exchange of archival information, especially in North America. It is probably true to say, however, that so far it has not been possible to produce a standard for archival description which is adapted from AACR2 or any of its derivatives, and which has been widely accepted by archivists as a useful tool for ordinary purposes within repositories. The Archival Description Project which worked at Liverpool University during 1984–85 took this view, and suggested in its report that there would be scope for further research on seeking to develop an AACR2-compatible standard. This is the background for the development of MAD2.

Some of the reasons for the difficulties encountered have been outlined in earlier parts of this chapter, and the fact that these difficulties are not always appreciated by librarians tends to make the problem more difficult. The increasing demand for international standards and provision for immediately accessible databases makes it important for us to reach for solutions. It is not acceptable that library and archival standards for the description of their materials should continue to be so irreconcilable.

◼ USER RESPONSE

User studies have traditionally received a low priority among archives services. In the present climate of opinion, where all services are being closely scrutinized for the value they offer to their customers, this subject has been rapidly revived. Even so, there have as yet been few systematic studies of the response of lay users to archival finding aids, in the context of any British archive service, nor have user organizations much concentrated on this aspect. Although there would be many difficulties in implementing it, an extensive user study is clearly overdue.[32]

It was mentioned earlier in this chapter that the main representation file should be a structural one, but that this type of finding aid was not usually user friendly. A structural finding aid is directly and immediately useful only to one type of user, a researcher who is studying the origin and central development of the organization whose archives are under inspection. Such a user will be looking primarily for evidential material. Other users who wish to use informational material will find the structural finding aid of marginal value, and may find the administrative history which it contains, necessary but tiresome.

On the other hand, it is not entirely clear that the majority of users would prefer subject-based finding aids. R.H. Lytle's 1979 study tested the reliability of retrieval from structural and subject-based descriptions (this, of course, is not quite the same question) and came to the conclusion that neither system had much advantage over the other.[33] This meant that since structural listings must necessarily continue to be the main description (for reasons of moral defence), there is no pressing reason why traditional approaches should be changed. Probably there is a need for more subject-based descriptions, so that finding aid systems should perhaps be designed with their possibility in mind. Subject-based finding aids (incorporating an element of the structural) may be produced by assembling sets of subgroup or series descriptions on a selective basis.

Users certainly need access points to find their way into finding aids, and would probably voice a preference for union indexes which integrate finding aid systems, provided these were properly designed.

Archival descriptions, at whatever level, should be formatted with user needs in mind. In particular, users need to scan lists for specific information and, therefore, the fields used in them should be laid out accordingly. A user scanning for relevant dates, for instance, would be grateful to have covering dates set out in a separate column on the left or right of the free-text field. Free text, on the other hand, lends itself to browsing, the main other user technique for dealing with the identification of material.

Finding aids are part of the outreach or publication programmes of the archives service. One consequence of this is that there should be a clear decision on their openness to users. Ideally, all finding aids should be classified as for free access, even where they relate to originals which are closed. (In this case, there would be a note in the finding aids stating access conditions.) Ideally too, a version of every significant description should be found in the National Register of Archives.

In practice, these counsels of perfection are probably unattainable, since it is sometimes necessary to conceal either the fact of custody of certain materials, or at least some details about them. It would still be preferable if the principle of openness were to be adopted explicitly, and provision made for certain exceptions.

NOTES

1. Cook, M. and Procter, M. (1989), *Manual of Archival Description*, 2nd edn, Aldershot: Gower. International Council on Archives (1994), *ISAD(G): Standard General Archival Description*, Ottawa: Secretariat of the ICA Ad Hoc Commission on Descriptive Standards. International Council on Archives (1996), *ISAAR(CPF): International Standard Archival Authority Record for Corporate Bodies, Persons and Families*, Ottawa: Secretariat of the ICA Ad Hoc Commission on Descriptive Standards.
2. Newton, S.C. (1969), *The Londonderry Papers: Catalogue of the Documents Deposited in the Durham Record Office by the 9th Marquess of Londonderry*, Durham: Durham County Council.
3. PRO (1971), *Records of Interest to Social Scientists 1919–1939*, PRO Handbooks 14, London: HMSO. There are many other examples in this and similar series.
4. Oxfordshire County Council (1963), *A Handlist of Enclosure Acts and Awards Relating to the County of Oxford*, Oxford.
5. Hampshire Archivists Group (1970), *Poor Law in Hampshire through the Centuries: a Guide to the Records*, Winchester: Hampshire County Council.
6. MAD2, para. 14.5; ISAD(G) 3.5.
7. The original article was Scott, P. J. (1966), 'The Record Group Concept: a Case for Abandonment', *American Archivist*, **29**, 493–504. See also Scott, P.J., Smith, C.D. and Finlay, G. (1980), 'Archives and Administrative Change: Some Methods and Approaches', *Archives and Manuscripts*, **8**, 51–69; Hurley, C. (1994), 'The Australian ("Series") System – a Revolution in Archival

control', in S. McKemmish and M. Piggott (eds), *The Records Continuum: Ian Maclean and Australian Archives, First Fifty Years*, Monash Occasional Papers in Librarianship, Recordkeeping and Bibliography No. 5, pp. 150–72, Sydney: Ancora Press in association with Australian Archives.

8.   Stibbe, H. (1992), 'Implementing the Concept of Fonds: Primary Access Point, Multilevel Description and Authority Control', *Archivaria*, **34**, 109–37.

9.   Walne, P. (1973), 'The Record Commissions, 1800–37', in F. Ranger (ed.), *Prisca Munimenta: Studies in Archival and Administrative History*, pp. 9–18, London: University of London Press.

10. *Government Publications: British National Archives*, London: HMSO, lists issued annually until 1984.

11. London: HMSO, Sectional List 17.

12. A significant pioneer was the project for imaging 10 per cent of the holdings of the Archivo de Indias at Seville, initiated in 1992.

13. (1970–83), *Constitutional Relations between Britain and India: the Transfer of Power 1942–1947*, vols 1–12, London: HMSO.

14. Taylor. H.A. (1984), *Archival Services and the Concept of the User: a RAMP Study*, Paris: Unesco.

15. Pugh, R.B. (ed.) (1964), *The Records of the Colonial and Dominions Offices*, PRO Handbooks 3, London: HMSO.

16. MAD2, section 14.3.

17. International Council on Archives (1996), *ISAAR(CPF): International Standard Archival Authority Record for Corporate Bodies, Persons and Families*, Ottawa: Secretariat of the ICA Ad Hoc Commission on Descriptive Standards.

18. Taylor (1984), p. 38.

19. Roper, M. (1972), 'Modern Departmental Records and the Record Office', *Journal of the Society of Archivists*, 4, 400–412.

20. Ranger, F. (1970), 'The Common Pursuit', *Archives*, **9**, 121–9.

21. http://www.nra.gov.uk/.

22. (1988–), *National Inventory of Documentary Sources in the UK and Ireland for Users of Archives and Manuscript Collections*, Cambridge: Chadwyck-Healey.

23. Listed at http://www.liv.ac.uk/~archives/home.html.

24. www.archivesinfo.net/.

25. ARCHON is at www.hmc.gov.uk/. The PRO mapping project is at www.pro.gov.uk/. The university funded projects, under the aegis of JISC.NFF are at www.kcl.ac.uk/projects/srch/reports/.

26. National Council on Archives (1997), *Rules for the Construction of Personal, Place and Corporate Names*, NCA, issued in disk form 1996; definitive publication 1997: www.hmc.gov.uk/nnaft.htm.

27. Black, E. (1991), *Authority Control: a Manual for Archivists*, Ottawa: Bureau of Canadian Archivists, Planning Committee on Descriptive Standards.
28. Gorman, M. and Winkler, P.W. (eds) (1988), *Anglo-American Cataloguing Rules*, 2nd edn revd, Part I, chs 3–11, London: Library Association Publishing.
29. International Federation of Library Associations and Institutions (1977), *ISBD(NBM): International Standard Bibliographic Description for Non-book Materials*, London: IFLA International Office for UBC. Simmons, P. and Hopkinson, A. (1984), *CCF: the Common Communications Format*, Paris: Unesco.
30. Hensen, S.L. (1989), *Archives, Personal Papers and Manuscripts: a Cataloging Manual for Archival Repositories, Historical Societies and Manuscript Libraries (APPM)*, 2nd edn revd, Chicago: Society of American Archivists.
31. Smiraglia, R.P. (ed.) (1990), *Describing Archival Materials: the Use of the MARC AMC Format,* New York and London: Haworth Press.
32. Forbes, H. and Dunhill, R. (1997), 'Survey of Local Authority Archive Services', *Journal of the Society of Archivists*, **18**, 37–57.
33. Lytle, R.H. (1979), 'Subject Retrieval in Archives: a Comparison of the Provenance and Content of Indexing Methods', PhD thesis, University of Maryland, p. 199. Ribeiro's study (1996), 'Subject Indexing and Authority Control in Archives: the Need for Subject Indexing in Archives and for an Indexing Policy Using Controlled Language', *Journal of the Society of Archivists*, **17**, 27–54, came to the conclusion that the most successful users were those who best knew the material they were studying, irrespective of the quality of the finding aids offered. See also Menne-Haritz, A. (1993), 'Appraisal or Selection: Can a Content-Oriented Appraisal Be Harmonised with the Principle of Provenance?', in *The Principle of Provenance: Report from the First Stockholm Conference on Archival Theory and the Principle of Provenance*, 2–3 September, pp. 103–31, Stockholm: Svenska Riksarkivet.

7

THE STRUCTURE AND FORM OF DATA IN ARCHIVAL DESCRIPTION

At least one of the British university training courses had begun to offer a course component in archival computing by 1970. The Society of Archivists began holding annual in-service courses in the subject in 1982. After these tentative beginnings groups of archivists began to prepare for what seemed the imminent age of the computer by preparing an analysis of the structure of data elements that were needed for archival description. The Methods of Listing working party (of the Specialist Repositories Group of the Society) had already been at work on this for a year. The working party produced a draft data structure, and this was examined at a series of open meetings held at a variety of places, and finally reached a sixth version. At this stage (1984) the Archival Description Project at Liverpool University, which was working on a standard for non-computerized archival description, took up the work and incorporated the data structure into the first edition of its *Manual of Archival Description* (MAD). This first edition was essentially a discussion draft. The project continued to hold workshops and discussion groups in different places, and when the (for the moment, definitive) second edition (MAD2) appeared early in 1990 it could be claimed that there had been wide acceptance in professional circles.[1] It was used as one of the three basic documents considered by the international commission that drew up the General International Standard Archival Description ISAD(G), published in its definitive version in 1993.[2]

MAD2 was prepared at a time when the only models available for comparison were the American standards adapted from AACR2. The Archival Description Project took the decision not to follow this approach, but to examine the descriptive practices of archivists in real life, and construct rules based upon this observation. In consequence, Part I of MAD2 is an important analysis of the essential nature of archival work in description, which makes clear (among other things) exactly in what ways it is different from the work of library cataloguing.

After some years' experience of working with MAD2, both in the writing of hard-copy finding aids and by using it as a basis for developing a computer package,[3] it has become plain that in its present condition the document will not serve as a general-purpose set of cataloguing rules. It will be necessary to continue development work, in particular so as to incorporate the international standards ISAD(G) and ISAAR(CPF),[4] to elaborate the specific rules (which could be derived in large part from AACR2) on the presentation of data, and to incorporate authority rules and files.

For the moment, however, it is clear that for British archivists the only effective and operational cataloguing rules are:

O   the two international standards ISAD(G) and ISAAR(CPF)
O   MAD2 in so far as it is usable in this way
O   for those working with the MARC AMC format, APPM.

In future, choices may be wider. The Canadian enterprise, RAD, will be completed. There is nothing in the design of this that would prevent adoption within Britain or Europe, but RAD is complex and would require an infrastructure of training courses and workshops. Other sets of rules may come from Australia or from outside the English-language tradition.

THE DATA STRUCTURE OF ISAD(G), ISAAR(CPF) AND MAD2

Despite the problems mentioned, it does seem likely that the data elements recognized by MAD2 are likely to prove a satisfactory list for most purposes. The grouping of these data elements into areas and sub-areas may have to be adapted in order to accommodate the international standards.

It is a general principle that data elements, or corresponding fields in a computer system, are not used unless there is a positive need for them. They can be omitted or left empty. The only field always required is one of those in the identity statement, since it is always necessary to identify the material being described. Setting out the full list of all possible data elements, therefore, gives a picture that for most purposes is unnecessarily complex.

In MAD2, data elements that relate to each other are linked into areas (which may be compared with the areas in AACR2) and sub-areas. There is, therefore, a hierarchical character in the list of data elements. In addition to the areas, the list of data elements is also divided into two major sectors, according to whether or not the data is to be regarded as being in the public domain. Archivists have always kept some information about the transfer and management of their holdings confidential, and MAD2 aims to retain this facility.

Figure 7.1 overleaf shows how the data elements in MAD2 compare with those in ISAD(G) and ISAAR(CPF), giving the specific paragraph references.

The archival description sector is intended to hold data elements that are directly required by users for retrieval of information, and is therefore intended to be fully in the public domain. The management information sector is intended to hold data elements that are needed for internal management purposes and are not open to public inspection.

It is not entirely possible to divide all the data elements neatly into these two categories: in practice, archival finding aids are often used both for internal administration and for providing a service to readers. One of the components of the archival description sector, entitled the access, publication and reference record, might be seen as belonging about equally to both sectors, and should perhaps have been treated as an independent sector.

It should also be noted that the archival descriptions (representations of the original), formatted to suit the appropriate level, are needed as much for management information as for intellectual control. The two sectors of the data element structure are interdependent in this respect.

THE ARCHIVAL DESCRIPTION SECTOR

This sector is divided into three areas, and so at first sight resembles the areas of information provided for bibliographic descriptions in AACR2.[5] After a closer acquaintance, the resemblance appears more and more superficial, since none of the data elements themselves really corresponds at all closely with those used in bibliographical cataloguing.

The procedure in an archival repository is broadly as follows. An accumulation of archives is sorted and arranged in component groupings according to level. The description process is then applied to these level by level. The group as a whole has a description proper to itself, which usually concentrates on the circumstances which brought the group into existence – contextual or provenance information. The historical survey continues through the subgroups. The description of series which comes next appears to move a little closer to bibliographical practice in that it is a set of series-by-series descriptions,

Structured data fields	MAD2	ISAD(G)	ISAAR(CPF)
Archival description sector	14.1		
Identity statement area	14.2	3.1	1.1
Reference code	14.2A	3.1.1	1.3
Title	14.2B	3.1.2	
Term for form/type/genre	14.2B3		
Name element	14.2B4		
Span dates	14.2B5	3.1.3	
Level number	14.2C	3.1.4	
Administrative and custodial history area	14.3	3.2	
Administrative or biographical history	14.3A	3.2.2	2.1–3
Source of administrative history			
Office holders/personal or corporate names		3.2.1	
Place of origin			
Previous administrative systems			
Significant dates		3.2.3	
Custodial history	14.3B	3.2.4	
Sequence of ownership			
Place of custody; sequence of location			
Method of transfer			
Date/conditions of transfer to archives			
Source references (see also Accession)			
Archivist's note	14.3C	3.6	3.1
Relational complexity and status	14.3C1		
Appraisal principle	14.3C2	3.3.2	
System of arrangement (see also	14.3C3	3.3.4	
Arrangement record; Appraisal review record)			
Content and character area	14.4	3.3	
Abstract	14.4A	3.3.1	
Date			
Site, locality, place			
Personal or corporate names			
Events, activities			
Subject keywords			
Diplomatic description	14.4B		
General diplomatic: form/type/genre			
Problem features			
Predominant language		3.4.4	
Script			
Special features			
Secondary characteristics			
Physical description	14.4C		
Physical character	14.4C1	3.4.5	

Figure 7.1   Data elements and areas in MAD2, ISAD(G) and ISAAR(CPF)

Structured data fields	MAD2	ISAD(G)	ISAAR(CPF)
Quantity, bulk or size (see also Location)	14.4C2		
Physical condition (see also Conservation)	14.4C3		
Access, publication and use area	14.5		
Access record	14.5A		
Access conditions	14.5A1	3.4.2	
Copying conditions	14.5A2	3.4.3	
Copyright information (see also Issue)	14.5A3	3.4.3	
Publication record	14.5B	3.5.5	
Citations			
Bibliographical details			
Related materials	14.5C	3.5	
Related materials elsewhere	14.5C1	3.5.1/3/4	
Existence of copies	14.5C2	3.5.2	
Other finding aids	14.5C3	3.4.6	
Lists deposited elsewhere	14.5C4		
Exhibition record	14.5D		
Circumstances (see also Loan record)	14.5D1		
Physical condition (see also Conservation area)	14.5D2		
Management information sector	14.6		
Administrative control information area	14.7		
Accession record (see also Custodial history area)	14.7A		
Number, code, reference	14.7A1		
Date(s) of accession/custody	14.7A2		
Method of acquisition	14.7A3		
Immediate source	14.7A4	3.2.5	
Conditions	14.7A5		
Deposit agreement (see also Location record)	14.7A5		
Future accruals	14.7A6		
Funding	14.7A7		
Location record	14.7B		
Place of storage	14.7B1		
Bulk (see also Physical description)	14.7B2		
Accruals (see also Accession record)	14.7B3	3.3.3	
Process control area	14.8		
Arrangement record (see also Archivist's note)	14.8A	3.3.4	
Sorting method	14.8A1		
Funding	14.8A2		
Dates of completion	14.8A3		
Description record	14.8B		
Description plan	14.8B1		
Funding	14.8B2		

Figure 7.1   cont'd

Structured data fields	MAD2	ISAD(G)	ISAAR(CPF)
Dates of completion	14.8B3		
Indexing record	14.8C		
Person responsible			
System, controls used			
Funding			
Dates of completion			
Issue for use record	14.8D		
Access status and policy (see also			
Access record)	14.8D1		
User's identity	14.8D2		
Time, date and issue of return	14.8D3		
Frequency of reference	14.8D4		
Enquiry record	14.8E		
Identity of enquirer	14.8E1		
Purpose	14.8E2		
Dates	14.8E3		
Loan record	14.8F		
Person/organization to whom loaned	14.8F1		
Dates of dispatch	14.8F2		
Dates of return/due for return	14.8F3		
Insurance or security details			
(see also Exhibition record)	14.8F4		
Appraisal review record	14.8G	3.3.2	
Procedure used	14.8G1		
Action taken/recommended	14.8G2		
Action date	14.8G3		
Appraiser (see also Archivist's note)	14.8G4		
Conservation area	14.9		
Administration (see also Physical			
description)	14.9A		
Conservation record	14.9B		
Conservation history	14.9B1		
Repairs required	14.9B2		
Level of priority	14.9B3		
Conservator responsible	14.9B4		
Start and finish dates	14.9B5		
Repairs carried out	14.9B6		
Recommendations for future			
conservation	14.9B7		
Materials used	14.9B8		
Funding (see also Administrative			
control information area).	14.9B9		

Figure 7.1   concluded

which might be compared with a library catalogue. Finally there are lists of items which do not look at all bibliographical. A completed set of hierarchical finding aids, therefore, consists of at least three (and probably at least four, in practice) levels of description, each of which has a model of its own.

The first area in the sector is compulsory for all archival descriptions, and is a statement of the identity of the archival entity (at whatever level, or of whatever size) that is being described. Generally, identity is established by means of an archival reference code, though there are cases when a plain language title could be used instead, especially for large groups. Reference codes usually contain a reference to the level of description being used. Titles can also suggest level, and indeed the importance of titles decreases, in archival description, as one passes from the higher to the lower levels.

The next area is the administrative and custodial history of the archival entity being described. One of the higher levels of description is usually envisaged here, though of course every archival entity has both an administrative and a custodial history, which may be important in its interpretation. This history can have two aspects, and both form a part of the full description. First, there is the administrative history of the organization which brought the archive group or series into being and, secondly, there is the custodial history – the history of the events which have occurred in the life of that archive between its original creation and its passing into the regular custody of the archives service (an important event which normally should always be recorded).

The various data elements which might go into an administrative history are set out in the rules. They include the name and function of the administrator or administrative unit, office or person who was responsible originally for creating the archive, the place where the creation and original storage was done (and if relevant, the department or suborganization which was responsible), and the authority under which the creators were acting at the time. This provision has in mind principally the case of records generated as a result of legislation or a formal decision of the governing body of an organization, but the provision could be relevant also to the records of a private individual. In this case, the authority statement could refer to an event or undertaking in the person's life, such as joining an official committee or taking up some enterprise.

The administrative history inevitably includes some description of the functions intended to be carried out (or actually carried out – this may be different) by the creating organization. This makes the administrative history an important first guide to the user, who can use it to assess the likely relevance of the group or subgroup to the intended researches.

The custodial history refers to the archive's adventures in the period after it ceased to be in current use as a business record until after its transfer to or deposit in the archives service. There will always be at least one event in this history, the transfer itself. Often, there will be much more. The adventures of many groups of British government archives in the long period between their currency and their eventual arrangement in a public repository were colourful, and had visible effects on the physical appearance of the material. Some of the State Papers (incontrovertibly government archives) ended up in the British Museum, and played a part in the development of that repository's successor, the British Library, as a centre of research, and as a national institution.[6]

The treatment of the archives in the course of their custodial history may also have a bearing on their value as primary evidence. We no longer believe, as Jenkinson did, that an archive's value in research or as legal evidence depends on our certainty that it has never left official custody. Primary sources are evaluated as to their authenticity (i.e. tests can be made to see that they are not forgeries, or have not been altered), not as to the purity of their custodial history.[7] Nevertheless the custodial history is of interest in the interpretation of the documents, and should be set out in the main description of the group.

Custodial history may record the sequence of ownership changes, both those which left the archive *in situ*, and those (such as changes by sale) which involved the material being moved, and perhaps its arrangement disturbed. The place of the owner's custody, or the sequence of these places, may be valuable information. Generally, there should be some information on the conditions under which the transfer to the archives service took place, whether by transfer under statute or official regulation, deposit by a private owner, bequest, purchase or rescue and, of course, the date of this transaction. Finally, the trail of clues which points to the course of the custodial history – the original or other obsolete reference codes which the documents may have borne – could be indicated. (The detail of this particular point might be more appropriate in a micro description.) It is possible that there may be cases where the transfer section of the custodial history may have to be kept confidential.

The administrative and custodial history area can be regarded as the main component of a macro description – particularly at group or subgroup level; or it may be an entry in a file of creator agencies. At group level, some additions on the physical character of the archive, and a reference to the whereabouts of appropriate micro descriptions would probably complete it as a working finding aid. Alternatively, though, the area can be regarded as forming part of an archival description, the most central part of which is the area which follows.

This area, the content and character area, is the one which corresponds most closely, in its general appearance and make-up, to a catalogue entry for books. Like all the forms mentioned in the data standard, this one can be used at any level, but takes its most characteristic shape at series level: that is, at the point where the micro descriptions meet the macro ones, the point of greatest importance where management needs are concerned.

The main content description is called the abstract in MAD2, because this part of a description normally consists of a summary of the matters dealt with in the original materials. It is a free-text field linked to a number of dedicated fields. Logically the content description field should be double, since we have to provide both a title and an abstract of the total content. Each of these demands some consideration.

Archival materials, whether they are items, series or groups, do not normally have titles in the sense in which published materials have: with these, the author or responsible originator has already supplied a title that goes at the top and can be copied out in representations. In describing archives, the title usually is derived by the archivist from the archive entity itself. Generally, this title will have a structure like this:

O a term suggesting the type of materials that are being dealt with, such as 'papers of....', 'maps and plans from ... ', 'letters between ... ', etc. A general default, which can often be omitted because it is self-evident, is 'archives of ...'
O the name of the principal creating organization or person, with suitable qualifiers
O simple covering dates of the material covered.

Examples are:

[Archives of] Smith & Co. Ltd, gunsmiths, 1799–1900
Personal papers of William Brown, psychologist, 1910–1970

Subgroups bear the names of the functional subdivisions to which they refer. When series are being dealt with it may be necessary to supply a title by examining their make-up and content. To find a suitable title, the archivists will first look for evidence as to whether the series had a title, or some sort of working label, when it was in current use. If this approach fails, alternative sources are form ('the Red Book/s'), function ('registers of vaccinations'), place of original custody ('Leahurst correspondence files'), name of original compiler ('Lord Smith's in-letters'). If these elements fail to produce a satisfactory title, then recourse can be had to the reference code. It is essential that an archival entity should be related to its context, particularly in regard to level, but it can if necessary do without a title.

MAD2 recommends that titles should contain at least two of the three possible elements noted above: a personal or corporate name; a term indicating the form of the material; and covering dates. This recommendation originated in proposals for cataloguing rules within a manuscript library, and one can see that they have in mind the kind of title often adopted by libraries for their manuscript collections. A typical example would be 'Alexander Hamilton papers, 175?–1804'. The recommendation is perhaps less suitable for a public archives service, since both the form and the date parameters may be unnecessary. Even so, a group title such as 'Borough of Borchester' (*sc.* official archives), *c.* 1560–1835' would be perfectly acceptable in this context. Close alternatives such as 'Borough of Borchester before the Municipal Reform Act' would satisfy the recommendation just as well. See the example of a series description in Figure 7.2.

After the title comes the body of the abstract, a free-text narrative description. It is important that the abstract should contain all the data items in the original which would be required for effective retrieval. It is likely that the abstract will be the source of any keywords used in a search, whether that were to be a manual or an online search, since these will be used as possible access points. To ensure that these keywords are included, it may be useful to provide the archivist with a series of prompts, in the form of dedicated subfields to be filled in with specific data where it occurs. These specific items might include dates (single or covering); site, locality or place (in some situations map co-ordinates could be used); personal names; events or activities; or subject terms drawn from an authority list. The data in these fields will provide access points for specialized finding aids, or for using in online searches, and will also be the source of any index. Because of this it is especially suitable for the terminology to be subjected to authority control. For instance, many local archives services provide a list of place names within their area, hierarchically arranged under ancient parishes. For personal and corporate names the NCA rules may be used. Subject wordlists or thesauri are less common, but sometimes a wider subject-term list can be used, such as the *Library of Congress Subject Headings* or the *Social History and Industrial Classification*.[8] Archivists often find it difficult to use authority lists compiled for library use.

The dedicated fields linked to the free-text sections are variable in their fullness. Some may have relatively lengthy entries, while some can be limited to a narrow range of possible data. Diplomatic description is a field which must allow considerable variation. It should give some information on the form of the record: at group level this will be brief, but at series and item levels some free text may be needed (e.g. series: correspondence filing systems, loose-leaf registers; item: mortgage, marriage settlement, letter). As mentioned above, a word or two from

Management group level: ECCLESIASTICAL COURTS

Management subgroup: PROBATE

Series:

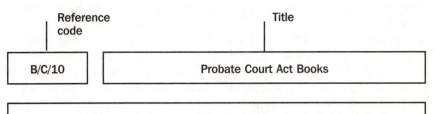

Reference code	Title
B/C/10	Probate Court Act Books

Daily record of the probate acts of the Consistory Court. Entries usually comprise only a brief note of the grant of probate or administration, with perhaps the name of a local clergyman before whom the executor or administrator was to swear the oath to administer honestly the good of the deceased. In the first four at least of these volumes, there are a few entries relating to court business other than probate.

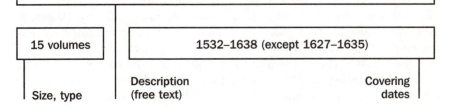

15 volumes	1532–1638 (except 1627–1635)
Size, type	Description (free text) / Covering dates

Source: Staffordshire Record Office.

Figure 7.2   The basic structure of a series description

the diplomatic description may be used as one of the elements in the title, and if this is done, then of course it need not be repeated. This section can be used to note the existence of any original indexes or finding aids, since these may be important means of access to the archive.

Another field allows for a note of problems encountered in relation to this archive, such as missing information, difficulty of interpretation, or the like. Narrower fields are those which can be used to note the predominant language used, and the characteristic script ('Chancery hand'), where this information is important. All these fields can apply to descriptions at all levels, though the way in which they are used varies according to the level.

The next area of the data standard contains a physical description. This provides space for a note on the formal character of the archive:

files, volumes, bundles (this may be replaced by or linked with the note on diplomatic character in the preceding section). Next comes data on dimensions, material, quantity, text (sometimes a link with the predominant script is indicated). A note of the existence of any copies, microfilm, photocopy, transcript, and so on, may appear here, and then a brief statement of the physical condition of the entity being described, especially where this might affect the archivist's decision on whether or not to allow access. The area is completed with entries containing information on special features, such as seals, watermarks. or any other physical feature which may be worthy of study or which might affect access. Once again, this area may be used at any level, but increases in specificity at the lower levels; and once again, any part of it may be omitted.

The next area is the access, publication and reference record. Logically, this is intermediate between the archival description sector and the management information sector. It contains data which is needed for the construction of publicly available finding aids, and also for the management of processes within the repository.

The access field is used to record any limitations on the openness of access there may be, either general limitations applicable to all users, or limitation to some particular group of users. These limitations may take the form of an action date associated with the general closure period. An example which is of value equally for public users and for archivists managing the user services is the case where access becomes open after 30 years, and the action date is 25 March 1970: the material becomes open at 26 March 2000 (or, more usually in practice, on 1 January 2001).

There may be restrictions on reproduction of the material, which again may allow for privileged users (such as authorized representatives of the originating department). Relevant data here has a management context: a cross-reference to correspondence files recording policy instructions on access and reproduction limitations may be useful.

A third field allows the extension of this information to the question of copyright. It may be necessary to record the ownership of the copyright, restrictions imposed on users through copyright, its expiry date, and cross-reference to the office's correspondence files.

Both intellectual and administrative control may demand that there should be information on the publication history of an archive. The reference may include a correct bibliographic description of a published version of an archival text, or a reference to a case where the archive has been cited. These are sometimes complicated questions, especially where the data item is being included in a group or subgroup description, and there may be need for some freedom to insert textual notes.

Linked with the publication record is a field which allows for a reference to associated materials: archives or published work, perhaps based on the holdings of a different repository, which bears upon the content or interpretation of the archives. This should hold at least the relevant cross-reference and a free-text note of the nature of the relationship.

Whether an archival entity has at some stage been lent out for exhibition may be a point of interest to public users, and is certainly a point which requires management information. Exhibition is a form of publication. A proper record of it might include the name of the person or organization to whom the material was lent, the dates of the loan and a reference to any formal publication or reference in the exhibition catalogue.

This completes the archival description sector, and the remainder of the data standard covers the management information sector. The main purpose of this is to record information useful for the internal management of the archives service, the establishment of administrative controls over the material and the control of the various processes through which the archives are put. Information in this sector is not regarded as being in the public domain: if there is a decision that any of this data should be published in the finding aids, then usually there is an alternative place for it in the archival description sector.

MANAGEMENT INFORMATION SECTOR

The management information sector contains three areas, covering administrative control information, internal movement control, and conservation.

Administrative control information has two sub-areas: the accession and location records. In the first, information about the acquisition of the archive is recorded. Fields are provided for data on its accession (this may refer to a separate accessions register). The date of this event is an important item, and so are its means of acquisition and its immediate provenance or source. Means of acquisition could include purchase, gift, loan, deposit, transfer or rescue; this field links with the final event noted in the custodial history. Because there will probably be data here which ought not to be published at first or without restriction, this separate section for management use is provided as an addition. It is important that there should be a permanent record of the transfer.

The second sub-area provides for a location record, and a tool for the management of the space occupied. The place of storage is obviously necessary as a management aid. The volume of storage or shelving occupied also suggests a need for information on the expected rate of accrual and the expected date of the next consignment. This may suggest a 'bring-forward' record reminding the staff to make contact with the originating organization at a certain date, giving a reference to the relevant correspondence files, and to the source of funding where this exists.

The process control area contains seven sub-areas, all concerned with the supervision of processes carried out within the archives service, and not of direct concern to users. The first division provides a control of the completion of the main processes: archival and physical arrangement of the material. Within this broad label are included a host of operations, ranging from initial registration, through fumigation, boxing, labelling, through to final storage and completion of the finding aids. The amount of detail given in the record depends on the level (primarily chosen for management convenience) and the nature of the material.

At the end of all this, the completion of the final archival description, with the name of the staff member responsible, a note of funding and the date, may be a useful record. A similar record may be provided for the completion of the indexing work, though this of course may be regarded as integral to the general description.

This part of the description could be used to provide a record of production of the material for reference by a user. There are fields for the user's identity and for the circumstances of the access given. The designers of the data standard intended that this part of it should be usable in the context of RM, and therefore there are fields covering the issue and return of material to internal users, and for recording the number of times a record entity is referred to in any given period. The number of times a series is accessed in a year, for instance, may be significant when it is being appraised, or when the retention schedule is being revised. Access to the record, and its issue to users, should be governed by a policy in regard to that actual category of record, and therefore it should be possible to include a cross-reference to documents or sources laying down what this policy is.

Another sub-area is used to record cases where reference to the archive has been made in order to answer enquiries from outside users. The full record could include the identity of the enquirer, the date of the reference, and a means of identifying the appropriate correspondence in the files. Perhaps it should be added that because the data standard makes provision for this kind of record, it must not be taken as advocating that this record should always be kept. Whether this is done or not is a question to be decided by the archives service itself, bearing in mind its general needs and resources. Many archives services do not record enquiry references to their material, and do not keep the enquiries themselves for any length of time. Other services find that recording this information helps to simplify the work of answering enquiries over time.

Loan of material for use in exhibitions or for reference in another repository, where it happens, may make it necessary to have a control record. Fields needed might include the name of the person or organization to which the loan was made, the dates of sending out and return (or the date on which return is due), and a note of insurance requirements. This division refers back to the record of exhibition loans which is part of the publication record.

The last sub-area is primarily for RM information and records appraisal reviews. It may be used to note the appraisal category or the action to be taken, the date on which action is due, and the officer responsible for it. There might well have been further provision here, for RM procedures in connection with review might include sending a disposal recommendation to the originating department, recording a disposal instruction, or varying the policy in special cases. If these items, or any like them, are to be included, they could come in this area of the data standard.

The final area is the conservation record, which would be a permanent part of the archive's custodial history, and also an administrative control over repair processes. This area could be used to preserve a record of previous conservation history, and of repair work needed and carried out. The conservator responsible, start and finish dates, and return to permanent storage, all have dedicated fields. Another field might be used to bring the item forward for inspection or further repair at a stated date. Another use of this record might be to help with stock control by recording the use of materials in repair: this may of course be cross-referenced to conservation registers in use in the service. If there is special funding this may be noted.

The data items in the management information sector can be applied to any level of arrangement or description, but a movement down the scale to series and item can be perceived in the later areas and divisions. It is probable that most physical controls are best exercised at series level, but that the conservation record may tend to concentrate on item level. Even here, however, it is worth recalling that environmental conservation, being a management function, should probably seek to find a level well above item for its main operation. Environmental conservators should look to series (if not group) as their main level of control and, therefore, will need to frame their finding aids and control instruments accordingly.

The full detail of the general structure of data elements, instructions on applying them to particular archival descriptions, a set of model descriptions and some examples, are given in MAD2, Parts II–IV.

STANDARDS, FORMATS AND RULES THAT APPLY TO ARCHIVAL DESCRIPTION

Most archivists working in the British tradition have been trained in an environment in which the only rules to be followed are those drawn up for use within an archives service: in-house rules and conventions. In some cases these are quite detailed, and are supervised strictly; but this is not common. Most archives services have a considerable backlog of finding aids drawn up in past years that do not conform to the current standards. There is therefore a re-cataloguing problem in the conversion of older forms, as well as (commonly) a cataloguing backlog in dealing with new materials that have been acquired but are awaiting treatment. These problems seem to exist everywhere in the world.

As the end of the twentieth century approaches, we must prepare ourselves for a world in which there is much tighter regulation of forms. Where networking of one kind or another is the norm, there must be rules that govern the structure and shape of data so as to ensure that exchange and integration is as easy as possible. In terms of archival description that means that there will be rules governing the structure of descriptions, the format of finding aids, and authority control over the data that is entered in these.

At the time of writing the following rules, formats and standards are in use in some places, and practising archivists must be aware of what they are, and of what their general shape and appearance are. Detailed knowledge will be needed by those who actually have to use them, but all archivists should know the general shape and purpose of established rules and standards, how to find the authoritative texts when required and the circumstances in which each will be needed.

There are a great many internationally recognized standards that might in some circumstances be needed. It is not always easy for unpractised readers to understand the difference between the kinds and types that they fall into, nor the precise functions of each one. The best way to come to an understanding is actually to start work with one or more of them. There is, however, a clear logical explanation of the different kinds of standard and the need for each of them. This is contained in a specialist report made to the Society of American Archivists in 1989.[9] A good grasp of logical thinking is necessary.

The following is a list of the most common standards in use at the present day or under active development (in addition to those dealt with earlier in this chapter). Other, more technical or more specialized, standards are listed in appropriate reference books, and are not dealt with here.[10] The question of authority control is considered in Chapter 8.

○   *Description (cataloguing) rules*
   – Anglo-American Cataloguing Rules (AACR2)
   – Archives, Private Papers and Manuscripts (APPM)
○   *Data exchange formats*
   – Machine-Readable Catalogue (MARC) and Archives and Manuscripts Control (AMC)
   – Standard Generalized Mark-up Language (SGML) and Encoded Archival Description (EAD)
   – ANSI/NISO Z39.50

AACR2

The Anglo-American Cataloguing Rules, developed and supported by librarianship bodies internationally, are the standard governing the cataloguing of books in most countries.[11] It is not suggested that archivists should use AACR2 in any of its forms (although it does have a chapter governing the cataloguing of manuscripts). It is a library standard and, therefore, loses efficiency when called upon to structure descriptions of collectivities with multiple linked levels. However, it is important that archivists should in future become somewhat more familiar with it because it underlies several of the standards and formats discussed below, and is so well-established internationally.

AACR2 sets a baseline from which developments in archival description can proceed. Catalogue entries in it have a basic structure that is virtually unassailable in the minds of all information users, even archivists. According to this all descriptions conform more or less closely to a structure like the very simplified version shown in Figure 7.3.

Heading: a name suggesting the authorship or creation of the material

Title: a succinct statement that identifies the material

Description: a summary of content and scope

Production details

Additional entries giving access points relating to alternative authors, content etc.

Details of whereabouts of the material

Figure 7.3   The structure of a bibliographic description

Like all other information workers, archivists use variants of this structure, but do not generally depart from the essential idea. AACR2 is therefore a kind of baseline from which, consciously or not, we all work.

AACR2 also contains elaborated rules for the formation of data content, including names, dates and types of material, and points towards authority controls for subjects. In view of this, the writers of archival cataloguing standards, notably Hensen and the National Council on Archives, have based their work strongly on what has already been laid down in AACR2. The standard is also well maintained, and is able to respond to changes as they appear internationally. For these reasons, it is desirable that archivists should include a knowledge of the standard as part of their professional toolkit. However, the National Council on Archives, in elaborating its rules for the formation of names, has decided that archivists should not use this aspect of AACR2 in preference to its own standard.

APPM

Developed by Stephen Hensen and others as part of the work of the Society of American Archivists, *Archives, Private Papers and Manuscripts* (APPM) was adopted by that Society as a standard in 1989, and is now maintained by its Committee on Archival Information Exchange.[12] APPM was devised within the general structure of AACR2 (replacing chapter 4). It is an adaptation of library-based cataloguing rules aimed to allow archivists to provide group/collection level descriptions to library catalogues or to bibliographic databases. The principal online databases of this kind – the Research Libraries Information Network (RLIN), the Online Computer Library Center (OCLC) and to a lesser extent the Western Libraries Network (WLN) – require participants to use either APPM or AACR2 when they compose material for entry to the database. This connection with AACR2 has proved to be an advantage for users of APPM, for they can use the former's rules and authority controls as a default, wherever a case is met where APPM has no specific guidance: for example, where an unusual name is encountered.

Despite its obvious origin within the world of librarianship, APPM has proved capable of allowing archivists to write not only group descriptions but also item descriptions, and to link them; it also allows provenance information. The rules are framed for application within a MARC environment, and so they provide dedicated fields that are to give access points to searchers. The text is therefore highly structured, and demands that cataloguers should be able to analyse their input in some detail. It is assumed that entries will be made by paraphrasing and restructuring internal finding aids. The direct purpose of APPM is to promote data exchange by allowing entries to be inserted into online databases or online public access catalogues (OPACs) that contain non-archival material.

There is now a considerable body of experience in the use of APPM, chiefly but not entirely American. A subset of the rules in APPM have been drawn up specifically for use in describing government records for inclusion in the RLIN database.[13] There is no formal reason why APPM should not be adopted in countries outside the USA, but opposition to it has gathered around its AACR2-like character. Elsewhere in the English-speaking world, as in Canada and Australia, archivists have preferred to develop their own specialized cataloguing rules, though as yet none of these is in daily practical use in a fully developed form.[14]

At the time of writing, APPM is the only case of archival description rules having been formally adopted by the professional body concerned (the Society of American Archivists) and by appropriate official organizations in public life (committees of the Library of Congress and others). The lesson to be learned from this is that no description rules, or indeed any other form of authority control, will be successful unless they have been formally adopted as a result of some agreed procedure, and so recognized nationally. It is noteworthy that at the end of the twentieth century few countries have procedures of this sort in place.

MARC AND AMC

MARC is a data exchange format. It is now quite venerable, and is regarded as a fundamental standard in most of the world of librarianship.[15] It is highly structured and nowadays looks rather clumsy and old-fashioned; but its universality as a format required for using bibliographic databases ensures that it continues as a valid standard.

There may be many reasons why archivists might want to participate in bibliographic databases. Archivists may choose to join one of the online bibliographic databases that accept archival descriptions. These databases are shared by organizations – mainly libraries – that wish to have access to the information, and to add their own information too. The largest of the shared databases include RLIN and OCLC, both of which have large numbers of (chiefly group-level) archival descriptions.

Other archivists might wish, or be obliged, to use the OPAC facilities provided by a library service. Several university archivists have sought to include their holdings in the general or special catalogues of their host libraries, and there are obviously strong reasons why these libraries should wish to include references to primary materials in their custody.[16] Although archivists do genuinely find difficulty in adapting library standards and procedures to their work, it would clearly be a valuable resource if their users could have access to these materials by way of the same catalogues and finding aids as they would use for secondary materials.

Virtually all library cataloguing systems and bibliographical data exchange systems are compatible with the MARC format, and many require it. No doubt new library systems will be developed in the future (and are actively being developed now) that do not require the strict use of MARC formats; but all such systems are designed so that they can accept and use data that is presented in that form. This is because the MARC formats are used so widely in the world and because there is such a vast mass of data already structured in that way. Archivists, therefore, should be open to the possibility that they may wish to participate in one or more of these systems.

There are many variations and differences in MARC. One difference is national: USMARC is different in a number of ways from UKMARC, and so forth. At the time of writing, there are moves to amalgamate these two national formats, and also the Canadian variant. Whether these efforts succeed or not, the problem presented by the difference is not enormous. There are software systems that are capable of translating data from one national format to another; and in any case it is not always necessary for an archives service to adopt the MARC format of its own nation if there are advantages in using another. For this reason, many British archivists who have opted to use MARC, have also opted to use the US version, because it provides better for archival descriptions.[17]

Other variations concern the type of material that is being catalogued. The data structure for books assumes that AACR2 is being used for data content. There are MARC formats for serials, music, manuscripts, visual materials, non-book materials, authority data and others. Plans are in hand to bring all these specialized formats into one single format.

The format for archives, Archives and Manuscripts Control (AMC) is one of these specialized formats.[18] It was originally devised by a working party of the Society of American Archivists in 1982, and this society has issued many of the instructional manuals and other material that makes the format usable. For several years, the format has been controlled by the governing body of MARC itself, so that it is a fully authorized and integrated part of the overall MARC format. The purpose of AMC, of course, is to give archivists a vehicle for structuring archival descriptions. Provision is made in it for provenance and archival management information, and the different levels of description are recognized. Multi-level linkages, and linkages between content and context information can be controlled in the format. See the example in Figure 7.4.

```
001$aLiv:RP XV A.2.26#
015.00$aPiece#
016.00$aRP XV A.2.26#
041.00$aeng#
080.00$aSpecial Collections:RP XV A.2.26#
100.10$aDawson, Flora#
240.00$aHugh Reynolds Rathbone and Emily Evelyn Rathbone – Additions . General
         Correspondence#
245.00$aLetter to Emily Evelyn Rathbone$bLetter from Flora Dawson#
260.00$aInverary$c1922 May 15#
300.00$f1 letter#
500.00$aapp. RP XV–RPXV A – PAPERS OF HUGH REYNOLDS RATHBONE AND EMILY
         EVELYN RATHBONE date from c.1841–1958 and include RP XV.1 – GENERAL
         CORRESPONDENCE, RP XV.2 – GENERAL PAPERS -including printed material,
         newscuttings and other papers concerning their public and private interests,
         RP XV.3–4 – ACCOUNTS, including papers concerning financial affairs of
         Rathbone Brothers and the family, RP XV A.1 – FAMILY CORRESPONDENCE,
         RP XV A.2 – GENERAL CORRESPONDENCE, RP XV A.3 – GENERAL PAPERS,
         RP XV A.4 – DEEDS AND ACCOUNTS, RP XV A.5 – STAFF RECORDS, RP XV
         A.6 – PROPERTY RECORDS, RP XV A.7 – BIOGRAPHICAL AND HISTORICAL
         NOTES. N.B. the group RP XV A represents material deposited by R.S.
         Rathbone in Dec 1987.#

506.00$aUnrestricted access#
520.00$aConcerning upkeep of gravestone at Inverary (possibly of Edward Reynolds
         Rathbone)#
524.00$aRathbone papers#
541.00$aDeposited by Richard Simon Rathbone in Dec 1987#
545.00$aHugh Reynolds Rathbone (1862-1940) was eldest son of Richard Reynolds
         Rathbone and Frances (n,e Roberts). Grain merchant, partner of Ross T.
         Smyth & Co. 1889-1924. Member of Mersey Docks and Harbour Board
         1905–1933, Royal Commission on Wheat Supplies 1916–1920, Liberal M.P.
         for Wavertree 1923–1924. Strong involvement with University of Liverpool:
         treasurer 1903–1918, president of council 1918–1924, Pro-chancellor
         1924–1930. Married in 1886 Emily Evelyn Rathbone (1862–1940), daughter
         of William Rathbone VI and Emily (n,e Lyle). Her public works included chair-
         manship of Crofton Recovery Hospital Committee, president of Liverpool
         Home for Crippled and Invalid Children, 1918, and of Robert Jones Memorial
         Workshops for Cripples, 1918–1939. They had three children, Hannah Mary
         (Nancy, later Warre), Richard Reynolds (Reynolds) and Hugo Ponsonby.#
656.00$aCorrespondent$bDawson, Flora#
700.10$aRathbone, Emily Evelyn and Rathbone, Edward Reynolds#
773$aRathbone papers – Hugh Reynolds Rathbone and Emily Evelyn Rathbone –
         additions – General Correspondence#
851$aDepartment of Special Collections and Archives$cLiverpool University Library,
         PO Box 123, Liverpool L69 3DA#
```

Source: Liverpool University.

Figure 7.4   Example of a MARC AMC record, showing system metadata and tagging

There is an active email list in which questions can be asked and answered and there is a least one published survey of experience in using the MARC AMC format.[19]

All versions of MARC are immediately recognizable, as, in them, data is structured into fields that are identified by numerical tags. These tags broadly follow the library convention that entries in a catalogue have a main entry, sorted under the author (statement of responsibility), and may also have added entries, sorted under headings that refer to other parties or subjects. Writing a MARC description therefore implies that the data to be input has already been analysed. It is generally assumed that the source for a MARC entry will be a finding aid already carried out to in-house standards. The purpose of a MARC record is that it is for export to an external system. The format is suitable for use in conjunction with other data transfer standards, such as SGML.

SGML AND EAD

The Standard Generalized Mark-up Language (SGML) is a well-established and widely used international standard.[20] Although strange at first to many archivists, the concept of a mark-up language is familiar. Those who remember preparing texts for publication in the days of hot-metal printing will recall that proofs had to be marked up by using a set of arcane symbols. The principle of SGML is similar in that it supplies a set of symbols, identifying field tags, that can be written into a document. SGML is dissimilar, though, in that it supplies tags that not only identify textual display, but also indicate the type of document that is being dealt with and sets out the structure of that document. Since SGML tags can be recognized by many systems, a marked-up document can be interpreted, transferred, output or searched to a great extent independently of the platform or system that was used to create it. In particular, it is easy to transfer data to and from MARC documents.

A generalized mark-up language can be used to describe the character and structure of any document at all. Since many documents actually fall into easily recognized categories, it is not surprising that specific applications of SGML have been developed which are ready-made for use with particular kinds of document. These specialized formats are called Document Type Definitions (DTD). Archival descriptions are a particular kind of document, and for some years groups of archivists have been working to elaborate a DTD for them. This is termed the Encoded Archival Description (EAD) (see Figures 7.5 and 7.6 on pp.178–9). The original development was done by a team at the library of the University of California, Berkeley, starting in 1993, but many experimental sites have been involved, and the work is now co-ordinated by the Library of Congress. Several participants have been outside the USA, and an application is now under active development by the PRO in London. An 'alpha' version of EAD was tested by many of these participants, and in the light of feedback from them a 'beta' version was launched in 1997. Although it is still regarded as experimental, it is thought that major restructurings are no longer likely. All the relevant texts are available online,[21] and there is an email discussion list.[22] The PRO version of EAD specifically assigns tags indicating up to seven levels of description to accord with ISAD(G).[23]

Archivists may also find it useful to know of another specialized application of SGML, used to encode the structure of full-length text. This is the Text Encoding Initiative (TEI), developed by a consortium of projects aiming to transfer large bodies of literature into electronic form. This application of SGML may be of interest to archivists who are concerned with putting full-text material online.[24]

Hypertext Mark-up Language (HTML), used for structuring documents for display on the World Wide Web, is a standard derived from SGML. This is the mark-up language used currently used to make archival descriptions and archives service publicity available on the Internet. It is a generally simple application that has made it possible for more than 200 repositories (at the time of writing) to mark their presence online. A working party of active archivists has published a guide to the good composition of web pages, using HTML.[25] A particular feature of this language is that it incorporates hypertext links, leading users directly from one page (or document) to another, irrespective of where any of these pages have been generated. HTML therefore offers a (perhaps deceptively) simple solution to the problem of multi-level descriptions, but leaves archivists with their constant concern of providing information on the context and origin of their materials.

ANSI/NISO Z39.50

The full title of this specification is Information Retrieval (Z39.50): Application Service Definition and Protocol Specification. It is also an international standard.[26] The current (1995) version is a refinement on the original, brought into use in 1988. The apparently curious code by which the standard is known simply indicates that it is number 50 in the sequence of standards issued by the American standards organizations to cover various aspects of information structure and transfer. Z39.50 is in effect a specific implementation of SGML.

The purpose of this standard is to specify the technical conditions needed to send a search request from one system or machine to another,

<c02><did>
<head>**D 709 2/8: Papers as member of the Opposition: Shadow Energy Spokesman 1979–1981**</head>
<unitid>D 709 2/8</unitid>
<unittitle> *Labour Party. Opposition – energy spokesman*<date>1979–1981</date></unittitle>
</did>
<scopecontent>
<head>Scope and content</head>
<p>The group D 709 2/8 contains a small amount of correspondence relating to David Owen's career as Shadow Energy Spokesman, dated 1980</p></scopecontent>
<bioghist>
<head>Biographical notes</head>
<p>On the defeat of the Labour Party in the General Election of May 1979 David Owen took the position of Shadow Energy Spokesman, until his decision to leave the Labour Party in January 1981.</p>
<p>During this period the Labour Party was experiencing serious internal disputes concerning the balance of its power; with increasing pressure from Tony Benn and the Labour Left to lessen the influence of the Parliamentary Labour Party and heighten the influence of Labour activists. The ascendancy of the Left wing of the Labour Party at this time was strongly opposed by Owen, and finally provoked him into the decision to leave the Party (see<emph>D 709 2/14 Papers on leaving the Labour Party</emph>).</p>
</bioghist><arrangement>
<head>Arrangement</head>
<p>The papers in group D 709 2/8 are arranged into the following groups:<list>
<item>D 709 2/8/1 General correspondence</item></list></p>
</arrangement><odd>
<head> Related materials</head>
<p>Several transcripts of speeches and articles on energy-related issues made by David Owen as Shadow Energy Spokesman can be found with general files of his speeches (D 709 2/9) and articles (D 709 2/10)</p>
</odd><c03><did>
<head>**D 709 2/8/1: General correspondence**</head>
<unitid>D 709 2/8/1</unitid>
<unittitle>*Labour Party. Shadow Energy Spokesman* Correspondence</unittitle>
</did><scopecontent>
<head>Scope and content</head)
<p>D 709 2/8/1 contains a small group of letters relating to David Owen's career as Shadow Energy Spokesman, dated May–Jul 1980.</p>
</scopecontent><c04><did>
<united>**D 709 2/8/11**</unitid>
<unittitle>*Correspondence concerning open cast coal mining*<unitdate>29 May 1980–30 Jul 1980</unitdate></unittitle><physdesc><extent>10 letters</extent></physdesc><note><p>Letters/copy letters between David Owen, <persname>James Callaghan</persname>and <persname Bill Tobutt</persname> of the<corpname>Transport and General Workers' Union</corpname> concerning the decline in the open cast coal industry.
</p></note></did><controlaccess>
<subject othersource='ICSSD'>Coal industry</subject)
<subject othersource='ICSSD'>Trade unions</subject>
<subject othersource='Owen autobiography'>Callaghan, James</persname>
<persname>Tobutt, William</persname><controlaccess></c04></c03><c02>

Source: University of Liverpool, David Owen papers.

Figure 7.5   Examples of a description marked up in EAD

**D 709 2/8: Papers as member of the Opposition:
Shadow Energy Spokesman 1979–1981**

D 709 2/8
Labour Party .Opposition — energy spokesman 1979–1981

Scope and content
The group D 709 2/8 contains a small amount of correspondence relating
to David Owen's career as Shadow Energy Spokesman, dated 1980

Biographical notes
On the defeat of the Labour Party in the General Election of May 1979 David
Owen took the position of Shadow Energy Spokesman, until his decision to leave
the Labour Party in January 1981.
During this period the Labour Party was experiencing serious internal disputes
concerning the balance of its power; with increasing pressure from Tony Benn
and the Labour Left to lessen the influence of the Parliamentary Labour Party
and heighten the influence of Labour activists. The ascendancy of the Left
wing of the Labour Party at this time was strongly opposed by Owen, and finally
provoked him into the decision to leave the Party (see *D 709 2/14
Papers on leaving the Labour Party*).

Arrangement
The papers in group D 709 2/8 are arranged into the following groups:
D 709 2/8/1 General correspondence

Related materials
Several transcripts of speeches and articles on energy-related issues made
by David Owen as Shadow Energy Spokesman can be found with general files of his
speeches (D 709 2/9) and articles(D 709 2/10)

D 709 2/8/1: General correspondence

D 709 2/8/1
Labour Party . Shadow Energy Spokesman . Correspondence

Scope and content
D 709 2/8/1 contains a small group of letters relating to David Owen's
career as Shadow Energy Spokesman, dated May–Jul 1980.

D 709 2/8/1/1
Correspondence concerning open cast coal mining 29 May

1980-30 Jul 1980; 10 letters
Note: Letters/copy letters between David Owen, James Callaghan
and Bill Tobutt of the Transport and General Workers' Union concerning the decline in the
open cast coal industry.

Subject heading: Coal industry
Subject heading: Trade unions
Personal name: Callaghan, James
Personal name: Tobutt, William

*Figure 7.6   The same description as in Figure 7.5, as it would appear
to users*

to respond to this request and to implement it by transferring the document required. By using this standard, therefore, information managers can take a step towards the free retrieval and transmission of documents across a variety of systems. Initially the main use of it was to facilitate the remote searching of databases, especially library catalogues, using a standard web browser. It would be normal, but not necessary, for the records searched and transferred to be themselves in a standard format, such as MARC. Z39.50, possibly with further development, forms part of large-scale projects such as the Virtual Electronic Library.[27]

Like SGML, this standard has been worked on by a specialist group of archivists in Britain and the USA with a view to exploiting its potential for the free search and interchange of archival descriptions.[28] Archivists planning a description system that aims to make information available electronically should include Z39.50 capabilities in the design.

The following chapter discusses some of the questions that arise from using these standards and formats, and brings in the subject of authority standards and controls.

NOTES

1. Cook, M. and Procter, M. (1989), *Manual of Archival Description*, 2nd edn, Aldershot: Gower. The book in fact appeared in 1990. Michael Roper, speaking as President of the Society of Archivists at its conference in 1991 gave it a degree of endorsement.
2. International Council on Archives, Ad Hoc Commission on Archival Description Standards. The commission's secretariat, from which its documents can be obtained is located at the National Archives of Canada, Ottawa.
3. Museum Documentation Association (July 1995), *MODES for Archives: a Concise Guide*, M. Cook (ed.), Cambridge: MDA.
4. See Chapter 4 in this volume.
5. Gorman, M. and Winkler, P.W. (eds) (1988), *Anglo-American Cataloguing Rules*, 2nd edn revd, Part II, ch. 1, London: Library Association Publishing.
6. The Grigg Report (1954), *Report of the Committee on Departmental Records*, Cmd 9163, pp. 12–15, London: HMSO.
7. Jenkinson, C.H. (1965), *A Manual of Archive Administration*, 2nd edn revd, pp. 37–8, London: Lund Humphries.
8. (1993), *Library of Congress Subject Headings*, 16th edn, Washington, DC: Cataloging Distribution Service, Library of Congress. Museum Documentation Association (1993), *Social*

History and Industrial Classification (SHIC), a Subject Classification for Museum Collections, 2nd edn, Cambridge: MDA.

9. Bearman, D. (1989), 'Description Standards: a Framework for Action', *American Archivist*, 52, 514–19. Reprinted in Walch, V.I. for the Working Group on Standards for Archival Descriptions (1994), *Standards for Archival Description: a Handbook*, pp. 5–8, Chicago: Society of American Archivists.

10. Walch (1994).

11. Gorman, M. and Winkler, P.W. (eds) (1988), *Anglo-American Cataloguing Rules*, 2nd edn revd, London: Library Association Publishing.

12. Hensen, S.L.(comp.) (1989), *Archives, Personal Papers and Manuscripts: a Cataloging Manual for Archival Repositories, Historical Societies and Manuscript Libraries*, 2nd edn, Chicago: Society of American Archivists.

13. Research Libraries Group Government Records Project (1992), *Report on Descriptive Practices for Government Records*, Stanford, CA: RLG

14. Bureau of Canadian Archivists, Planning Committee on Discipline Standards (1990), *RAD: Rules for Archival Description*, Ottawa: Bureau of Canadian Archivists. Australian Society of Archivists, *ACPM: Australian Common Practice Manual*, in progress.

15. Gredley, E. and Hopkinson, A. (1990), *Exchanging Bibliographic Data: MARC and Other International Formats*, London: Library Association.

16. For example the Universities of Hull and Aberdeen. A full list is available at www.archivesinfo.net/.

17. FitzGerald, S. (1995), 'Archives Cataloguing on Computer at the Royal Botanic Gardens, Kew: Using MARC, International Standards and Unicorn', *Journal of the Society of Archivists*, **16**, 179–91.

18. Sahli, N. (1985), *MARC for Archives and Manuscripts: the AMC Format*, Chicago: Society of American Archivists. Evans, M. and Weber, L.B. (1985), *MARC for Archives and Manuscripts: a Compendium of Practice*, Chicago: Society of American Archivists.

19. See Smiraglia, R.P. (ed.) (1990), *Describing Archival Materials: the Use of the MARC AMC Format*, New York and London: Haworth Press. Hensen, S.L. (1991), 'RAD, MAD and APPM: the Search for Anglo-American Standards for Archival Description', *Archives and Museum Informatics*, **5**, 2–5.

20. ISO 8879: 1986.

21. Documents are maintained at http://sunsite.berkeley.edu/FindingAids/. Substantial files can be downloaded from the Library of Congress by using ftp.loc.gov. For a general explanation see also

Higgins, R. (1997), 'Standardised Languages for Data Exchange and Storage', *Business Archives: Principles and Practice*, **73**, 33–47, which gives an example of a legal title deed encoded into EAD.

22. The list is EAD, supported by Listserv@loc.gov.
23. www.pro.gov.uk/.
24. Text Encoding Initiative (1994), *Guidelines for Electronic Text Encoding and Interchange*, available at http://www.uic.edu/orgs/tei.
25. Society of Archivists Archives and Internet Group, *Writing Web Pages: Guidelines for Archivists*, http://www.archives.org.uk.
26. ISO 23950 Search and Retrieve Service Definition and Protocol Specification. See NISO/ANSI (1989), *Information Retrieval Service Definition and Protocol Specification*, New Jersey: Transaction Books.
27. This application is promoted by the Committee on Institutional Cooperation. See http://www.cic.net/cic/.
28. Watry, P.B. and Watry, M.M. (1996), 'Automating Archival Collections Using MARC-AMC and Z39.50 at the University of Liverpool: a Case Study', *Journal of the Society of Archivists*, **17**, 167–73.

CHAPTER

8

THE ORGANIZATION OF INFORMATION IN ARCHIVAL SYSTEMS

It was seen in Chapter 6 that archival description involved the creation of representations of the original archives. These representations could then be used to carry out the various tasks that are required in order to ensure that the original materials and the evidence they contain can be put to every appropriate use. The whole range of activities involved in this work, from the design of the system to the sorting orders of the finding aids can be pulled together under the general title of organization of information, thereby underlining the parallels there are between this work and tasks commonly carried out in the world of information management. Information organization includes the whole range of activities: indexing, abstracting, description, classification, records management and data exchange.

In information theory a document consists of a combination of text, representing a message, and a medium. In archival theory, there is an additional element, which has been labelled 'recordness'.[1] This means that records and archives, besides being documents (in whatever medium) in the general sense, also have a special character that arises from their context. They have been created and used in the course of some actual business, and form part of that business. They can never lose this contextual dimension, or if they do, then a significant part of their value is lost. Context, or provenance, therefore must be recognized as a fundamental part of the definition.

An additional distinctive feature of archives, different from many other aspects of information management, is that what are referred to generally as 'documents' may be groups, subgroups, series, items or pieces: that is to say, aggregate archival entities have to be treated as units according to context.

In the wider world of information management, the organization of information (often called the organization of knowledge) is the organization of documented messages in which information is contained.[2] The organization of archival information is the same, but refers to the way in which archivally documented messages are managed. For present purposes this definition also covers the organization of records by a records management system. This is because archives are a subset of records, and the two categories share the quality of 'recordness'.

Archivists are accustomed to organizing the representations they have made into finding-aids systems. These finding aids perform a function similar to that of indexing, cataloguing and classification in library systems, use some of the same procedures and technologies, and can be considered in the same general context. It may therefore be convenient to consider these similarities (and differences) under the same headings.

Indexing is a term that covers a set of procedures for providing access to bodies of information – these can be descriptions of groups, series or items, or parts of any of these – without regard to the actual location of the materials. Cataloguing, in library terms, is the indexing of documents in particular collections. Classification is the arrangement of index entries in accordance with a scheme of relationships between them, as opposed to alphabetical or numerical arrangement of the entry headings. Classification categories and the headings of descriptions within them can be arranged according to broader-narrower or whole-to-part hierarchical relations, chronology or any other systematic method.

Archival description can be regarded, like cataloguing, as a specialized case of indexing, and that archival descriptions can be sorted into an order, or orders, dictated by classification. As was seen in Chapter 6, mainstream archival practice is that the main set of descriptions should be sorted into a structural order, reflecting the original system under which the materials were created, but any other sorting order can be set up for secondary sets of finding aids.

Many ready-made classification schemes exist, and are widely used in the field of librarianship. Although there are also some classification schemes commonly used to some extent in archivology, archivists generally feel that there are serious objections to using ready-made schemes. Nevertheless we can accept the general principle that archival descriptions can and should be classified, even if special classification schemes must be created for them. The general principles for the use of classification schemes in archives are that:

○   no classification scheme should be adopted that does not preserve some link with provenance information
○   classified sets of finding aids should always be linked to the main set, which is arranged in structural order.

Archival descriptions are suitable for treatment as forms of indexing, because of their structure. As we have seen in the previous chapters, archival descriptions consist of specific data items in dedicated fields, and also have blocks of free text. The free-text areas are again divided into those representing contextual or provenance information, and those representing the information contained in the documents. Each description (each representation of an original) has a structure that consists of a heading followed by fields containing an expansion or qualification of that heading (see Figure 8.1)

```
Heading

    Reference code

    Description
```

Figure 8.1   The structure of an index entry

If this general structure is valid, then in any particular case archival descriptions can be sorted into an arrangement determined by the heading. Headings of descriptions are access points, by which users can find a way into the finding-aids system.

ACCESS POINTS

Different sorting orders, and hence different classification schemes, may be adopted by using different fields as the heading that is to be sorted. The generic term for the headings used in any particular context is 'access point'. There is a growing body of theory and practice that governs their use, and though the term is not yet generally familiar to archivists it will become so.[3] There is a general presumption that access points are normally governed by authority control.

In librarianship the principal catalogue or index is sorted according to the main entry heading. This heading serves to provide a definitive description of a message as contained in a document, and so permits the recognition and gathering together of all other manifestations of the same message. Where there are variant forms of the message these may be gathered together by using a uniform title.[4] Although the concept of the uniform title barely exists in archives management (because each archival entity is unique), this principle still holds in archival usage, since there are many occasions on which it is desired to bring together different archival entities (for example, to reconstitute a scattered group). In archives work, we can assign the term 'main entry heading' to the headings used in the main (structural) finding aid, and use other headings for finding aids that are organized in different ways.

The body of an archival description then attempts to give information on context, content, meaning, purpose and related features of the messages found in groups, series or items. Indexes can be set up so that these items of description can be accessed, and these methods of access involve the use of information retrieval techniques, two aspects of which can now be considered: indexing as a technique, and online searching of textbases.

▉ INDEXING

The distinction between specific and general indexes may serve to introduce some further discussion of access points in archival description systems. Users beginning a search must make their entry into the finding aids either from the top (the widest possible view of the subject) or from the bottom (the narrowest and most specific view). Entry from the top means using the guide first, with its index; the terms searched for may be the broader ones in a structured indexing scheme, and the user will be looking for the most appropriate groups to search. Entry from the bottom would mean searching for specific or narrower terms in the index to a particular group or archival entity as a way of scanning the item or series lists: the user's objective would be the identification of individual documents (see Figure 8.2). These two approaches are not total alternatives, for the user's strategy is determined by the nature of the search being undertaken, and the amount of background knowledge the user already has. Indexes are available as a starting-point in both strategies.

The difference between library and archive practice is particularly obvious here. In libraries, the subject index normally forms part of the principal representation file, the catalogue, or else is a separate and parallel catalogue of equal status. In an archival finding-aid system, the principal representation file is normally something quite distinct. The guides, catalogues and lists of an archival finding-aid system are different in format and intention from the indexes which provide one way of entry into their textual contents. An exception to this is the one mentioned below, the case where the index is itself the main finding aid to a particular group.[5]

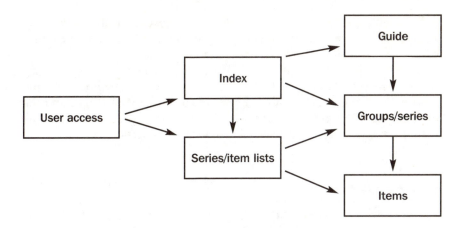

Figure 8.2   User access via access points

Another point of difference is that in archival searching the names and designations of particular persons and administrative structures in the originating organization are especially important as guides to the whereabouts of subject information. To identify which subgroup or series is most relevant to a search, a user often needs only to establish which office or person was responsible for a relevant function during the period of currency. The administrative or biographical history ought to reveal the most useful names. After discovering these, the user may be able to build a search strategy on retrieving the names of functionaries, wherever they occur at appropriate dates. It follows that many subject enquiries can be answered, at least for skilled users, by reference to institutional or personal name indexes.

> The arrangement of archives by provenance goes a good deal of the way to narrow the field in record enquiries. In respect of any one enquiry nearly all administrative departments can be ruled out on chronological grounds, or those of area of competence in a way which is not paralleled in the library field.[6]

Index headings are normally keywords or phrases that appear in the main finding aids, and are not derived directly from the content of original archive materials. The MAD2 data structure for archival description proposes that the central descriptive feature of the content of archives should be a free-text abstract. Free text also occurs in context descriptions (administrative/custodial histories) and in headnotes – that is, they form the bulk of all macro descriptions. They also appear in some fields in micro descriptions, for instance where there are item titles. All these fields should be capable of providing material for index construction, which means that they should ideally be written with the aid of a thesaurus or permitted vocabulary, and should contain all the necessary terms for transposal to the index.

Special indexing problems arise where medieval or other early archives are the subject of the index. These include spelling variants, obsolete or changing name-forms, illegible or difficult readings, and the need to identify obsolete names or places and specialized terms. The main problems here are discussed in specialist studies.[7]

VOCABULARY CONTROL

The best principle is that archival descriptions should be written using the terms that will match the terms that will be used by searchers when they embark on a search of the finding aids. Unfortunately it is difficult to achieve this degree of perfection. The terms used by archivists when compiling finding aids will be influenced by (a) the terminology of the original documents, which may tend to use technical terms (many archives are legal or quasi-legal in context) or what is now archaic language; and (b) terms common in professional discourse, which may not easily fit with ordinary outside language. Users, of course, come to the search with varied backgrounds. It is quite rare, in practice, to find much correspondence between what might be seen as natural search terms by users and those generated by professional staff.

The most common approach to solving this problem has been to require the use of a restricted set of terms, perhaps with some cross-references to alternative terms. In an archival context, this method has been much more common in connection with indexes than with the textual elements of archival descriptions, but the principle is the same. Controlled lists of terms may cover names, places and subjects.

Although there are many difficulties in setting acceptable rules for personal names that will work for all or most archives services, these are the ones that have been tackled by the profession first. It is important that in future archivists should not set about deciding personal name rules for themselves ('reinventing the wheel') but should rather seek to negotiate variations in what is now the UK national standard: the National Council on Archives Rules.[8] These were based on the rules current in librarianship (AACR2), but there are significant variations, introduced because of the special needs of archival description.[9]

Corporate names are included in the NCA rules. These, more than personal names, will usually need several 'see' and 'see also' references, because organizations have always tended to change the specific forms of their name over time. Archivists will need to establish a preferred form of the current name (or the name that is to appear in the heading), and of previous names; and will wish to establish references to alternative names that were used at particular times, and to alternative names that belonged to subordinate, linked or related bodies.

With place names, territorial groupings can be preserved by determining a hierarchical order of names, for instance based upon ancient parishes, and within these, townships and other areas of decreasing size or increasing specificity. In view of the difficulty of spelling variants over long periods of time, this choice would be a sensible one for a territorially based archives service. Rules as to the use of standard spellings and transcribed spellings might appear in the staff instructions: in the index the standard modern spelling should normally be used. Many archives services find it useful to index boundary changes in graphical form, by drawing up maps of the territorial situation at different periods. At least one computer graphics system exists for this.[10]

Archivists have often taken the view that they cannot use library-based compilations of subject terms, and it is generally agreed that this is the most difficult area. Most archives services have tended to avoid the problem, or have developed only very simple locally compiled lists of preferred terms. Here again it is important to avoid duplicating work that has been done elsewhere, and to adopt general standards if at all possible. The most widely used authority list is the *Library of Congress Subject Headings* (LCSH).[11] There are, however, reasons why archivists find it difficult to use library-based authority lists. The most prominent of these is that they need to use names and terms that were once current but have either passed out of use, or have even become offensive. A British example would be 'Poor Law', which during most of the nineteenth century and earlier was the natural term for the public assistance to the poor. It would be inaccurate and offensive to use it now (variants of 'welfare' or 'social security' would be used) but it is necessary to allow users to search for the term in archival finding aids.

Despite these difficulties, the NCA is currently working on a list of subject terms, and archivists will find it useful to negotiate their own input into this work.[12] Nowadays subject-term lists tend to prefer single-concept terms rather than complex subject headings.

In archival finding aids, subject indexes will not normally occupy the important place held by these in library systems. This is because of the nature of the media. It is quite normal for archival documents, at any level, to refer to many subjects. At group level, take the example of the archives of a landed estate. The whole group might appear in finding aids that gather together material bearing on land use, but there may be documents within the group that deal with a large range of other subjects: social or political activity, religious observance, population movements, climate, etc. At item level, a single letter, the importance of which must depend on its context, may refer to any topic that exists, or any combination of them. The value of subject indexes therefore depends greatly on the consistency and level of the entries in it. Few archivists can seriously attempt a full subject indexing of their material.

INDEX PLANNING

Most archivists have some practical familiarity with making indexes, and with the difficulties that come with them. Although many of the older indexes in use today have derived from *ad hoc* and relatively unplanned initiatives, there would be general assent to the proposition that index planning is desirable: that is to say, some degree of authority control is needed. An unplanned and undisciplined index is only useful until a certain size and/or degree of congestion is reached. After that, radical reform, including reform of the language used and the terms chosen, is needed. In fact, planned decisions are needed on other points as well. Some of these are listed in the following sections.

There are well-established standards, as well as a considerable literature, covering all aspects of the planning and control of indexes.[13] Some familiarity with this is indispensable, especially as there is a large number of technical terms and concepts.

Three characteristics of indexes need to be addressed at the planning stage:

1. *Exhaustivity*. Automated systems are the most exhaustive, since they can patiently compile lists of all the terms available. These lists are consequently difficult to use precisely because they are too exhaustive.
2. *Selectivity*. Human indexing systems tend to be best at selectivity, but they may have the fault of omitting significant references. MAD2 has a recommendation against bias.
3. *Specificity*. As a general principle, index entries should be as specific as possible. This means that the list of terms will be long, which can be a difficulty. Indexing to quite a high specificity is often more natural with archival materials, since subject references tend to be quite specific in the documents themselves.

The underlying structure of the index needs to be determined. Is it to be an alphabeticized list of terms chosen freely from the natural language (but containing cross-references) or is there to be some authority control over the terms and concepts to be included in it? If the latter, then is the index to be an application of a general classification scheme or, as an alternative, is it necessary to compile a special scheme for it?

All human knowledge, which must be expressed and recorded by using words, can be organized into coherent schemes. Any particular term can relate in various ways to other terms, according the context in which it is used. These relationships can be reduced to three basic ones:

O   synonyms: words that mean the same
O   broader terms: where the term selected covers many more specific terms
O   narrower terms: where the term selected refers to something that fits within a broader category of things.

A common form of authority control that recognizes and uses these semantic relationships is the thesaurus, which is a dictionary of terms arranged to show these relationships. A thesaurus can be used to control the terms used as headings in any index.[14] It is fairly common for archives services to develop simple thesauri for use internally.

Indexes arranged under keywords taken from natural language are alphabetic, and those arranged in accordance with a classification scheme are systematic. There has been at times a considerable debate among archivists as to the desirability of each, but it appears that today the profession is fairly generally in favour of the alphabetic. On the other hand, there is a strong and probably growing under-current of opinion in favour of some degree of authority control of the language used. Most archivists' opinions are formed from their own experience.

Attempts in the past to construct or adapt general classification schemes to govern archival indexes have not succeeded in attracting general support from archivists, nor have there been widely used adaptations of classification schemes devised by other agencies: 'in library catalogues general ideas not only govern the layout of the classification but provide pegs on which to hang references to general works, including the most general of all, such as encyclopaedias. There are no general records [i.e. archives] in this sense.'[15]

All logically structured indexing schemes share the same defect, which is that the indexer has to work with a copy of the scheme on the desk, and has to check each term that has not become familiar. If the scheme is a notational one, the notation has to be learnt and entered, and can often look very odd, as the following entry from the Classification Research Group's scheme, as used by *Library and Information Science Abstracts* shows (see Figure 8.3 overleaf).[16]

While it is true that indexers can quickly learn the meaning of most of the principal notational codes, nevertheless to use them would still require constant reference to the book, users would need instruction, and there is often a rather cumbersome appearance in the final result.

QiNbmGkD2 9–

  Buildings

    Planning

      Teacher training college libraries

        Cardiff College of Education

Source: LISA.

Figure 8.3   Example of an entry in a notational classification

Another difference between archives and library practice is important here. In libraries, indexing (like cataloguing) is often a specialist job. Those who practise it can therefore reasonably be expected to be familiar with appropriate schemes. In archives, description, the construction of finding aids, and therefore indexing, is usually regarded as something that every professional should do. It is not so easy to assume that all archivists are familiar with technical schemes, or that they are prepared to become so.

In any case, a scheme cannot be adopted unless it is available in a finished form to start with, which at present is not often the case. It is worth considering whether one of the specialist schemes, such as CRG[17] or SH1C[18] can be adapted for use in an archives service. Even if a suitable scheme is available, the authority control must still provide for new terms to be included as the work of indexing proceeds. This is a bigger difficulty than it sounds, since new terms have to be slotted into the correct place in the hierarchy, and the correct related terms, at higher and lower levels, must be in place to receive them. Many terms have more than one possible place in the scheme, because they have more than one facet. The operation requires knowledge and judgement, and also consumes time. One cannot expect indexing work to be completed on schedule if the indexer has got to break off constantly to operate authority control procedures. There is always the difficulty of lack of consistency when more than one worker is involved at any stage. This kind of problem has certainly caused many indexing schemes to fail, and in doing so has brought their designers into the natural language school of thought.

But then, natural language indexing also has serious problems. The main one is that of synonyms and near synonyms, and behind these lie the array of syntactical and semantic problems which the logical classification schemes attempt to solve.

The indexer has two choices: either to accept any word as a possible heading in the index, no matter what synonyms exist, or to adopt a system of 'preferred terms', and list these in an authority file or thesaurus. Both courses have difficulties. The former introduces endless complications into the index, which if continued unchecked will eventually make it difficult to use.

In an uncontrolled natural language index, concepts that are related logically but unrelated alphabetically are randomly scattered. References to an important theme will be divided through all the terms encountered. Bridge construction may be such a theme in local government archives. The index terms within it might cover planning, procurement, legal provision, transport of materials, the actual building process, maintenance, use by passengers, and so on. Even terms relating to a single level and a specific activity may be scattered: stonework, mortar, bonding, etc. A systematic scheme would be able to bring these together in a logical sequence, and would also direct the mind of the user to new divisions of the scheme which might otherwise have been disregarded. The more specialized the archives on which the index is based the more complex these problems become.

The second course is also difficult. The list of preferred terms, simple enough at first, soon grows to look like a systematic classification scheme or thesaurus, but without the worked-out hierarchical analysis that the latter has. The need to enter preferred terms ('use for'), non-preferred terms ('see') and cross-references ('see also') to their alternatives at all the appropriate places means that instructions to the working indexers must become increasingly elaborate, and so must the checking process.

The biggest problem in indexing is probably that of maintaining consistency. So many variations in style, choice of terms, the modification of terms, depth of indexing, etc. are available, that even when the index is the work of only one member of staff over a period of time (the best way), inconsistencies come in. Classification schemes and thesauri can certainly be a help, and are sometimes perhaps even indispensable, in combating inconsistency. The golden rule is that any scheme which is adopted should be adopted for the benefit of the user, not directly for that of the indexer.[19]

An important experiment on the effectiveness of controlled vocabulary in finding aids was carried out in the City Archives of Oporto.[20] This study is particularly useful because it includes a summary of the published literature on information retrieval, but it is worth observing that the main finding was that the most important factor in retrieval was the familiarity of the users with the material they were working with.

The physical form in which indexes are presented has some importance. In the past, most archives services have tended to use indexes of the end-of-volume type, and indexes on cards. Other physical types, such as sheaf indexes, have been less common, and the use of electro-mechanical card systems has been negligible. Automated indexes of any kind are still not common, but deserve discussion because of their potential for the future.

Irrespective of their physical form, indexes are a necessary component of any finding aid and, therefore, of any finding-aids system. A finding aid may therefore normally consist of a list or inventory (the essential representation of the originals) and an index that provides a means of access to it. The distinction between an index and a list is important, for on the conceptual level there are clearly two kinds of index to be met within an archival system. One kind is the index to a particular list or set of descriptions (note that in some cases the index may itself be the principal finding aid to some part of the holdings: this is considered in a separate section in this chapter). The other kind is the index to the macro descriptions generally. An example would be the index(es) to the guide to the overall holdings of the archives service. These two kinds both provide possible initial access points for users, and are an essential linkage between parts of the system. The first kind has to be very specific in its construction and its entries; the second must be constructed on a broader model, so that the amalgamation of different indexes of the same kind can be considered. Some mechanical aspects of index construction are also worth considering.

Whatever mode of indexing structure is adopted, there must be a decision on the filing rules to be used to place headings in order, whether 'letter by letter' or 'word by word'. In some cases, this choice can have important consequences. The rules must allow for headings that are numerical (either Roman or Arabic), spaces or other special characters. Librarians have been accustomed to these rules for many decades, but there are still no uniform schemes in general use. Archivists may find the rules published by records managers are the most suitable for the present.[21] The rule in use should be explained to non-expert users in the explanatory material attached to finding aids.

The choice of typefaces is important. In the past, indexers have had a tendency to insist on using a large number of type variants – capitals, lower case, italic, etc. – each style representing some feature inherent in the term used for it. The fullest instance of this is perhaps the earlier indexes to manuscripts in the British Library.[22] Theoretically, this is a device to bring another channel into use: the type character gives information to the user about certain qualities in the term. Thus, in a personal name index, honorific titles might be given in italic. Elsewhere, capitalized words might indicate those which are included at a certain hierarchical level in the classification scheme.

The index planner must decide whether it is necessary to include this extra channel. Is it important to the user that this type of information should be given in the main alphabetical sequence? If the information is important, then perhaps a separate place could be found for it. More important than this nowadays is a decision as to whether the cost and difficulty of using a variety of types in one piece of print is justified. For most of this century, features like this had come to be regarded as an expensive luxury, but now that most written material is produced by word-processing, it has once again become easy and cheap to introduce textual variations. Nevertheless, the result is fussy and not particularly friendly to users. The practice is not generally recommended. In any case the relevant standard should be followed.

AUTOMATIC AND INTELLECTUAL METHODS OF INDEXING

Indexing still remains overwhelmingly a human activity. Selection and interconnection of terms is essentially an intellectual activity. It is likely to remain at the core of professional study and procedures. Nevertheless, it is natural that attempts should be made to use the power offered by computers wherever possible. In the context of archives, it has so far rarely been possible to use a completely machine-generated index, but it may be possible to include an element of machine-processing.

Indexing by human agency is of course much more common and is a traditional activity in an archives service. There are two steps in it: identifying topics, features or applications, and describing these in terms that can be used for retrieval. Experience has shown that choosing terms is very idiosyncratic, and that it does not seem possible to regulate the activity very closely, even by using controlled vocabulary.[23] On the other hand, human indexers are better at recognizing the presence of themes and subjects where these are not explicitly referred to in the text.

Not much space need be given to considering human-generated indexes, for here the computer does not introduce an essentially new feature. It is merely a device for reducing the clerical work involved in organizing the index entries once they have been written. Even so, the efficiency and speed with which this is done may well make the difference between success or failure of an indexing scheme, especially when considered from a budgetary point of view.[24] At the present time, most human-generated indexing will be done as part of a finding-aid system that requires the selection of access points.

Human-generated indexes may operate in one of two ways. In the first, the indexer scans the textual descriptions and marks in tags which will instruct the system to extract the tagged terms as index headings. It is possible to use different tags so that the system can differentiate between different indexes (place, persons, subject), or between headings, qualifiers and linking terms. The example shown in Figure 8.4 is from a page of listing for a large manuscript library.[25]

Throughout please divide text as follows. [2]MS no.[2]

[3]BIB.REF.[3] [4] *incipit*[4] [5] Sends[5] [6] other title[6] [7] language[7]

[8]keyword[8] [9] authentication[9] [10] date[10].

Figure 8.4   Tagging to select index headings

In the second way, the indexer may extract the terms to be used in the index, and write them separately into an input field, or traditionally on to an index card. Finding-aids worksheets or input documents might provide a box for index keywords; most specialized computer software includes sortable fields for this data. Most data exchange formats also include similar retrievable fields. It might be thought that this method demands an unjustifiable input of skilled labour. Certainly it must be a relatively expensive method, since it involves rewriting some of the material. On the other hand, this is an approach which gives the maximum amount of control over the generation of the index, which in turn means that there is less likelihood of the index becoming choked with useless or unintelligible entries. This approach may be advisable where the index is a complex one, carried out at some depth on important documents. It makes it directly possible for multiple or user-selected index entries to be generated in anticipation or response to a search.

Most user enquiries are for subject information which can only be expressed by combining keywords or by using syntactical links between keywords. Neither the requirements of the user nor the concepts contained within documents are likely to be simple. Looked at from either point of view, a typical subject statement might consist of three elements, linked by connecting words.

(Out-relief) of (agricultural workers) by (Poor Law unions)

might be an example: the brackets indicate that a compound term is being used as a search element.

This statement may be made into an entry in a preco-ordinate index by simply writing it out together with the appropriate reference. It can then be rotated, or permuted, by bringing each of the main terms in it to the front:

> **Agricultural workers**, out-relief of by Poor Law unions(ref)
> **Out-relief** of agricultural workers by Poor Law unions.(ref)
> **Poor Law unions**, out-relief of agricultural workers by.(ref)

Such an index is called preco-ordinate because compound terms are co-ordinated before any search is made by the user: each entry consists of a statement which brings together a number of elements to create a complex but precise subject heading. The user's problem with such an index is to identify the combinations of headings which will identify the entry required and exclude all others.

The example illustrates that permuting the terms increases the number of entries in the index, but makes the problem of identifying correct headings simpler (at the expense of multiplying entries). Even so, it is clear that not every substantive term appears as a heading in the three entries. Some means of access is still needed to:

> relief (as a term in Poor Law administration)
> unions (as units of administration in the Poor Law)

There are also possible synonyms, such as 'poor relief', 'farm workers' or 'boards of guardians' (and many others). These may be covered by a previously determined vocabulary or by cross-references. Notice, too, that several of these terms are obsolete, archaic or technical when seen from the point of view of a modern reader. Archaic technical terms may also at times include terms that might be seen as politically incorrect nowadays, but which must clearly be used if they are needed to provide access to primary sources.

Another approach would be to make the index a postco-ordinate one, in which the headings represent only one concept (linked to a reference). Co-ordination of these concepts is then done by the user during the course of a search. The example would read as follows:

> Agricultural workers (ref)
> Out-relief (ref)
> Poor Law unions (ref)

The problem of synonyms or archaic terms, as before, can be dealt with by vocabulary control, or by see/see also references.

In this index, the user must find a way of combining the separate entries so as to identify the subject statement that is being searched for, and to exclude others. The main problem can be seen from the example: the concepts which are used as headings are unqualified, and one cannot see their precise use in the context except by retrieving the documents they refer to. Combining the headings may make a search more precise (thus in the present example, it is possible that only one reference may have entries for all three terms), which makes this type of index better for mechanized systems.

All three headings in the example are terms which occur at different levels in a classification scheme, and are also terms which have more than one facet: that is, they have a place in more than one hierarchical classification.

Figure 8.5 suggests the possibility of an alternative form of index, the chain. In this system, all the relevant terms at different hierarchical levels are displayed, in such a way that the terms at levels below the one being used as a heading are given. In the example, possible chain entries would be:

> **Poor Law**. Unions. Relief. Out-relief
> **Unions**. Relief. Out-relief
> **Relief.** Out-relief
> **Out-relief**

When sorted alphabetically this would become:

> **Out-relief** (ref)
> **Poor Law.** Unions. Relief. Out-relief (ref)
> **Relief.** Out-relief (ref)
> **Unions.** Relief. Out-relief (ref)

The principle is that terms below the lead terms in hierarchical level are all repeated, but not those above it. It is still necessary to use

Agriculture	Population	Primary production
Labour	Rural population	Agricultural prdn
Farm workers	Farm workers	Labour
Employment	**Poor Law**	
Wages	Unions	
Agricultural wages	Relief	
Supplementation	Out-relief etc.	
Out-relief		

Figure 8.5   Examples of subject terms in hierarchical order in facets

vocabulary control to deal with the problem of synonyms and archaic terms.

Chain indexes are preco-ordinated, so that they will be judged by their ability to bring together linked concepts in a useful way. They also need a classification scheme or thesaurus which provides the necessary hierarchy of terms. If there is no previously established classification scheme, staff have to invent linkages or replicate terms uselessly. In an archival context, the approach is likely to interest only specialist archives services which cover technical fields and have written or can use a suitable classification scheme.

The assumption so far has been that there is no real alternative to using humans to select the entries in an index, even though their freedom of choice might be limited by using authority controls. As far as the ordinary user of computers is concerned, no machine available to us yet is able to exercise the necessary judgements. However, some of the more routine procedures may be relegated to the computer. These are some possible ways of doing this:

O   listing each word in the text in alphabetical order
O   permuting each word in selected parts of the text
O   extracting words or phrases placed between tags
O   sorting words written into dedicated fields.

Automatic indexing systems such as these are provided as part of several information or text management packages, and are often readily available without special programming. They can also be used to provide concordances (lists of terms, with or without a count of the number of times each is used) to texts, which in turn can be an essential tool in composing classification schemes or thesauri. A number of computer packages can also incorporate and apply locally constructed thesauri.[26]

Computerized indexes, whether machine-generated or not, can be formatted to provide output in convenient ways. Some early systems provided for the computer to print out index entries on cards, which could easily be duplicated for cross-referencing, and which could be inserted alphabetically in the existing files. This operation is wasteful, since computers are well able to print out updated indexes at convenient intervals, and can also combine two or more indexes provided that they are held in structurally compatible files. In most cases they can also be searched, so the printout index is not necessarily the most useful format for the resulting work. Indexes can be used, for example, as a structure for user-operated interfaces.

Computer systems cannot exercise judgement in selecting preferred terms, but they can very easily count the occurrence of terms within a text. They can also easily, quickly and accurately check terms against a list held in memory. Such a list can also point to synonyms and alternatives. More complex systems may be able to include some elements of syntactic parsing in order to identify and include phrases that should be treated as a unit. Computer systems can link terms that occur in similar situations or in proximity within text. At their most complex, these methods merge into expert systems, in which a body of expert knowledge is organized into interlinked sets of terms, so that a search for one or more terms can be led, by means of answers to questions, to higher and higher degrees of refinement. Expert systems have been tried out by archives services (usually as part of larger public information systems) but they demand very much preparatory development, and their use is not widespread in this context.

Unless we consider some of the most advanced and expensive systems for language analysis, developed by large-scale textual computing projects, there are only three ways in which computers can effectively be used to create and present an index. These all depend on the computer's ability to list and arrange the terms held in a textbase. They are known as Keyword In Context (KWIC), Keyword Out of Context (KWOC) and Keyword Alongside Context (KWAC).

In KWIC indexes, a separate entry is created for every word held in the text, except for those excluded by a stop list ('the', 'of', etc.). The keywords are arranged in alphabetical order down the middle of the page or screen, with the surrounding text preserved around them. Each entry has a location indicator.

Figure 8.6 shows the advantage of the system. By preserving the immediate context of each keyword much syntactical structuring is

Information science and archives **administration**

Information science and **archives administration**

Plans and the structure of **behaviour**

Education, its **data** and first principles

Education, its data and first principles

Education, its data and **first principles**

Information science and archives administration

Plans and the structure of behaviour

Education, its data and first **principles**

Information **science** and archives administration

Plans and the **structure** of behaviour

Figure 8.6   Example of a KWIC index

avoided. Note that the terms 'information science' and 'archives admin-istration' appear both as two-word phrases and as separate words. The method is particularly useful for indexing documents like a list of file titles, where a useful contextual statement is contained in the title. A drawback is that, since every word appears, the index can be very large.

KWOC indexes operate in a similar way but in this case each word, as it appears as a heading, is placed in the left margin, with the whole of the indexed line appearing as a subheading below and to the right. This method can also produce very large indexes and, as can be seen in Figure 8.7, the two-word phrase is not presented as a unit.

The compound phrase problem is solved in KWAC indexes. Here the lead term still appears on the left margin, but the remainder of its context is set out in the same order as in the original text. Word pairs and phrases beginning with the keyword are preserved but, on the other hand, the words that originally appeared before the entry are not kept in that order (see Figure 8.8 overleaf).

---

administration
  Information science and archives administration
archives
  Information science and archives administration
behaviour
  Plans and the structure of behaviour
data
  Education, its data and first principles
Education
  Education, its data and first principles
first
  Education, its data and first principles
Information
  Information science and archives administration
Plans
  Plans and the structure of behaviour
principles
  Education, its data and first principles
science
  Information science and archives administration
structure
  Plans and the structure of behaviour

Figure 8.7   Example of a KWOC index

administration
  Information science and archives
archives
  administration Information science and
behaviour
  Plans and the structure of
data
  and first principles Education, its
Education
  its data and first principles
first
  principles Education, its data and
Information
  science and archives administration
Plans
  and the structure of behaviour
principles
  Education, its data and first
science
  and archives administration Information
structure
  of behaviour Plans and the

Figure 8.8   Example of a KWAC index

INDEXES AS THE PRINCIPAL FINDING AID

The possibility that indexes might be used as the principal finding aid deserves discussion. There are certainly cases where indexes can refer directly to the original archive, and so may be regarded as the principal finding aids to that entity, rather than as retrieval aids in support of a textual description. There seem to be three main instances:

1. If there is an original index, which was compiled and in use during the period when the materials were still current, this index (although itself archival) becomes a useful means of access.

2. Sometimes an index, rather than a description, may be the most natural finding aid. The example given by Bell[27] is that of the British government's Cabinet Papers from 1938. A structural description for this series can be based upon the administrative

history of the cabinet office, plus a note of the chronological sequence of meetings. Since many subjects would be raised at any meeting, the chronological list is not a useful finding aid except to those whose search is narrowly chronological. A subject index to matters considered at each meeting is needed and is, in effect, the main finding aid for most users. There are other comparable cases: for example, where items in a series are arranged (whether in the original system or not) on alphabetical or numerical references, as with a sequence of case files. Wills are a good example of this type, and these are held by many archives services. Some of these sequences could also be regarded as being self-indexing, in that the reference code by which they are filed are also index headings.

3.   Some larger repositories based in libraries have the custom of indexing collections of private letters, the index referring directly to the original, and not being derived from, or referring to, terms which appear in the textual description.[28] Since it is possible to write abstracts of letters, or to incorporate names into summary descriptions, this method of operation may be said to be based on the design of the finding aids in that repository, and not necessarily on the character of the original materials. Outside the context of manuscript libraries the practice is not common.

Indexes are also systems in which textual structures may be used to sort access points into an agreed order. There are many ways of doing this, but there always remains a possible alternative, which is to leave the main text of a finding aid unstructured and to rely on a computer system to search it for specific keywords or character strings. Modern systems, both hardware and software, make it possible to search very large textbases in reasonably short stretches of time. Some may therefore feel that the effort put into analysing and designing databases with specialized (sortable) fields, not being always necessary, is a waste. In real life, a compromise is probably best: choose a system that will provide dedicated fields (and which therefore can make indexes) but will also allow users to search the text online.

INTERACTIVE SEARCHING

Up to the present, automated systems for archival description are commonly designed on the basis that the output is to be assimilated to traditional hard-copy formats. In systems like this, computers are being used as tools to produce the same kind of finding aids as were produced by manual methods in the past. Although it might seem wasteful, there are still good reasons for sticking to this method at least for a time. New finding aids have to be added to existing finding-aids systems, and there may be no immediate prospect of converting the backlog of these. Archivists on duty in the searchroom must be able to answer readers' enquiries intelligently and fully. The day when readers can access electronic finding aids directly has, in most cases, still not arrived.

In this context, archives services have tended to see their best policy as being one of continuing existing series of finding aids (particularly where these took the form of published volumes). The largest of these services outside the PRO, the Manuscript Collections of the British Library, explicitly took this view. Their policy during the 1980s was to use computing services to reduce the burden of clerical and other routine work involved in the production of their published catalogues. Other main repositories, such as the London Metropolitan Archives, took a similar view. In other cases the computer was used to introduce a new type of finding aid – for instance the West Sussex Record Office's index to wills – but here, too, the emphasis was on the production of updatable hard copy formats.

However, by the early 1980s it became clear that computers would be available cheaply for interactive facilities, especially the storage and searching of databases, and from this point it has become necessary for archivists to include this possibility in their planning for retrieval strategies in the future. The first voice to be raised to this effect was D. Bearman's in the USA, who met with considerable resistance.[29] Since then the spread of powerful, small computers (and even more by easily constructed networks) has rendered his view less unfashionable. Some description of the procedures and difficulties of interactive searching is therefore necessary here.

It is, of course, possible to use a computer to search a database held within its memory, even if interactive facilities are not formally available. This would involve the user in framing a question, the answer to which would be the information required (assuming that this information was actually held in the database). The trouble is that, for reasons discussed in the earlier part of this chapter, it is not easy to formulate a complex question, using exactly the right keywords and linked combinations of keywords, so that they match exactly the index headings held in the system (or strings of characters in the text). Usually it is necessary to make several attempts, modifying the terms used in the light of results obtained. This means that offline access to the computer is frustrating, and retrieval by this means is likely to be inaccurate, unreliable and slow.

Interactive facilities, in which the user can directly question the computer and get an immediate answer, transform this situation. Users can now ask for the retrieval of data identifying electronic documents which contain their specified keywords. The reply may suggest that a different keyword or combination of keywords should be tried: this can be done, and another answer received. The process of question and answer can be carried on, the questions becoming more and more refined each time, until the user can be satisfied that all relevant information has been retrieved. The final version can then, if required, be printed out.

If any database can be searched in this way, it is easy to see that the index format, involving the preliminary selection of terms, may perhaps become redundant, for computers can just as easily search for specified terms within the body of a piece of text, as in an alphabetically selected and arranged list of headings. The only requirement is that the original programming, or software package, provides the facility for this kind of search, the system is large enough to hold all the data, and fast enough to be able to search the whole text in an acceptable time. Users (whether staff or members of the public) should be able to identify a set of keywords, and the logical connections between them, which the machine can use as the keys to its search.

Early computer systems had the drawback that keywords entered for a search had to be exactly matched in the text. Capital letters or plural terminations, for example, might cause a search to fail. Modern systems do not usually suffer from this defect, as they allow the user to override capitals or lower-case differences, and to specify alternative termina-tions (or prefixes) to words. Thus the search term 'train+' could produce a response to 'trains' and 'training' as well as to the string specified. More sophisticated ways of linking terms which are related linguistically but which differ in some way from each other also exist but are probably not especially relevant to archival management.

Computer systems which provide searching facilities may require that the user should be able to use a command language, which consists of a sequence of commands chosen from a permitted range, and which cause the system to work in the required way. Command languages vary a great deal in complexity. Some are quite simple and knowledge of these can easily be acquired by users. More complex command lan-guages need more study, and these would be better used by trained staff. The standard for such languages, Structured Query Language (SQL) is widely used by systems designers. Naturally, the more complex the lan-guage, the more elaborate the search procedures that are possible. This may be a limiting factor, especially if the searching is to be done by external users or relatively inexpert people.

It is possible to overcome these problems in some cases by under-taking extra programming, and adding a 'front-end' to the programmes being used. There has been much development of these of recent years. Early versions might prompt the user by writing out a sequence of plain-language questions to which an answer is required. A sequence of questions and answers might be as follows:

> User: 'Search'
> Computer: What is the name of the database you wish to search?
> User: 'Strangford papers'
> Computer: OK. What is the first keyword?

More recent versions use graphics, so that users can choose appropriate databases, and then appropriate indexes by clicking the icons relating to them. There has been extensive development of user interfaces by museums, in particular, and users are now often accustomed to methods such as touch-sensitive screens.

Special programming of this sort can often make a complex system more user friendly, but it does also have drawbacks. Users rapidly become expert in the system they have learnt. When this happens they become impatient with the constant repetition of prompts, and it may be useful to introduce an optional choice of level, which allows the expert user to switch off prompts which have become too elementary.

Keywords to be searched for may be linked by logical operators, based upon Boolean algebra. For most purposes there are three of these: AND, OR and NOT.

literacy AND Rutland	instructs the system to find every instance in which a record contains both terms.
literacy OR Rutland	finds every record in which one of the terms occurs.
literacy NOT Rutland	finds records in which one of the terms appears but leaves out those in which they both appear together.

The logical operators can be used to link three or more terms in any combination:

> literacy AND Rutland NOT newspapers.
> literacy OR Rutland OR reading books.

Keywords may also be combined into single compound terms, and two or more of these compound terms can also be combined in a search:

> (literacy AND Rutland) AND (newspapers OR (reading books)) NOT writing.

Additional operators control the way the search is conducted. The most common ones are:

=	(the search terms must appear exactly as specified)
<,>	(smaller than, larger than: these can often be used for alphabetical strings as well as for numbers)
*	(contains)

Particular software systems have other operators.

As databases get bigger, the results of a single search, or of a series of searches, get bigger. A hit list containing many hundreds of retrieved references presents the enquirer with a difficult task. Some modern systems can apply weighted term vector or probabilistic techniques. In these, the system checks the results against the list of search terms and assigns each one a weighting, based on the degree to which it matches all the search terms, or how many instances of the search terms are found in the text. The resulting hit list can then be arranged in order of probable relevance.

As far as the mechanism of searching is concerned, these command facilities are flexible and intelligible, and allow a very wide range of search enquiries to be made. Difficulties experienced in carrying out a search usually derive far more from the intellectual difficulties inherent in formulating a search request than from the difficulties of interpreting it for the computer.

These difficulties, however, are considerable. The problem is to match the descriptions of archival entities which have been put into the database with the ideas formulated by users. If this match is to be made, there must be compatibility between the terminology (and even between the habits of thought and background knowledge) used by the archivist and by the user. This is asking a great deal even if one could assume that most users could formulate their enquiries in clear terms. Most often users need the stimulus of contact with the material before they can devise meaningful keywords for a retrieval strategy: browsing may be the best introduction for them.

There are many possibilities for failure. The user may not succeed in thinking of and then asking for the keywords which are present in the database (a synonym may have been used); the system may not have recognized the keyword asked for (some difference in format may not have been discounted); or the keyword combinations asked for may produce a flood of positive replies which take great labour to distinguish from each other. There may be too few hits, or too many. The possibilities of refinement of searches which are inherent in interactive searching may reduce this hiatus between the system and the user, but it is a gap which is always likely to exist. Even more is the gap between the thought and language of the archivist who originally devised the description which is being searched and those of the users of it. Ultimately it is a question of bridging the gap between minds. In some respects computers have reduced this gap, because they can sometimes minimize the labour involved in checking possibilities. In other ways, though, it is possible that they have increased the gap, because they tend to shield their holdings behind technological screens.

Online searching can be done remotely where the texts to be searched are held in a network. Large international data systems, such as the World Wide Web, depend on it, and it is likely that the expertise of many users in approaching textbases will grow.

◼ NOTES

1. Terry Cook (1996), 'Keeping Our Electronic Memory: Approaches for Securing Computer-Generated Records', lecture given to British government senior establishment officers at the Public Record Office, 4 October.
2. Anderson, J.D. (1997), 'Organization of Knowledge', in J. Feather and P. Sturges (eds), *International Encyclopedia of Information and Library Science*, pp. 336–53, London and New York: Routledge.
3. ISO 5963: *Documentation – Methods for Examining Documents, Determining their Subject, and Selecting Index Terms*, International Standards Organization. ISAAR(CPF) glossary.
4. The agreed standard form of a title where there are variants in use: AACR2.
5. Bell, L.(1971), 'Controlled Vocabulary Subject Indexing of Archives', *Journal of the Society of Archivists*, **4**, 285–99.
6. Ibid., p. 285.
7. Cox, N.S.M. and Davies, R.S.(1970), *The Indexing of Records in the PRO*, Newcastle upon Tyne: PRO. Hunnisett, R. (1972), *Indexing for Editors*, London: British Records Association.
8. National Council on Archives (1997), *Rules for the Construction of Personal, Place and Corporate Names*, London: NCA. Also Gorman, M. and Winkler, P.W. (eds) (1988), *Anglo-American Cataloguing Rules* (hereafter *AACR2*), 2nd edn revd, Part II, ch. 22, London: Library Association Publishing.
9. Relevant standards are listed in Rhoades, J.B. (1982), *The Applicability of UNISIST Guidelines and ISO International Standards to Archives Administration and Records Management: a RAMP Study*, Paris: Unesco. V.I.Walch for the Working Group on Standards for Archival Description (1994), *Standards for Archival Description: a Handbook*, Chicago: Society of American Archivists.
10. In use in the Riksarkivet (National Archives) of Sweden, Stockholm.
11. Library of Congress, Subject Cataloging Division (1993), *Library of Congress Subject Headings*, Washington, DC.: Library of

Congress. See also Chan, L.M. (1986), *Library of Congress Subject Headings: Principles and Applications*, 2nd edn, New York: Libraries Unlimited.

12. At the time of writing, co-ordinated by the Royal Commission on Historical Manuscripts, Quality House, Quality Court, Chancery Lane, London WC2A 1HP.

13. British Standards Institution (1988), *British Standard Recommendations for Preparing Indexes to Books, Periodicals and Other Documents*, BS3700, London: BSI. International Standards Organization (1993), *Information and Documentation: Guidelines for the Content, Organization and Presentation Of Indexes*, ISO/DIS999, Draft International Standard, ISO/TC 46/SC9, Geneva: ISO. A general introduction to indexing is Lancaster, F.W. (1991), *Indexing and Abstracting in Theory and Practice*, Chicago: University of Illinois and Library Association.

14. ISO 2788, *Documentation – Guidelines for the Establishment and Development of Monolingual Thesauri*, Geneva: International Standards Organization.

15. Bell (1971), p. 286.

16. Edwards, T., 'Indexing LISA ...', cited in Harrod, L.M.(1978), *Indexers on Indexing*, pp. 304–16, New York: R.R. Bowker.

17. Classification Research Group scheme.

18. Museum Documentation Association (1993), *Social History and Industrial Classification (SHIC), a Subject Classification for Museum Collections*, 2nd edn, Cambridge: MDA.

19. Bell (1971), p. 287.

20. Ribeiro, F. (1996), *Journal of the Society of Archivists*, **17**, 27–54.

21. Association for Records Managers and Administrators (ARMA International), Standards Advisory and Development Committee (1989), *Filing Procedures Guideline*. Also ARMA (1990) *Alphabetic Filing Rules*, (ANSI/ARMA International 1/1990; and ARMA (1989), *Numeric Filing Guideline*; and ARMA (1988) *Subject Filing Guideline*: all available from ARMA. A draft American standard is in progress: ANSI/NISO (1993), *Proposed American National Standard Guidelines For Indexes And Related Information Retrieval Devices*, Washington, DC: National Information Standards Organization Press.

22. British Library, Department of Manuscripts (1982), *Guide to the Catalogues and Indexes of the Department of Manuscripts*, M.A.E. Nickson (ed.), London: British Library. British Library, Department of Manuscripts (1985), *Index of Manuscripts in the British Library*, London: Chadwyck-Healey. www.bl.uk/collections/manuscripts/.

23. Leonard, L.E. (1977), *Inter-Indexer Consistency Studies, 1954–75: a Review of the Literature and Summary of Study Results*,

Occasional papers no. 131, Chicago: University of Illinois Graduate School of Library Science.

24. British Manuscript Collections (1989), *Automated Cataloguing: a Manual,* London: British Library.

25. Hibbins, R.V. (1981), *Cataloguing in the Department of Manuscripts, a Feasibility Study and Proposal for the Introduction of Automation,* London: British Library.

26. Mallinson, P. (1993), 'Developments in Free-Text Retrieval Systems', *Journal of the Society of Archivists,* **14**, 55–64.

27. Bell (1971), p. 296.

28. Hudson, J.P. (1979), *Manuscripts Indexing,* London: British Library Department of Manuscripts.

29. Bearman, D. (1979), 'Automated Access to Archival Information: Assessing Systems', *American Archivist,* **42**, 179–90.

CHAPTER

9

COMPUTING FOR ARCHIVAL MANAGEMENT

 BACKGROUND

Information management cannot be carried on without using computers, which today are the essential and universally used machines for the capture, storage, processing and transfer of information. The ready availability and growing capacity of personal computers, and the general introduction of online multi-terminal networks in administration mean that computing services of some kind are within the reach of most administrative or research departments, however small and isolated they may be. Archives services are not excluded from this generalization, even though at the time of writing, the majority of established archives services are still, at least in part, being run manually.

The history of archival computing in Britain has been recorded in a series of surveys. These have charted the rather unsteady progress of new automated systems in this field. The first, edited by L. Bell and M. Roper,[1] was the report of an international seminar held in 1974. Most of the participants represented major national archives institutions – Britain, Canada, USA, Belgium, France, West Germany, Italy, the Netherlands and the USSR. There was only one contribution from a local archives service. This was the East Sussex Record Office (ESRO) which has the distinction of being the first non-national archives service to undertake major automation.

A second survey by Lionel Bell in 1974 was almost contemporary with the first, and led to the report of an enquiry into current systems in use in Britain: at that time it appears that there were some 15 active archival computer applications.[2] However, six of these were within the PRO and five of them might properly be categorized as programs for aspects of historical research. Many of the systems noted were for the production of indexes.

Cook's survey published in 1980 was partial, but broke new ground in noting the arrival of automated systems in records management. It was still assumed at this date that most archival automation was occurring in the big national archives institutions, libraries and museums.[3]

R. Bartle and M. Cook carried out a more detailed survey of computer applications in Britain, outside the PRO, in the latter half of 1982. This found that there had been considerable new work, and that new developments were coming to light very rapidly. Seven organizations (including four county archives services) were operating automated systems for RM; 18 were developing them for archival management; and there were a few other cases of specific applications such as the indexing of particular series. A feature of this report was that a majority of systems noted had been introduced since 1980, and that interactive and personal computer schemes were beginning to predominate.[4]

Since then there have been no systematic surveys, but the Information Technology (IT) Group of the Society of Archivists has made spasmodic attempts to keep track of the systems in use. The database of their findings has been published in electronic form, and is available as one of the Society's publications.[5]

It would be wrong to give the impression that this series of surveys shows an uninterrupted progress in computer development. On the contrary, development has been patchy and prone to setbacks. Most of the systems introduced with high expectations in the 1970s either failed entirely or have been silently replaced: this includes the first local archives service scheme, ESRO, which was withdrawn in stages during the 1980s. Some development activities have been substantially curtailed as a result of difficulties encountered: this includes the most innovative home-developed system, that of the Somerset Record Office.[6]

The reasons for the failure of these early systems can give us some clues as to what is needed for a successful one. The pioneering systems were defeated by the limitations of the hardware and software. Methods of data capture and input were at first much too cumbersome. Input by punched cards was especially inappropriate, for it required that all data should be broken down into units of not more than 80 characters. But even when this difficulty was overcome, serious problems remained: data had to be typed in and constantly checked. Validation and verification emerged as major problems and causes of expense. In many systems, data was first written out by archivists, then typed by clerical staff, checked and retyped, offline. In some cases data was typed twice routinely, by different typists, and the two versions checked for discrepancies. Offline data capture and input always represented considerable cost elements but, even more importantly, they were constant causes of delay and dissatisfaction.

Although online data entry is now normal, and does not present the same cost problems, the questions of validation and verification still remain. Validation procedures test that the data is the right kind for the situation, and that it is presented in the right form. For example, dates, and only dates, should be entered into dedicated date fields. Automatic validation has always been possible but is generally not much use in an archival context. For example, systems can easily check whether numerical or alphabetical data are being entered, and will prevent letters being put into number fields. But in archival description data is normally alpha-numerical and so this particular check is often not available. Verification is more fundamental: this checks on the truthfulness or aptness of the data presented. It is hard to imagine how this could be removed from the intellectual control of the material exercised by professional staff.

The other main problem was the size of the data store required. Archival systems do not demand any great computing power or complexity, as far as the operations are concerned, but they do always contain a large amount of data. To be useful to archivists, the hardware must be able to contain large databases, and the software must be able to work with this at high speed. Both these requirements are now available, but until the early 1990s they were expensive special features.

Despite these difficulties, the pioneers of archival automation saw that it was not impossible to design systems that would be suitable. The difficulty was to obtain the funding and technical support. In 1983 the Society of Archivists Computer Applications Committee conducted a survey to establish what funding would be possible.[7] They found that a significant number of archives services would be prepared to collaborate and to pay an annual subscription. This finding suggested that a service on the model of the Museum Documentation Association (which at that time was funded largely by subscriptions from participating museums) could be feasible. The plan was not proceeded with because in the circumstances of the time it was not possible to find the necessary technical support. Computer bureaux were then not prepared to work for small markets.

The next best thing was to adapt an existing system to archival needs. There were several attempts to do this, working from different bases. One approach was for an individual archivist to build up specialized programs on the basis of a commercially available database system. The outstanding example of this approach was the work of Adam Green, applied eventually at the Somerset Record Office, developing the package, Advanced Revelation. Another approach was for a group of archivists, working in collaboration in their spare time, to adapt a parallel system. The best example of this was perhaps the group based at the British Antarctic Survey in Cambridge to adapt the museum's cataloguing package, MODES.[8] Other similar groups worked at adapting widely used packages. Indeed this approach still continues, the most outstanding example possibly being the CLIO system developed at the Scottish Record Office.

The third possible approach was to seek to develop a larger library management package. This resulted in the development of the package, ARCHWAY, developed by a specialist bureau and subscribed to by a small group of archives services.

Because of the general lack of resources to support these developments, the third approach was the most promising. It was made possible by a change in the strategy of computer firms, which began in the mid-1990s to take an interest in small technical markets, together with the increasing flexibility of library systems. What defeated the ARCHWAY project was the failure of the backing firm to maintain itself commercially, in a very slow and difficult market.

All these efforts to develop archival automation systems, or to adapt other systems to archival use suffered from the same basic defect. Too much work was needed for development, while the eventual market would be too small. In addition, the failure of the profession to adapt quickly to computerized methods destroyed the possibility of a standard, or generally used system. The lack of standards and agreed formats underlined this difficulty. At the present time, although the power and range of computer systems has grown enormously, problems of this kind still exist and are positively hindering the successful automation of archives services everywhere.

A somewhat similar situation has existed in connection with online or networked services. There has so far been no serious attempt in Britain to create a central online database of archival information, comparable to any of the bibliographic or documentary databases. In North America, the RLIN and OCLC networks have been including substantial numbers of archival descriptions since the mid-1980s. It was once widely expected that archivists would follow this route and that there would be a gradual convergence of library and archival practice. This expectation now appears to be false; if anything, the two bibliographic traditions have tended to separate.

Some of the reasons for this separation are obviously based in the nature of the material. There are three characteristics of archives that create difficulties:

O   Provenance: because archives are managed as fonds, that is under the headings created by the organizations that created them, there is less need than with books to provide access points under subject headings.

○   Many of the creating organizations are territorial. To search for the archives of a county education service, for example, users will naturally turn to the appropriate county record office, and there is no obvious need for a general description available on an expensive network.

○   Reference rate: archives services generally hold bulky materials which (although there is a high demand overall) have a low reference rate. Much of the expected realizable value of archival information resides in their use in the future – often the remote future.

Perhaps it will always be difficult to justify the use of database systems whose main virtue is rapid retrieval. We should remember though that there are other uses for long-distance data exchange: the reintegration of scattered fonds, finding and enlarging new user groups, exploiting the content of archival holdings in new ways. The overall aim of an archives service should be to make its material as generally usable as possible.

There are, however, special cases where the very rapid retrieval of information from older records or from archives may be essential. The easiest example might be a medical records system, in which patient records that had lain unused for decades might suddenly be urgently needed. Other examples generally concentrate on the archives of science, where a new project may urgently need access to data held over from long previous experiments. In cases like these the rapid retrieval facility offered by computerized databases becomes a significant advantage.

ARCHIVAL DESCRIPTION

Computerizing archival description is a much more complicated process than computerizing the cataloguing of books. Despite the publication of MAD2 in 1990 there is still no established cataloguing standard for British archivists. The problem of description at several levels, each of which has its own distinctive character, makes it difficult to devise record formats which will suit the realities of archival management. There has been insufficient preparatory work on the problems of authority control, indexing or searching free-text descriptive entries. In addition, there have been problems of staff retraining, or of the hostility of some existing personnel, and there have been problems of access to computing services.

DATA CAPTURE

The first difficulty in introducing automated description systems is how to assemble the data which is to be written into the descriptions. This problem, of course, exists also in non-automated systems. Bartle and Cook noted that archives services rarely sought to alter their existing administrative arrangements: the thinking was that computers could perhaps be used to streamline existing processes, but should not seriously influence the methods of work of professional staff, or the way duties might be delegated within the office. Until very recently this immobility was a strong feature of the larger as well as of the smaller archives services.

The conservatism which is evidenced in staffing structures and procedures is based on the view that data capture is a matter of writing notes or filling in paper forms, which are adaptations from, and represent, traditional listing stationery. Where batch-mode working was the norm, this is not surprising. Archives services have designed input data forms which are versions of their usual listing stationery, but which represent on paper the field structure of the system into which the data will be input. In earlier days, input forms were generally set out with individual character spaces. This was because many systems allocated set numbers of characters to each individual field. Variable field lengths are normal today, and indeed are a requirement for successful archival databases.

Data input forms are designed in the light of the office procedures they are to be a part of, and in the light of the methods by which the data is to be processed. Usually this has been by keyboarding the data remotely, so that clarity of instructions to the operator is an important feature. The other main features are:

1.   The description is broken up as far as possible into clearly defined fields, the contents of which are restricted by the current standard.
2.   As far as possible the work processes are reduced to a sequence of narrow choices.

These points may be illustrated in turn.

A reasonably strictly controlled input data form, where such a thing is necessary, might allow a variable-length free-text description in its central fields but would provide tight control of the peripheral fields (see Figure 9.1). For example, entries in the 'date' field are limited to those which conform to a list of possibilities set out in the system manual. The range of possibilities allowed demonstrates the difficulty archivists have in establishing definite descriptive usages: the range of information and format in archives is too great. The purpose of this kind of field limitation is to reduce the possibilities of error where the data processing is to be carried out by inexpert clerical staff at a distance from the workbench.

An important problem is to find a way which is perceived as clear and natural for both archivists and the clerical staff of the archives service. It is desirable for the success of the system that data input and processing should be done as close to the site of the professional work as possible. Physical remoteness of data processing services has been an important factor in the failure of some systems in the past, and a cause of staff hostility.

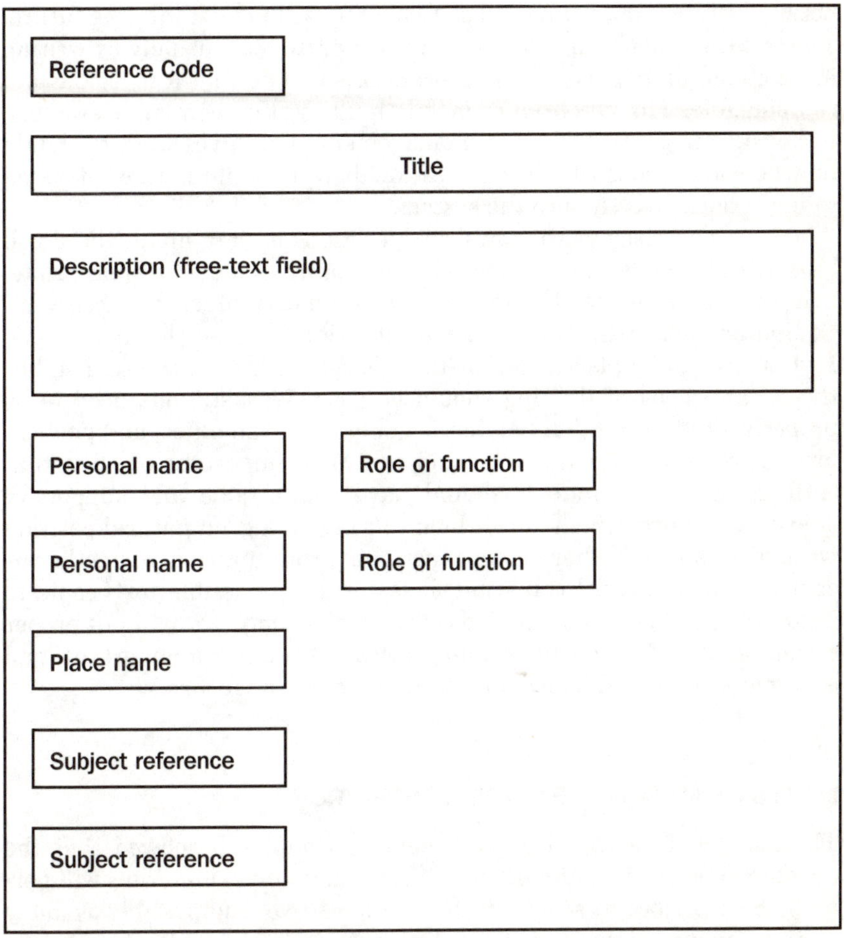

Figure 9.1   A simplified pattern for a structured data input screen. The fields for access points (personal name, place name, subjects) may be multiplied as many times as necessary

There is an alternative to filling in input forms, which is to use formatted screens on a conveniently situated computer, or on a laptop. What is required for this is front-end programming, so that the input of data into a system is governed by a subordinate program, the user interface. In the formatted screen labelled spaces will appear corresponding to the fields into which data is to be entered. Alternatively, a series of prompts can be supplied, and the operator will have to provide data in answer to these. Without such user-friendly devices, it can be difficult to control the entry and checking of data, and on this will depend the success of the whole system.

Many data entry systems assume that the existing relationship between professional staff and clerical staff will persist into the future. The tradition has been that archivists generate text (usually by writing in longhand on paper); typists process this text so that it is legible and reproducible. The potential of mobile multi-station computer systems, however, is so great that senior management of archives services should now be considering whether professional staff should not be retrained to input data directly into the system.

Whoever carries out the physical operations of data input, there will be cost and design implications. The environment must be appropriate, and the relevant health and safety standards must be observed.[9] Computers generally need a clean situation, and so do their users. Lights have to be placed so that they do not reflect on the screen, but the general level of lighting should be good. Workstations need to be properly sited in relation to what is going on in the office, and particularly in relation to doors and windows. Most important of all is that staff using the computers should have comfortable and supportive adjustable chairs, which allow them to work in a good natural position without strain. Whether or not repetitive strain injury is correctly categorized as a medical condition, it is certainly possible for people to injure themselves by long periods of work at a computer without proper supports. This factor will certainly become even more important, and even more regulated by legal requirements, in the future.

LEVELS OF ARRANGEMENT AND DESCRIPTION

The analysis of archival arrangement in Chapter 5 showed that the question of levels is fundamental. In general archival materials will normally be described at several levels – at least two, and possibly as many as eight or nine. Descriptions at different levels have different characteristics and are treated in different ways. Macro descriptions may be grouped together in horizontal collections, to produce guides. Micro descriptions are less frequently gathered together, but are often lengthy and may be assembled as a collection of lists. Most descriptions at all levels, but especially at micro levels, consist of a headnote or introduction that is free text, followed by a structured list. Vertically connected descriptions at several levels are published as catalogues.

Guides and handlists

Group/subgroup descriptions do not in themselves pose much of a problem for automation, since they are relatively homogeneous, and generally consist of a title (heading) followed by connected narrative (body). Automated systems could treat these through word-processing, much as any text for publication is treated. Indexing, if required, can be provided for by tagging, or by a concordance facility in the software. Archivists always have a tendency to use footnotes or endnotes in any body of text.

More serious problems arise when series descriptions are added, as they normally are. Series descriptions consist of some free text, but always with associated dedicated fields, and present a much more structured picture (see Figure 9.2 overleaf). They contrast clearly with descriptions at a higher level, and it is difficult to conceive a system which will contain both types of data structure within a single processing system.

It is now common or even standard procedure to separate guides, with their descriptions of groups, subgroups and sometime series, from item lists. The arrangement of the reference area of the reading room may well reflect this. This separation solves the problems posed by the (normally) different structure of item-level finding aids. The international standard ISAAR(CPF) provides for group-level descriptions that are so separated (dealt with in Chapter 6). If this or an in-house standard is used, provision might be made for including EAD tags.

For the production of guides, a system is needed which will allow freedom in the construction, length and content of fields, and permit the combination of long free-text entries, followed by the more structured sequences of series descriptions. The index should be capable of drawing keywords from both parts. The system should allow retrieval of data by sorting any of the distinguishable fields. These specifications are nowadays provided by most commercial software packages.

Lists and inventories

Micro descriptions, being essentially lists, do not present quite the same characteristics. The increasing flexibility of computer systems have reduced any difficulties there may have been in using variable length and free-text fields within structured databases, so that considerable variations in, for example, the length of file titles or additional notes,

---

BOROUGH COUNCILS

The Municipal Corporations Act 1835 abolished the many borough councils with various constitutions that had existed previously. New councils elected on a wider franchise were set up with improved financial regulation and police forces. This measure removed several ancient boroughs from that status, but thereafter populous settlements acquired borough status as they grew. Garworth was created a municipal borough in 1866, and Inchley in 1877. The larger towns became County Boroughs in 1888, including the county town of Denton. Wider responsibilities were given to the boroughs as the century progressed. They provided services in areas such as policing, refuse disposal, schools, museums, libraries, public health, water, gas and electricity, slaughterhouses, markets, highways, public transport, housing, building regulation, baths, town halls and other public buildings.

The Local Government Act 1972, effective from 1974, abolished borough councils. Their powers were taken over by the County Council and newly formed District Councils, the latter usually based in former municipal boroughs but with different, wider boundaries. Dentonshire Record Office became the archive authority with responsibility for the archives of superseded bodies.

Belfield: Borough Council minutes 1917–1974; committee minutes and papers 1917–1974; licensing registers 1930–1969; and other matters.

Charnley: Borough Council minutes 1946–1971; rate books 19–20 century; valuation lists 1854–1954; accounts 1835–1974.

Denton: principal committee minutes 1848–1963; childcare committee minutes 1948–1967; town planning scheme 1929.

Figure 9.2   Specimen Guide page, giving an administrative history of the (management level) Municipal Boroughs, followed by a brief notice of the main series held for each archive group

can easily be accommodated. Dedicated fields to contain reference codes, dates, location and other information can be created or deleted quite easily in many systems.

The headnote which many lists require might perhaps bring in some of the problems experienced in the macro descriptions. In practice, however, several database systems available now will provide for headnotes and column headings of at least moderate length (see Figure 9.3). This will probably be sufficient for most archivists, especially if an office

---

DDX9999 *Letters of Alexander Smith at London*

/5	John Isaac at Preston congratulating him on taking his degree	1859 May 1
/6	Isaac Nash at Blackburn concerning the death of Nash's parents	1859 May 2
/7	Alan Liddel at Blackburn about insanity amongst librarians	1862 Jun 2

Source: Lancashire Records Office.

Figure 9.3   Specimen item list with three tabulated columns

rule is introduced which will encourage general information on an archival entity to be put into the macro descriptions rather than into a headnote governing a micro description. Indexing should not present any new problem.

Vertical descriptions

When vertical sets of descriptions are considered, complications once again begin to appear. A catalogue of a collection or group, ranging through perhaps four, perhaps six levels, will include so many different description structures that one might be tempted to treat the question as one of text processing. Is a catalogue not to be treated as a kind of publication? Certainly many catalogues have been published, either as bound books, or in some less formal way. The preparation of texts of this kind would be a suitable job for automated publication systems.

Such a suggestion, though certainly feasible, skirts around the possibility of a central electronic database for an archives service. Moreover, there are different kinds of finding aid possible, other than guides, lists and catalogues. Handlists of selected types of document; subject guides selected from various parts of the collection; location lists, microform catalogues, lists by date, physical condition, language, possession of seals – these are all examples of the possible output from an archival database. If this kind of selection and ordering is to be possible, the system must be able to recognize appropriate field labels, index tags and other control symbols, when they occur throughout a range of record structures.

Except in the case of published catalogues, finding aids that take this form may perhaps be considered an obsolete form. In repository management, the more modern practice of separating group/series descriptions from item descriptions is preferable. Figure 9.4 shows an example of multi-level descriptions.

SYSTEM SPECIFICATION

Software

The first need is for a systems analysis which will make clear the aims and objectives of a proposed archival automation, which in turn will make clear the professional aims that have to be reached and the categories in which the necessary information will be managed. Formal analyses of this kind have been undertaken by a few archives services, including the PRO and the Suffolk and Somerset Record Offices (among others), for their own use. We still lack a generally usable study on this, so that archivists faced with planning for their own service still have to learn by examining case studies.[10]

It is fairly safe to say that no software house has yet produced a system which is capable of solving all these problems. Text management systems are being actively developed, as are searching facilities, and it is possible that archivists may find that they can devise a way of bringing their description formats and methods within the ambit of a loosely controlled free-text package. At the moment, however, this prospect looks unlikely. It is more likely that, by adapting their own formats of description, archivists may respond to the increasing availability of software systems that give rapid search facilities to long textual files.[11]

Pending such radical new developments, it is more practical to consider limited computer service. All successful systems of today have done this, whether they use purpose-designed software or whether they have adapted commercial packages. Limited systems are those that are intended to carry out only a specified set of operations within the archives office, and do not aim at providing a completely integrated service. In this discussion it is assumed that the operations generally collected under the heading of description (the provision of finding aids) is the aspect most likely to be taken on.

The main problem is, of course, finding a system that will allow multi-level descriptions, in which the entries at different levels have different structures but in which both vertical and horizontal linkages must be provided. This requirement at once rules out all 'flat file' systems which emulate card indexes. The linkages between levels must operate in a way that will allow output that is clear to users, and must avoid repeating tediously long strings of connecting data.

```
JRL/          JOHN RYLANDS UNIVERSITY LIBRARY OF MANCHESTER

EGR3/7        Papers of Mary Countess of Stamford                    1744–1772

              Mary Booth, only child of George Booth, 2nd Earl of Warrington, married Harry
              Grey, 4th Earl of Stamford, on 18th May 1736. In default of male issue, her
              father bequeathed the Booth estates to trustees, George and Thomas Hunt,
              in trust for his daughter, with a remainder after her death to the use of her
              son George Harry Grey. While the trustees held the estates in law, Mary
              Countess of Stamford appears to have assumed full responsibility for the
              administration of the estates, dealing with such matters as the negotiations
              over the construction of the Bridgewater Canal (EGR3/7/2). Her husband had
              no legal interest in Booth estates, and there is no documentary evidence that
              he had any personal involvement in their administration.
              For the probate copy of the will of Mary Countess of Stamford see
              EGR1/8/12/4.
              3 series

EGR3/7/1      *Financial and estate papers*                          1745–1772

              The papers below reflect the active involvement of Mary Countess of
              Stamford in the administration of the estates. The several summaries
              of property leased for lives, of rental income and of estate income in
              general, many drawn up in Lady Stamford's own idiosyncratic hand,
              indicate a wish to acquire for herself a knowledge and understanding of
              the estates' overall financial position, necessary for the effective man-
              agement of the estates. Nor was Mary Booth unwilling to involve herself
              in the minutiae of estate administration: witness her own notes on the
              terms of a lease (EGR3/7/1/4/2), and the correspondence relating to
              the felling of trees on the Caverswall estate, co. Staffs, in which her son
              had an interest (EGR3/7/1/4/8).
              12 items, 119 pieces

EGR3/7/1/1    *Bundle of financial papers*                           1757–1770

                  The papers below include statements of the Earl of Warrington's
                  and Mary Countess of Stamford's accounts with John Jackson esq,
                  solicitor (EGR3/7/1/1/1), papers relating to Mrs Jane Gastineau
                  and miscellaneous bills and receipts.
                  1 bundle, 11 pieces

EGR3/7/1/1/1 Statement of account                                   23 May 1757

                  Account of George [Booth, 2nd] Earl of Warrington with John
                  Jackson esq [his solicitor]. Provides detailed information on
                  financial transactions conducted by Jackson on the Earl's
                  behalf, Aug 1756 to May 1757.

EGR3/7/1/1/2 Papers relating to Jane Gastineau              Jun 1757–May 1759

                      Letter from John Jackson to Mary discussing various legal
                      business: Mrs Gastineau's letter of attorney, charging the
                      personal estate of Mr Walton with disbursements for
                      taxes, and a draft release for John Walton; dated at Great
                      Queen Street [London], 4 June 1757
```

Note: The margin indents indicate dependence according to level.

Source: John Rylands Library of the University of Manchester.

Figure 9.4   Specimen page of multi-level descriptions

This requirement is not beyond the capabilities of computer systems but it is one that needs special programming. There are several commercial database packages that are commonly available that do have the capability, but they must be specifically adapted. The skill needed to do this is not beyond the capacity of ordinary archivists, but it does take time both to do the adaptation, to produce input forms and output reports and to experiment. These needs are likely to put the enterprise beyond the resources of most archive services at the present time.

In addition to this central requirement for multi-level descriptions, there should be provision for archival materials in special formats. MAD2 provides outlines for several of these: title deeds, letters and correspondence, photographs, cartographic archives, architectural and other plans, sound archives, film and video archives, and electronic (termed machine-readable) archives. Each of these presents the possibility of using different computer facilities and description structures. In each case MAD2 demands that the principle of the multi-level rule should be asserted: no matter what the format, all archives need to be described in the light of their context or provenance and in linked sequences representing the different levels of arrangement. This applies equally to even the most technically distinct forms, such as title deeds or technical drawings. At item level these materials can benefit from specially designed input screens that provide appropriate dedicated fields, as suggested by MAD2. These may perhaps be used in conjunction with specialised input forms.

Letters are among the more complex of the special formats, for although they are very common there is as yet no generally accepted standard for their description. The catalogue of Nelson's letters, produced by the National Maritime Museum, might be regarded as an interesting model. Data is structured into dedicated fields, and the resulting database is used to produce six differently sorted lists: in order of record number, series mark, date, recipient, place of writing (alphabetically), and place of writing by date (this produces an itinerary of Nelson's movements). This imaginative project illustrates the great potential there is even in restricted computer systems, but it must be remembered that since this is a single-level item-by-item list of documents, all problems of multi-level descriptions have been side-stepped.

It is not surprising that it is the letters or correspondence of the famous that have received the most thorough treatment. Behind this work there is the problem of the enormous bulk of similar material that exists in virtually every archive group. There will never be enough time and money to exploit these to the full, though it will only be through computer retrieval that this will be done, if ever.

Photographs have always been managed separately from their associated paperwork, though it must be emphasized that this association must always be maintained by appropriate linkages. Everyone is able to understand that a photograph can usually only be understood in terms of its context.[12] Nevertheless, photographs are best managed and retrieved for use if they are represented in a dedicated subject index. In modern conditions, the value of this index is vastly improved by using a system that will allow a visual image to appear on the screen. In fact, since otherwise large numbers of photographs might have to be brought up and replaced in the course of any enquiry, it might be said that photographs have been a difficult or unusable source until visual images in CD-ROM or similar formats became possible. These images can also of course be accessed remotely. The same remarks might as well be made in connection with architectural and technical plans and drawings, though in the case of these microforms have provided a similar retrieval facility for many years.

Sound and electronic archives do not seem to present any particular difficulty in the demands they make for their description. Apart from the models in MAD2, both have established practice in specialist institutions.[13]

The main choice facing archive managers is between purpose-designed systems and adapting generally available commercial systems. There are arguments for and against each of these.

Until recently it was widely assumed that a purpose-designed system was necessary for all but the smallest archives service, and that a suitable system would appear in due course. At the end of the century this is no longer so clear. There are some half a dozen systems available, but all have some defect. This might be the expense of buying it (which may include the cost of buying the underlying software platform) and the continuing cost of maintenance over time; or it might be that the package demands hardware that does not conform to the requirements of the employing body of the archives service. Training and 'hotline' problem-solving facilities are needed.

The main factor in the advance of commercial packages is the user interface. Users are now accustomed to graphical interfaces and, in particular, variants of Windows. Specialized software generally does not use Windows (although some may have alternative graphics). As is widely known, the Windows interface, which incorporates the underlying operating system, is constantly being developed and extended. This means that the designers of specialized software are under the constant need to develop the user interface aspect of their systems. The cost and resources needed to do this are beyond all but the largest suppliers.

The problem of this choice is sharpest in the universities that train initial entrants to the profession. Students come to the course already accustomed to using Windows-based systems and other common packages, and there is likely to be insufficient time (and perhaps not enough computer availability) to teach them alternative ways. If specialized software is thereby ruled out for the training courses, it is not possible for them to prepare newly qualified entrants for the systems they will meet in their jobs.

Finally, all archivists are under greater or lesser pressure to follow the systems and standards used by their employing agencies. They have always been faced by this choice: whether to follow their employers' methods and be different from the cognate world outside; or to follow professional standards and be different from the other departments of their home organization. This dilemma will continue and become more intense as specialist networks become more prominent.

Other computer applications in archives are supported by in-house programming or in-house computer facilities, particularly those of local government. All the established RM systems and some of the archival systems which are operational today in fact depend on the active co-operation and close liaison with the employing organization's computing or technology staff. Any archivist wishing to plan for a computer application would be well advised to start by establishing such a connection. The success of a system depends so much on local technical support.

Hardware

Archival management requires relatively little operational complexity from a computer: entry and editing text, sorting on specific fields, searching within text and indexing specified terms. These are relatively simple operations for most modern computer systems and, indeed, many of them can usually be provided by the resident operating system without any special software. The main problem with archival computing in the past has been the large amounts of data storage required, and of course the cost of this.

This problem has largely been solved by the progress of technology. As far as storage capacity is concerned, some personal computers can now store virtually as much data as a medium-sized archives service needs, on their own hard disks. A stand-alone personal computer system for an archives service is not outside consideration, especially since personal computers can be networked to provide multi-site access. Equally, very capacious online data storage is now normally provided with the aid of servers on a local network, so that archivists can use their employers' machines without causing congestion.

In the same way, the expense of data storage is much reduced. In the case of hard disks on personal computers, the cost is little more than the initial purchase price of the disk and its drive, which is a sum within the normal range of prices charged for office equipment. The development of online storage within larger networks has meant that the practice of writing data files on to magnetic tape for longer-term storage has now declined. Archivists should suggest to their computing service that an 'archiving' facility should be installed. This term is well understood in the computer world, and means the practice of moving data files which are not in immediate use away from current storage devices and writing them on to a backup system maintained by the computing service. Files are then stored in a separate library and can be brought back online, after a little delay, if the necessary command is given through the terminal. This facility may be planned in association with the general security backup that is part of any large system.

The term 'archiving' as used in the context of computer systems does not have the same meaning as it might have in other fields: computer archiving facilities generally only seek to retain data for limited periods. Nevertheless the concept is useful and it is the natural function of archive or records managers to promote archiving facilities within their organization.

The drift of this discussion is that while there is no unusually demanding hardware requirement for archive work, a suitable system will have close access to its database through a terminal (whether that be a personal computer or a dedicated terminal). Further reflection may suggest that a desirable extension should be towards multi-site access by other terminals: this would be useful in RM, and in archives management might cause a valuable change in work habits. The preparation and input of data will remain one of the main difficulties in any computer system, so that if terminals were to be available to members of the archives team, they might find it most convenient, after some practice, to enter their own data direct via their own keyboard.

Word processors are ideal for certain aspects of archives work, whether they stand alone or are linked to computer systems as input/output devices. Archival descriptions are ideal material for word-processing: they have to be edited on input, are constantly liable to correction and updating, have to be printed out anew on the appearance of a new demand, and have to be published or at least produced for the use of readers in-house and remotely. These operations are what word processors were designed for. Tagging for alternative methods of output, including remote access by computer networks, can also be provided through word-processing. Archivists may rejoice at the final departure of typewriters from their technologies.

OUTPUT

The output from any system should be considered at the design stage. Output can be to computer screens locally or remotely, or on hard copy.

Output to screen may be for internal users, who will be trained and prac-
tised, or to external users, sometimes untrained and unfamiliar, perhaps
even hostile. There is no doubt that over the next few years most users
will come to expect, or at least to tolerate, that they will have to use computer facilities themselves. At the present time there are few or no satisfactory user outputs in use in archives services, or at least ones that go
beyond the simplest preliminary steps. Much development of graphical
user interfaces will be needed before there is any real progress, but here
the systems being developed by museums will be very useful.

The PROMPT system at the PRO demonstrates a successful system
for the control of movement of archival materials within a large office,
using a restricted form of access by the public. Any user (staff member
or public) obtains access to an archival entity by using a terminal to key
in his or her identifying user number, followed by the reference code of
the document asked for. The system checks that the document is
available (and is not out to another reader, subject to closure or undergoing repair) and reports the request, together with a location reference, to the repository staff. The system works well (with the proviso
that computer breakdown is always possible and a backup service must
be ready), and can be used to provide statistics on document use. It is
enormously faster than manual call systems, and allows users to ask for
many more documents per day than in the past, without a corresponding increase of manual staff to satisfy the demand. The system
also reports the replacement of the item when it is finished with.

In other cases the service may still rely on hard-copy finding aids. Any
data that is entered into a computer file and stored there can be printed
out in some form of hard copy – usually on paper, but alternatively on
some other medium such as microfiche. Several archives services use
microfiche for their output, especially where there is a need to send the
information through the post or to remote users, and where network
connections have not yet been set up.

In the conditions of today, a computer system ought to be able to print
out material to a standard which will permit publication, or at least distribution directly to users. Ideally, output print ought to be camera-
ready for duplication in numbers. This means that it should have access
to a range of fonts (this is standard for virtually all systems today), and
printed out on a good quality ink or bubble jet or laser printer. It is often
possible to use a quicker and cheaper line printer for day-to-day
working printout in the office, and to channel the work to a more
expensive machine for special output. Data can be sent to remote users
on diskettes or by telephone link, though the latter does not appear to
be commonly used as yet.

If the system provides search facilities, it may well be that the
database will gradually (or even suddenly) be used less to provide

hard-copy versions of the archive lists, and more to provide the specific responses to search enquiries. A good approach that is practical at the present time is to allow searches by the archives staff, who will provide the appropriate responses to the users on paper or by word. For the moment, then, this will remain the task of the searchroom supervisor or staff, but the pressure on these is often so great that a rapid move to user-friendly searching facilities is much to be desired.

Some archives services stock their searchroom with pre-prepared search responses (frequently asked questions – FAQs), generated as the result of predicted enquiries. The final situation will be one where users have direct access to a terminal, together with simple instructions on the command language, and hard-copy finding aids will be phased out or at least be reduced to backup reference.

OTHER APPLICATIONS IN ARCHIVAL MANAGEMENT

The data structure for archival description (Chapter 7), provides for data elements which are useful in two quite different ways, the description of the archives themselves as a means of intellectual control, and the management of the processes which the archives have to be subjected to. It is probably rather important that these two uses should be clearly distinguished in the design of any particular control instrument. So far, in this chapter, the question of automating the archival descriptions has been the subject discussed. It should also be possible to use computers to control the physical and managerial processes.

The most generally useful process to be computerized first is probably accessioning. The accessions register itself is a database that can easily be structured. A flat-file system can be used for this because each accession (though it may be connected with groups or series already held) is an independent entity equal in value to all other accessions. The data entered in respect of each accession should of course contain a reference to the appropriate groups or series, if relevant. The database can easily be extended by linking with it an associated database of donors or transferors of accessions, which can in turn be used to develop a mailing list for outreach purposes.

Many archives services use their computer facilities to provide a selective mailing list for their publicity material, publications and reports. Combined with a word-processing facility, a mailing list system can be used to write out and send form letters (solicitation, replies to enquiries, user information, societies of 'Friends').

The reports generated from the database can include printed receipt forms for dispatch to the donor, returns to the National Register of

Archives, information notes to associated archives services, or specially formatted printouts for use by the staff who are to sort, list and store the material. Other internal reports are possible, for example a location register to manage the use of shelving and repository space.

Computerized accessions registers can be very powerful instruments for the management of the service. Problems, however, may arise when it is desired to link them to the databases needed for archival description.

The separation of contextual and content information that was referred to in Chapters 6 and 7 offers the possibility of databases to hold information on creator (or potential) creator bodies in the organization. This usage resembles the data held on donors in the accessions register, especially in that it can also be treated as a flat-file database. The data structure should follow that laid down in ISAAR(CPF). There should be horizontal and vertical references in appropriate fields, as well as linkages or references to groups or series held. See the example of an accessions register entry in Figure 9.5.

Any administrative process can be controlled by a computer system. RM systems provide, for instance, for checking records out to users and their return; for recording periodical reviews and their outcome; counting the number of references there have been to documents in a particular series over time; and recording the overall statistics of the system. In archival management, systems can be designed for the control of conservation processes and repair, which would include booking documents out to the repair section, recording what was done,

---

387BOO. Accessions nos: 1592, 2760

Booth Steamship Co. Ltd, 1866–1971

Deposited by the Company Secretary [name recorded], Cunard Buildings, Liverpool 3 on 3 Mar 1966, with a further accession in Feb 1975. The deposited was arranged throught Mr Albert Smith [address...].

See also Alfred Booth & Co., Booth Iquitos Line, Manaos Harbour Co.

Incorporated 24 June 1881 with Alfred Booth & Co having a majority shareholding. Archives cover services to northern Brazil, imports of leather and rubber; tours to Lisbon and Madeira; war service; West Indian trade.

Detailed lists.

Source: Adapted from Liverpool Record Office list.

Figure 9.5   An accessions register entry

and the return of the document. Bringing up documents periodically for inspection could be included, as well as stock control of repair materials. In the same way, the issue and return of archive materials which have been lent for exhibition can be controlled, and a record made of when and where they were exhibited and whether they were recorded in a published catalogue. References to archival materials in published work can be recorded and the record annexed to the archival description.

There is a difficulty with some of these processes, such as issue and return. This difficulty is that it is usually not easy to find an simple way to enter details of the documents issued that can be mechanized. If the data has to be entered manually in each case, the value of the system is much reduced and there is probably no point in introducing this element of automation unless the computer terminals are so conveniently placed that the extra work of entering issues and returns is easy and natural. What must be avoided is writing out the details, carrying this to an office and then getting it entered separately. It is also necessary to mechanize, if possible, the identity of requisitioning officers or those to whom the issues are made. There are, of course, ways of doing both, but they are costly and difficult to install. As regards the documents issued and returned, the best way is by attaching barcodes that can be read by an infra-red reader. This is easily done on the outside of a storage box, but to attach barcodes to actual files or documents is both costly and open to objections. Users can be identified by giving them a machine-readable identity card: but here again there are associated difficulties, especially where users are occasional or from other departments. The reader's card issued to members of the public can be used for this.

DISCUSSION

Staffing issues

One of the most important factors which must be taken into account when planning the introduction of a computer system is the question of staff attitudes and the need for training. Those who have been responsible for the planning of new systems are usually very enthusiastic about them, whereas those who have had new systems thrust upon them are usually hostile, at least to some degree. Staff indifference or even hostility are often sufficient to cause failure of the system. If a new system is under consideration, the minimum consideration for the staff would be that they should all be consulted at an early stage, and at later critical points. The effect of the new system on the work habits of each member of staff should be considered, and allowance made for necessary adjustments.

However, an even more positive approach than this is possible. This is to involve all members of staff in the analysis required for the design of the system, and to influence the design in the direction of providing a new area of responsibility, or a new area of work, for each member of the team (not only the professionals). If the new system can move the team in the direction of more collegiality, it is likely to improve its collective performance. At their best, computer systems have an ability to arouse enthusiasm and catalyse new approaches.

The problem of backlog conversion

The other general comment to be made concerns backlog. Backlog accumulation is a problem endemic to all archive work: the mass of uncatalogued material that has come to the repository in a large consignment; or the mass of material which has been processed and described inadequately or to obsolete (or just different) standards in the past. There are rarely sufficient resources to deal with backlogs, even if there is no question of introducing new systems.

There is no easy solution to this problem. In some cases it may be possible to take on extra temporary staff to deal with it, perhaps with the aid of a grant. In other cases, less satisfactory expedients might include making summary descriptions in the hope that eventually full ones can be made. Cataloguing standards do not specify depth of description, so that summary descriptions may be fully in accord with them: this is, of course, a requirement for any future work. In any case, when a new description system is adopted (whether manual or automatic) the decision must be made whether to attempt the conversion of the old finding aids, or to cover the uncatalogued backlog, or whether to leave this area for separate treatment.

No general advice can be given on this, except to point out that it is a common practice to begin new description systems at a specific point, and leave the old finding aids as a non-accruing file. Users must then consult two sets of finding aids in order to be sure that they have checked everything, but (in a library context) the relative activity of the old catalogue declines with time. In the case of archives, the old catalogue probably retains its importance indefinitely, so it is a balance of inconvenience. Difficulties with backlogs exist also with manual systems.

It is hoped that the development of EAD may help with the backlog problem to some extent. It would be an easier task to edit old finding aids while writing in SGML tags than it would be to recast the whole text. This still leaves the problem of inputting the data to a new system.

In 1998 the National Council on Archives launched a project for setting up an online archival network for the United Kingdom.[14] The project planners also decided to recommend EAD as a data standard since, as they remarked, it is not software-dependent, displays the hierarchical structure of archival data well and is easy to use. As against this they pointed out that the standard had not yet been tested against large quantities of data, and that search facilities might need further development. The project gave much attention to the question of backlog conversion. This problem was quantified when the costings for the proposed national network were presented. It was considered that the infrastructural work would cost between £6.1 million and £9 million, but that retrospective conversion of all the nation's backlog of non-standard archival descriptions would cost between £33 million and £38.5 million. The report contains a statistical attempt to quantify the extent of outstanding unconverted archival lists and inventories. Those held by the HMC were estimated at 3.5 million pages. The main causes of poor representations was considered to be:

○   poor palaeography – misreading original texts
○   incomplete and inconsistent data
○   inconsistent use of abbreviations, especially in personal names.

The application of national authority rules was therefore regarded as of equal importance with the observance of cataloguing rules and standards. The quantity of backlog conversion that would be required was so great as to unbalance the whole project.

NOTES

1.   Bell, L. and Roper, M. (eds) (1975), *Proceedings of an International Seminar on ADP in Archives*, London: Public Record Office, HMSO.
2.   Bell, L. (1974), 'PRO Survey of Computer Applications', *ADPA* (the ICA's journal on automation), **1**, 11–14.
3.   Cook, M. (1980), *Archives and the Computer*, London: Butterworth.
4.   Bartle, R. and Cook, M. (1983), *Computer Applications in Archives: a Survey*, British Library Research and Development Report 5749, Liverpool University.
5.   Chell, R. (1992), *Directory of Computer Applications in Archives*, London: Society of Archivists, IT Group. There have been periodic revisions.
6.   Information from the County Archivist and system designer, J.A.S.Green.

7. Carried out at a training workshop at the University of Cambridge.

8. The most recent edition is Cook, M. (1994), *MODES for Archives, a Concise Guide*, Cambridge: Museum Documentation Association.

9. Health and Safety (Display Screen Equipment) Regulations, 1992. Childs, R.J. (1996), *Health and Safety: a Guide to Good Health and Safety Practice in the Record Office*, Best Practice Guideline 3, London: Society of Archivists.

10. Phillips, C.M. and Woolgar, C.M. (1984), *Computerising Archives, Some Guidelines*, London: Society of Archivists, is an interesting pioneer study. IT Group (1993), *Criteria for Software Evaluation: a Checklist for Archivists*, London: Society of Archivists, is a more recent attempt.

11. Society of Archivists, IT Group (1993), *Criteria for software evaluation: a checklist for archivists*, London: Society of Archivists.

12. 'The Analysis of Visual Images for the Purpose of Cataloguing a Specialist Collection', *Methodologies in Specialised Archives*, London: Society of Archivists.

13. Ward, A. (1990), *A Manual of Sound Archive Administration*, Aldershot: Gower. The Data Archive (including the History Data Service) is at dawww.essex.ac.uk/. See also Roberts, D. (1993), 'Managing Records in Special Formats', in J. Ellis (ed.), *Keeping Archives*, 2nd edn, pp. 385–427, Sydney: Thorpe, in association with the Australian Society of Archivists.

14. 'Archives On-Line: the Establishment of a United Kingdom Archival Network', National Council on Archives, 1998. Comments were invited to the Hon. Secretary, c/o Birmingham City Archives, Central Library, Birmingham B3 3HQ.

10

ACCESS AND USE:
FACILITIES AND RESTRICTIONS

By comparison with other information services, archives have some-times tended not to give much emphasis to the study of user needs.[1] This is probably due to the nature of the materials: to a certain extent the management of archives cannot be influenced by a perception of user interests. The archives are what they are: if researchers come along who are interested in them, so much the better; if not, then pos-terity may be assumed to have needs. There are also two aspects to archives service that have had an important influence. During most of the twentieth century, many archivists have been profoundly influenced by the writings and traditions of Sir Hilary Jenkinson, who declared without equivocation that:

> the duties of the Archivist ... are primary and secondary. In the first place he has to take all possible precautions for the safeguarding of his Archives and for their custody, which is the safeguarding of their essential qual-ities. *Subject to the discharge of these duties* he has in the second place to provide to the best of his ability for the needs of historians and other research workers.[2]

This proposition would still gain general assent among archivists. In addition, many archives services were founded as an adjunct to, or in close association with, movements in academic study that implied that the archivists and their users were in close association.[3] All the assump-tions behind these traditions can now be tested against the require-ments of employing agencies and user groups.

In the first place, the archives of today are chosen from an increas-ingly huge mass of records by an increasingly stringent process of appraisal.[4] It will always be true that appraisal can only select from pre-existing records, and therefore cannot shape the content of an archive with complete freedom, but it can establish definitions, (or impose a bias) which ultimately must be affected by some perception of user needs. There is often some room for change in defining which record-creating bodies come within the service's collecting area. Archives services will increasingly follow the example of the PRO and establish an agreed acquisitions policy.[5] Under this they may choose their sources of intake with an eye to completing their holdings in subject areas they feel to be in need of reinforcement. Local archives services set up fieldwork projects which cover landed estates, manufacturing businesses, churches, political parties, and so on.[6] Their aim is to provide an archive which documents the life, or widely ranging and mutually balanced aspects of life, in their region. Modern documentation strategies tend to concentrate on this type of approach.

Specialist archives services do the same. Fieldwork projects are set up with the aim of finding accumulations of additional materials to reinforce their holdings, and to strengthen the value of those holdings for research. Archives services which relate only to one organization, such as those of research institutes or governments, may at first sight be in a more limited situation. In practice, many of these do in fact accept, or even seek, accessions of reinforcing materials from external sources. The PRO, for example, has accepted the private (or at least semi-official) papers of public personalities, and the archives of public institutions not covered by the public records Acts. They do this in order to improve the subject coverage of their holdings, and therefore, ultimately, to respond to the estimated needs of their users.[7]

The close association between academic users and archivists which existed in the heyday of interest in early medieval administrative studies has largely faded away, but it has been replaced by a wider and looser association with academic groups. The main archives services are important agents of research, and put significant efforts into research projects. The most important of these projects involve publication of archival texts, or of lists of sources for specific subjects. Other projects, however, are aimed at developing user services. The US National Archives conferences of the 1970s are a good example of this kind of activity,[8] but many other kinds can be observed. In Britain the annual sequence of conferences organized over many years by the British Records Association could be said to perform a similar function.[9] Despite the relative lack of systematic user studies, there is a great deal of user-related activity in the archive world.

ACCESS FACILITIES

A searchroom in which archival materials are produced for study by external readers is a standard provision in any archives service. The great expansion in the numbers of users which has occurred over the last couple of decades in Britain means that there is now much experience in running searchroom services. These services have changed and adapted under pressure, but still remain recognizably the same kind of thing as they were originally designed to be. The searchrooms at the new PRO in Kew are lighter and larger than the old ones in Chancery Lane. The finding aids have been moved out into a reference room nearby, so as to reduce noise and movement. Readers are offered electrical power points and network links at their desks. Otherwise there has been no essential change. The searchroom remains what it was: a reading room supervised by an invigilator, and with a counter where staff can control the issue and return of documents. As far as design and construction are concerned, there has been no radical alteration. Changes, however, there have been.

First, there are now more searchrooms than there were. It has increasingly become accepted, for example, that records centres may need a searchroom, and should therefore offer basic access facilities for users, whether internal or external. The federal records centres in the USA led the way in this, and the design was taken up by large-scale records centres, where they existed, in Britain.[10]

Secondly, searchrooms have customarily been given much more technology. In the PRO the processes of document production have been automated; elsewhere materials may be produced in microform. Copying projects and the sale of microfilm copies of important sources have increased the opportunities for access where microfilm readers may be used. Many records now exist only in microform, or in machine-readable media. Microfilming for purposes of conservation is now common. Self-service facilities for microforms and photocopying facilities for users are taken for granted. The public has become accustomed to using all these forms and facilities.

Thirdly, there has been erosion of customary standards for the production of archival documents. The practice of issuing them for access by certain users at places other than the supervised searchroom has grown with the development of RM services. In RM it has always been customary to issue records to their originating departments on request. It is hard not to extend this service when the records have become archives; indeed it was always accepted in principle in manuals of archive administration.[11]

Fourthly, archives in specialized formats are now increasingly managed by both general and specialized archives services. Film, videotape, audio materials and photographs have all developed such services. The access facilities demanded of a photographic archive are typical of the new approach. The users of these, which include television producers, journalists, research teams supporting media projects, and other people in a hurry, have quite different expectations of the services provided by the archives, than have more traditional users. These expectations cover all aspects of the service: acquisition, arrangement, storage, access facilities, finding aids, supporting services, and expert advice. These users are accustomed to pay for the service they receive.

THE CONTROL OF ACCESS

Because they are created as part of the transactions they record, there must always be the possibility of some restriction on access to archives, and even more on access to records. This does not mean that archives and records services do not have to provide access at all stages to certain classes of user. The traditional view, that archives become open for access after the lapse of a pre-established number of years (currently in very many countries 30 years for most records), has now been considerably eroded by the admission of special cases and exceptions; and in any case there is seldom any certain legal backing for this time limit in the case of non-government archives and records.

In 1997 the International Council on Archives was commissioned to make recommendations to the Council of Europe on a regime, applicable over the whole Region, for access to archives.[12] The main points covered are that:

O   each country should set out its access policy in a legal text, harmonized with laws covering related areas
O   access should be accorded equally to all, whether citizens or foreigners
O   access should be free of charge
O   exceptions to the normal closure period should be based on law
O   finding aids should cover material subject to closure (with notes on the effect of this closure) and not only material that is open
O   there should be provision for special access in particular cases (if necessary to specified parts of it only)
O   there should be an appeals procedure.

These points are all currently covered in some way in the archives legislation of the member countries, but what is new in the proposal is that they should become explicitly co-ordinated over the whole Region, and that they should confer legally enforceable rights. Even if this were not so, users would gain from the co-ordinated common policy on closure periods.

However, there are three areas in which legislation does, may or should impinge on the general opening date of archives. These are: confidentiality and sensitivity; data protection and the right of privacy; and freedom of information. These three are closely interwoven, and usually conflict (or at least overlap) with clauses in the national archives legislation.

Records are confidential where the data they contain has been created or acquired under the terms of an agreement, perhaps implicit, with interested parties at the time of origination, that they should remain closed to general access. The secrecy accorded to records in order to protect national security falls, in principle, within this category. It is generally agreed that national archives (or similar) legislation should contain provisions for the declassification of security records. Procedures like this are feasible because declassification can usually be carried out by an established process within government administration. But in the broader context of confidentiality this is not feasible because the interested parties may be many, dispersed or hard to find. Confidential records also may tend to overlap with another category, that of sensitive records – those that contain data that is personal, sensitive or bearing upon the private life and interests of individuals or groups. There is a need for lawfully defined rules on access to these materials.

In the case of sensitive and confidential records access must be delayed, perhaps for a very long period. A consensus seems to be growing around the figure of 100 years, which has a long tradition in Britain as it has been applied to the original returns of the national census for more than a century. This closure period, of course, applies to the records containing detailed personal information. It is also widely agreed that records containing personal data may be aggregated, and the data interpreted for general use. Archivists, particularly those who hold electronic records, may find themselves implementing systems of this kind. There is one principle to which they should remain constant: this is that the original nominal linkages in the data should be preserved for long-term archival use (subject, of course, to closure controls). The loss of nominal linkages in demographic (or similar) databases must necessarily change the meaning of the data in research.

Data protection is a special case in the control of sensitive records. It and freedom of information are discussed in a separate section later in this chapter.

Records management services must of course aim at maximizing the use of their material, by authorized users for legitimate purposes, at as early a stage in their lifetime as possible. These privileged users ('compiler-users' in the phrase of B. Delmas[13]) may not be confined to officials of the creating organization, but may include members of current research enterprises. Similarly, archival material to which access is restricted because of the special confidentiality of the data, may also be the subject of specially authorized research. It would be desirable if the archives service were to be involved in such projects at the planning stage, and if this particular use of the archives were to be conceived from the beginning as one of the reasons for the existence of that service.

These intrusions into the traditional pattern of access control have tended to lessen the idea of archives as purely historical. Archives do, of course, give a retrospective view, but not necessarily more so than many other information media. Once a thing is recorded, by whatever means, it passes into the realm of historical (or at least retrospective) research and reference.

The ICA recommendations on access include the principle that archival finding aids should normally be open to users and should contain references to all relevant material that exists, whether or not this material is at the moment subject to closure. According to this view it would be unethical for archivists to conceal the existence of archival material merely because it was within the closed period. An additional principle might be that finding aids intended for use by the public are to be regarded as being in the public domain. Ideally, archival finding aids should be published (nowadays perhaps by way of the Internet), and it is useful to consider them in this light. Material mentioned in them, but actually closed at any particular moment, can have a note attached to their descriptions to this effect.

The principle that all finding aids that contain reference to material that is open, should themselves be in the public domain, has never been formally established. The ICA has recommended that

> Finding aids should cover the whole of the records that they describe, and make reference to those which may have been withheld. Even if they make known the existence of withheld documents, and with the reservation that they do not themselves contain information protected by virtue of legislation, finding aids are freely accessible in order to permit readers to be able to request special permission for access.[14]

Questions of access should be dealt with in agreements for the deposit of archives. Traditionally, archivists have sometimes accepted deposited material with the stipulation that access should only be given when explicitly authorized by the donor. In accepting this clause, they have no doubt felt that in the long run the lapse of time would ensure that eventually there would be open access. This is a fair point; but we should remember the principle of open access to all. Access granted on the basis of partiality would offend an important ethical principle.

Laws covering copyright and intellectual property bear upon archival practice. Unfortunately recent revisions of the law on these topics have not addressed the problem as it relates to archives. Since the writer of a text, not whoever owns the medium on which it is carried, is the one who possesses copyright, the laws hitherto have been virtually unenforceable in many cases.[15]

THE RIGHTS OF USERS

It has never been questioned that users have rights, which may be exercised by and through the user facilities provided by an archives service. In practice, these rights are limited not only by shortage of resources – short opening hours, for instance – but by the perceived needs of the service. If the searchroom is closed temporarily so that the archives staff can complete some cataloguing task, that is to limit the rights of one set of users with the aim of serving another, possibly overlapping, set. Users' rights over the service are therefore negotiable. It may be important to try to define them.

First, users (or some users) may have defined legal rights. There are some categories of public archive to which there is a legal right of access. As S.C. Newton has pointed out, there are few of these, and the right is less well established on examination than it might have appeared.[16] Legal rights are tending to be strengthened by recent or proposed legislation on freedom of information and data protection.

Outside central government, there is legislation that gives rights of access, either generally or to data subjects, to the records of bodies other than the government itself. Although Britain is not a leader in this field, and has had an unfortunate tradition of secrecy in government, there is legislation covering some aspects.[17] There are rights of access to health and education records. In both of these the law has caused a noticeable change in the general culture. Patients in hospital can now expect routinely to see their daily medical reports and data, whereas formerly these were always kept secret. In schools and universities students now expect access to their marks and to comments on their progress. Since teachers and administrators know this they have changed their recording habits and modified the use they make of the records. Access rights extend to local government proceedings such as the conduct of business in councils and committees, and includes planning applications and decisions thereon. There is the possibility of judicial review, and this has notoriously been exercised in many contentious cases, including right of appeal to the Court of Human Rights. There is case law that covers some situations: the right of government to refuse access to documents has been successfully challenged in several cases during the 1990s, particularly where firms were prosecuted for allegedly selling arms to Iraq in defiance of formal prohibitions.

■ FREEDOM OF INFORMATION

Freedom of information has become a technical term that describes a particular class of legislation, that defines and supports the rights of citizens to demand access to specified types of document. The distinction between systems that allow citizens to have access to documents that contain information on themselves, and those that allow access to any documents over broad categories is the basis of the distinction between FOI and data protection. However, DP and FOI regimes should dovetail into each other, and should be consonant with relevant archives legislation.

Freedom of information is surrounded by a grey area where rights are uncertain and difficult to define. Much can be done to improve and safeguard the public's rights of access to documents of general public concern without enacting laws specifically labelled as FOI. A good deal of this work is being done in the former Soviet bloc countries, assisted by Unesco, the Council of Europe and by such bodies as the Open Society Archive.[18] The opening of the records of the former Communist Parties and in some cases of those of the secret police in those regions are a classic instance of how a degree of freedom of information might be obtained in these rather extraordinary situations, without specific FOI legislation.

About a dozen countries have enacted formal FOI laws. The classic case, usually quoted first, is that of Sweden, where the Freedom of the Press Act, dated 1766 but most recently amended in 1949, is a fundamental law under the Constitution of the state. This and other laws give the National Archives a very prominent role in implementing the procedures required to give access.[19] These laws essentially provide that any government record that is not specifically exempted shall be made available to public inspection. Recent revisions apply this principle to electronic records, and provide for public-access terminals in each ministry, the registration of all government databases or recording systems, the provision of metadata required for understanding the record, and arrangements for appraisal and (for records chosen for the archives) long-term preservation. In this enterprise the National Archives has a key position, being effectively the government body that supports and maintains this facility. It has a close association with the Data Protection Agency, and considerable powers to instruct ministries in the way they design and use their record systems.[20]

Strong FOI legislation has existed also for some time in the USA, and as a result of several high-profile investigations has become rather well known to the public.[21] A particular point of interest here is the explicit extension of the duties of the National Archives to the records of the President.[22] The great variety of state and local laws bearing on the subject, however, make this a difficult model, except that there is a procedure by which members of the public may make FOI searches by using remote terminals.[23] Useful FOI laws or regulations also exist in Canada, Australia, the Netherlands and Denmark.[24] A debate is being carried on in many countries on the subject, and is particularly active at present in the UK, where legislation is in progress.[25]

A good FOI law may be expected to deal with the following:[26]

O   It defines what records are included, defining both what is a record and what organizations are covered. Electronic records should of course be brought within the scope of the law.
O   It requires the government to explain clearly what records are held by its agencies.
O   A clear procedure for obtaining access to documents is laid down, nominating responsible persons or offices, and defining methods.
O   Time limits and fees are defined (and here the temptation to allow significant delays and heavy fees should be avoided. Democratic governments provide structures for elections and access to law courts without charge, and these are comparable services).
O   Exemptions should be explained, to allow necessary safeguards.
O   A procedure for separating exempt and non-exempt records should be set up and explained.
O   There should be an appeals procedure.

There is by now enough experience to show that FOI has a respectable history and is a workable project. It is natural and useful to make the National Archives a principal centre for implementation of the law, because underlying it there is the need to ensure that relevant records are in fact kept in usable form, appraised and retained over time. Probably it is best to specifically refer to FOI provisions in the Archives Act, and vice versa (as in Sweden).

Where there is no FOI legislation as such, there is sometimes a published code of practice that goes some way in the same direction. This was done in Britain in the 1980s (the code is soon to be replaced by an FOI Act). The example of Hong Kong is relevant, declaring that the government exists to serve the community and recognizing the need for the community to be well informed. It 'authorises and requires civil servants, routinely or on request, to provide information unless there are specific reasons for not doing so'.[27]

It would also not be unreasonable to think that a well-designed National Archives Act may be as generally useful to the public as the more high-profile FOI legislation. A survey of modern archives legislation might suggest that the following principles should be included in this:

○ The scope of the Act should be clear: we should know how public records are defined and controlled; the law should apply over the whole range of public service including para-statal bodies.

○ Access rules should be uniformly applied over this range; they should protect confidential and sensitive records but should give a general right of access otherwise.

○ Access to records and archives that are open under the law should be granted equally to all (some countries restrict access to foreign nationals, but this is a distinction difficult to justify in the modern world).

○ There should be positive methods to give access to records that are open, including remote access and the publication of finding aids.

○ The law should also cover the provision and retention of appropriate metadata, so that electronic records do not become unusable over time.

An important distinction between FOI and access to archives legislation, however, is that the former gives an enforceable right to citizens, rather than providing a service to them; and extends that right to records still held by the agencies in which they were created and used.[28] The case for FOI laws is much stronger when records are held in electronic form, because the traditional lapse of time definitions of closure period are no longer relevant.

There seems little doubt that the pressure on governments to codify and extend this sort of legislation and regulation will continue. A possible area into which it will extend is that of financial management and investment. Policy covering pensions in all sectors of society and the investment of pension funds is a case in point, particularly after the notorious malversation of these funds by Robert Maxwell and the disastrous effects of some stock market operations. Presumably the custom of funding pensions by way of private investment firms operating in the free market will grow, and with this the need both for strong supervision from government and transparency to the clientele.

The spread of electronic networks following the growth of the Internet has given a powerful boost to questions of public access and FOI. We now have quite a new situation, strongly underlined by the Singapore initiative to promote public access to the Internet.[29] This form of access naturally stimulates the supply of documents and information, and the habit of consulting them no doubt grows quickly. There do have to be some ground rules, enforceable by law, that ensure that there is equal access by all, that there is a sound procedure for declassifying confidential records, and that there is specific FOI right of access to certain types of records at least.

DATA PROTECTION

In the case of DP there are already international standards. These were made necessary by the need to control transborder flows of information through electronic channels, but there has also been a strong impulse to adopt them because so much personal information was being accumulated by private databases.[30] If anyone is frightened by the prospect of huge interrelated databases (no doubt increasingly held by multinational bodies) containing details of his or her private affairs, it is as likely that it is private rather than government databases that are in mind. A threat to one's credit rating is likely to be more immediately disturbing than the prospect, still rather remote, of a Big Brother type of surveillance from the authorities. However, the latter does give rise to public service protection issues, as recent developments with the *dangan* system in China show.[31]

Since personal data is stored in every country, and electronic transborder information also exists across every frontier, however undeveloped the region, it is not surprising that there is international pressure to establish DP legislation and to police it effectively. (A rather similar international situation exists in respect of copyright and intellectual property legislation, though this tends to be poorly policed.) The ordinary pattern is that there should be a DP Registrar, whose duty it is to see that all personal databases are known and not misused. Such an official is of course a public figure administering a public service. In this respect a DP Registrar is not different from, say, a chief inspector of standards of hygiene, or of weights and measures. It is interesting to see, though, a tendency of DP registrars to speak out not only against ill-doers but also against government proposals, where they seem to interfere with the oversight of personal data. There are proposals for setting up international DP regulatory bodies.[32]

Different from DP, but with a parallel effect, is legislation aimed at defining and protecting rights of privacy of individuals. The rapid growth and penetration of international news media has made this necessary, and the events surrounding the death of Princess Diana in 1997 has brought the matter to the forefront of public concern. International news media moguls are of course against it, and we have seen the spectacle of Rupert Murdoch bringing pressure on governments not to bring in privacy legislation. The owners of news media are often, as has been noticed, more powerful than the governments of smaller countries. In future, privacy and DP legislation should no doubt be integrated into a coherent code, which should in turn be integrated into the archives code.

In some parts of the world, DP provisions are undergoing a period of change, and further change is likely. The events in the European Union (EU) bring the issues well to the surface. The European Commission's Data Protection Directive 1995 has caused all the member countries of the EU to formulate legislation which must be in effect before October 1998.[33] European archivists and records managers are much disturbed by some of the provisions of this legislation, particularly since new concepts are being introduced which at present have not been well defined. If, in future, definition is to be by rulings of national or international courts of law, some of the effects on archives services may be considerable.

The new rules extend the coverage of DP to records and archives held on paper or in other non-electronic forms, wherever there is a set of records that might be defined (by whatever terms) as holding personal data. Generally DP provisions mean that data subjects or their representatives can have access to any data held that refers to them, may complain of misuse and may in some cases demand that the data be altered.

The core legislation requires that there should be a stated purpose for every personal database, and that the data should not be held after the period of its currency. Exceptions are possible in some cases where records can be held for purposes of historical, statistical or scientific research. These exceptions should cover the operations of the national and other archives services, and indeed suggest that (as in the leading countries) the National Archives should be closely associated with the DP agency. This is the more so as DP law also requires that all databases that hold personal data should be registered. Unfortunately in most parts of the world we do not have good enough legal definitions as yet, so that there are serious doubts as to whether personal databases will undergo a proper appraisal procedure, or stand any chance of being considered for research purposes in the long term[34] These imprecisions are side effects of a defective perception of the role of archives and records management in government and in society.

Overall, it is clear that archivists and records managers must see their mission as one that operates in alliance with DP agencies. The general aim is the same – the protection of citizens' rights – but the means by which this aim is achieved can be very different in the different services.

Beyond these legal rights, actual or desirable, users have other rights based on general ethics. They have a right to expect that publicly provided archives services should provide a suitable system of finding aids, and suitable conditions in which to consult archives that are open. These broad statements have never been defined, and existing standards are very variable. A suitable finding-aid system would presumably include explanatory material to help users understand it. Users, or potential users, might also have some basis for expecting that finding aids should use established terminology and standards of layout, procedure and design. The development of networks of and between archives services of like kinds might also be seen as the legitimate expectation of users collectively.

■ USER STUDIES

It has been noted that archives services have often displayed a 'suicidal urge ... to co-operate most when the co-operation benefits the researchers and least when it benefits our institutions'.[35] While archives services are generally willing to share information about holdings, they are unwilling to co-operate in acquisition policies or in the standardization of finding aids.

Examination of the position of user studies in the training of information professionals has tended to emphasize the relationship between these studies and aspects of management, particularly of marketing studies.[36] This suggestion is something quite new in the context of archives services, though there is a well-established tradition of it in librarianship.[37] The link between marketing studies, the investigatory techniques developed by the social sciences, and the study of user groups is one that certainly should be used by archivists. The users of archives, like those of library and documentation services, must belong either to unspecified and general social groupings, to organized and labelled specialist groups, or to invisible colleges which can be at least broadly defined. They are therefore suitable for study by research projects using established research techniques. At present user relations represent a serious difficulty to archivists. The great pressure for user facilities, coming at a time when resources are particularly scarce, and when the archive materials themselves need more careful management, is leading to a crisis. Existing services and facilities are becoming less efficient as a result.

The greatest pressure from users comes from loosely recognisable groups such as family historians or genealogists. It is curious that archivists have been, on the whole, slow to accept any of these as completely legitimate or worthy user groups. Possibly this may be because some of them are interests which have developed independently of the initiative of archivists in the past, or have had some element of competitiveness. Where effort has been put into developing such subjects as academically based local studies, or demographic history, the public has taken the matter into its own hand and decided to look up its ancestors instead. The problems imported by pressure from these users, however, will not be solved until the archivists decide to participate in the research. There are three aspects to the problem: the organization of the user services within the archives; the education and disciplining of the user group; and the provision of resources. These three problems are interrelated and will be solved, if at all, together.

USER EDUCATION

User education, as an aspect of extension programmes, is a very traditional part of archival activity. Most archives services have put out some material aimed at improving the response of users.[38] The tradition has been extended into specialist areas, for example into the development of archives services for schools.[39] Experience has tended to show that these efforts are better rewarded when they are undertaken co-operatively or jointly with the user education of other services. In school education, the movement, which in the 1960s led to greater use of archival material in teaching, has to a great extent merged into the much larger movement, for the provision of all kinds of resource material for teachers. The occasional publication of archive teaching units has now become the widespread provision of teachers' resource centres, and the general adoption of revised syllabuses.[40] The educational use of archives is now a recognized speciality.

User education is not confined to the outreach or extension aspects of an archives service. It should also cover users who are to a greater or less extent already inside the system: administrative users of records; professional or skilled researchers ('regular customers'); and the staff of the archives service itself, considered as users.

The first of these groups, the administrative user, is probably the most urgently in need of an education activity. Some of the techniques of information specialists may prove suitable for extension to archives or RM services. For example, a selective dissemination of information (SDI) exercise might well be suitable at least for specialist archives services. This technique consists in matching document and user 'profiles'.[41] The profile of a document, for this kind of purpose, would be composed of keywords derived from its archival description. A user profile could be constructed from appropriate keywords after an interview or after studying job descriptions. User profiles can also be made up from questionnaires, and this would allow the technique to be extended to users other than those who are officers of the employing organization. The matching process should provide for flows of information in response to user requests, but also in response to unsolicited notification by the archives service. Matching profiles can be done by computer, but also manually. This type of service is best done in close association with the other information services of the organization.

Users who are already members of invisible colleges associated with the archives service may also be the subject of SDI operations. In addition, the archives staff may seek to develop these colleges by participation in them: indeed, this is widely done. One outcome may be to get additional resources to undertake a publications programme or to organize seminars or conferences at which the research content of the programme can be extended. A logical development would be that the archives service would edit a periodical, either of the newsletter type, or a professional/scientific journal. This possibility is recognized by many archives services, which issue newsletters or – less frequently – journals, but a common fault is lack of close association with relevant research groups outside the service. The more specialized the archives service, the more likely it is to be closely in touch with a user group.[42]

Staff users are the least likely to receive specific training in the skills appropriate to them as users rather than as practitioners. The proper area of investigation here is the interface between the archivist designing finding aids, and the user seeking for information through them; in other words, the match between data derived from descriptive work and the subject enquiries met with in the searchroom. It is in this area that research is particularly needed. 'We have to match requests for information with patterns of retrieval designed to have application and relevance to as many cohorts of users as possible.'[43]

TOTAL ARCHIVES, FUNCTIONAL ANALYSIS AND THE IDEA OF PLANNED DOCUMENTATION

None of the problems discussed in this book will be solved in traditional terms. This is because the concepts of the archive and of archives services are in the process of changing radically. Traditionally, archives were textual documents, mainly on paper, which had undergone a period of maturation. At the end of this period they had become apt material for historical studies. The new concept of the archive embraces new media does not depend on a period of maturation and involves a process of conscious selection. The archive is then seen as something chosen by society, acting through its appointed agents. In the same way, where archives services were primarily seen as places where old documents were made available, they are now becoming centres for the management of particular kinds of data, within a context of groups of interlinked information services. The main business of the service may be seen as setting out the subjects to be documented and applying the resulting appraisal decisions.

Some of these changes were foreseen in Canada, where the administrative and constitutional position of the National Archives stimulated integrated user-oriented activities more than elsewhere. In the 1980s they formulated the concept of total archives. Hugh Taylor summarized the aims of this programme in this way:

1.   The acquisition of documents to reflect all aspects of social activity.
2.   Acquisition of all media of record.
3.   Involvement in the entire lifecycle of records, through a records management programme.
4.   Involvement in expanding networks for the interchange of information and strategic planning.[44]

The concept of 'media of record' would cover, in particular, photographs, film, sound media, paintings, drawings, prints, maps and machine-readable archives. This list should be extended to include books and documents which have passed an appraisal test and have been acquired by libraries of record. The accumulation that results would merit being called the national archive, but the relationships between the services which would maintain the totality of this archive would also give rise to some complex planning programmes.

The central principle of archives administration remains that of delegation. This was discussed in the early chapters of this book. The principle requires that archival series should be managed as a continuous operation. This places archives services of the PAT type in strong contrast with libraries and archives services of the HMT type. In the context of total archives, the distinction remains important since it is the archivist's contribution to emphasize the value of provenance and original context. If the media of record are separated and administered independently by specialist institutions, there will be loss. Here is yet another argument for the close association of information services.

If the medium on which a record or an archive is held is not important, then the main point is selection. Archives are on different media, and are produced by different organizations; what is common to all is that they have been selected from the great mass of records because they are worthy (within the terms of some criteria) of being kept for future use. The whole point of the enterprise, therefore, is appraisal and the criteria that are developed for it. These matters were discussed at length in Chapter 4.

At the present time it is hard to imagine an appraisal scenario that does not involve a reasoned documentation plan, based on an analysis of the functions of the organization whose records are to be appraised. Documentation plans look at the range of information that should be collected and conserved, and the uses to which it would be put. Devising the plan means that the planners will look first at the aims, purposes and intentions of the creating organization(s) and not simply at the physical records that may have been created: the point is to ensure that those purposes and that work are recorded as fully as is required. Documentation plans can also cover areas that are not confined to the work and purposes of a single organization, for example a territorial region.[45] This, too, is a context where archives services will have to co-operate with other information services because only thus will the achievement of the plan be possible. The future is with integrated information services rather than with specialist operations. That is the single most significant message of this book.

NOTES

1. McCrank, L.J. (ed.) (1981), *Automating the Archives*, p. 229, White Plains, New York: ASIS
2. Jenkinson, C.H. (1965), *A Manual of Archive Administration*, 2nd edn revd, sect. 5, p. 15, London: Lund Humphries. Emphasis in the original.
3. Galbraith, V.H. (1934), *An Introduction to the Use of the Public Records*, Oxford: University Press.
4. International Council on Archives (1980), *Constitution et reconstitution des patrimoines archivistiques nationaux*, Actes de la 19me conference internationale de la Table Ronde des Archives, Cagliari, 1977. Canadian Council on Archives (1990), *Guidelines for Developing an Acquisitions Policy*, Ottawa: National Archives of Canada.
5. Public Record Office (1998), 'An Acquisition Policy for UK Public Records', consultation document issued 20 January.

6. Cox, R.J. (1996), *Documenting Localities: a Practical Model for American Archivists and Manuscript Curators*, Lanham, MD and London: Society of American Archivists and Scarecrow Press.

7. Galbraith, V.H. (1948), *Studies in the Public Records*, London: Nelson.

8. Fishbein, M.H. (ed.) (1973), *The National Archives and Statistical Research*, Columbus: Ohio University Press.

9. Proceedings of the BRA conferences are published in their journal *Archives*, 1948 ff. See also the Business Archives Council's regular periodical *Business Archives, Sources and History* issued half-yearly.

10. Gondos, V. (ed.) (1970), *Reader for Archives and Records Center Buildings*, Chicago: Society of American Archivists. Whittick, M.H. (1986), *Guidelines for the Compilation of a Record Centre Users' Guide*, London: RMG, Society of Archivists.

11. Schellenberg, T.R. (1956), *Modern Archives, Principles and Techniques*, p. 234, Chicago: University of Chicago Press.

12. 'Draft Recommendation for a Standard European Policy on Access to Archives', submitted by the ICA to the Cultural Committee of the Council of Europe, January 1997: http://www.archives.ca/ica/.

13. Delmas, B. (1977), *User Needs and Archive Facilities: a Tentative Typology and Analysis*, Paris: Unesco.

14. Council of Europe (1997), 'Draft Recommendation for a Standard European Policy on Access to Archives', draft developed by the International Council on Archives, III. 8.

15. Post, J.B. and Foster, M.R. (1992), *Copyright: a Handbook for Archivists*, London: Society of Archivists is the most current text available at the time of writing.

16. Newton, S.C. (1977), 'Selection and Disposal: Legal Requirements', *Records Management I*, pp. 43–51, London: Society of Archivists, RMG.

17. UK Consumer Credit Act 1974; Local Government (Access to Information) Act 1985; Access to Personal Files Act 1987; Access to Medical Reports Act 1988; (Social Services) Regulations 1989; (Housing) Regulations 1989; Education (School Records) Regulations 1989; Access to Health Records Act 1990: all published in London by HMSO.

18. The Open Society Archive project is explained at www.osa.ceu.hu.

19. Freedom of the Press Act 1766/1949; Act on Secrecy 1980; the Archives Act 1990. The relevant clauses are published in International Council on Archives (1996), *Archival Legislation 1981–1994, Archivum XLI*, pp. 187–201, Munich: K.G. Saur.

20. Holmgren, M. (1994), 'The Swedish Principle of Public Access to Official Documents in Relation to Archival Theory and Electronic

Data Processing', in K. Abukhanfusa and J. Sydbeck (eds), *The Principle of Provenance: Report from the First Stockholm Conference on Archival Theory and the Principle of Provenance*, pp. 65–73, Stockholm: Svenska Riksarkivet.

21. For example the specific provisions relating to the Kennedy assassination: President John F. Kennedy Assassination Records Collection Act 1992, *Archivum XLI*, pp. 249–53, Munich: K.G. Saur.

22. Presidential Records Act 1978, *Archivum XLI*, pp. 244–7. Section 2202 reads 'the United States shall reserve and retain complete ownership, possession and control of Presidential records ... ' Private records and the records of presidential election campaigns are exempted but there are tightly expressed definitions.

23. www.milnet.com/milnet.fia.htm. Canada has a similar arrangement at http://qsilver.queensu.ca/~foi/legis.html.

24. Texts available in *Archivum*, 17 (1971), **19** (1972), **20** (1972), **21** (1973), **28** (1982), **40** (1995), **41** (1996).

25. *Your Right to Know: the Government's Proposals for a Freedom of Information Act*, Cmd. 3818, London: HMSO, presented to Parliament by the Chancellor of the Duchy of Lancaster, December 1997.

26. McMahon, T. (1996), 'Access to Government Information: a New Instrument for Public Accountability', *Government Information in Canada*, **3**, (1). Published at http://www.usask.ca/v3n1/mcmahon/mcmahon.html.

27. Government of Hong Kong (1997), *Code on Access to Information*, October, Hong Kong: Government printer.

28. Some national archives legislation does give the public an enforceable right of access: for example in Ireland, National Archives Act 1986, section 10.

29. http://s-one.net.sg See also http://picas.nhb.gov.sg. I am indebted to Dr Pitt Kwan Wah of the National Archives of Singapore.

30. Office of the Data Protection Registrar, *Data Protection Act 1984, Guidelines*, successive series. Office of the Data Protection Registrar (1994), *Open Government: Code of Practice on Access to Government Information*, London: HMSO.

31. 'Big Brother Goes to Market', *Guardian,* 31 January 1998, p. 17.

32. *Privacy in the European Union,* Conference of EU Data Protection Commissioners, Manchester, April 1996. Specifically the proposal is for a specialized Data Protection Supervisory Body to help develop and audit the system for maintaining criminal intelligence files in the new European Policy Office.

33. EC Data Protection Directive 95/46/EC. I am indebted to Paul J. Sillitoe for permission to use his thesis 'Public Access to Personal

Information', submitted as part of the (UK) Society of Archivists Diploma in Archive Administration, 1995.

34. The situation in France is perhaps a good model: Law 78-17 of 6 January 1978. There is a National Committee on Computers and Liberty to which the National Archives can appeal for the deposit of data.

35. D. Bearman (1982), *Towards National Information Systems: Opportunities and Requirements*, Chicago: Society of American Archivists, cited by Taylor, H.A. (1984), *Archival Services and the Concept of the User: a RAMP Study*, p. 74, Paris: Unesco.

36. Sene, H. (1984), *The Teaching of User Studies as a Subject for the Preparation of Librarians, Documentalists, Archivists and Other Information Specialists*, Paris: Unesco, international symposium on harmonization of education and training programmes in information science, librarianship and archival studies, October.

37. Ford, G. (1977), *User Studies: an Introductory Guide and Select Bibliography*, Sheffield: University of Sheffield, Centre for Research in User Studies.

38. Iredale, D. (1973), *Enjoying Archives*, Newton Abbot: David and Charles. Kitching, C. (1996), *Archives: the Very Essence of our Heritage*, London: HMSO.

39. Society of Archivists, Education Services Committee (1980), *Statement on the Educational Use of Archives*, London: Society of Archivists. Thompson, K.M. (comp.) (1982), *The Use of Archives in Education: a Bibliography*, London; Society of Archivists.

40. Schools Council (1976), *History, Geography and Social Science 8–13*, London: Schools Council.

41. Vickery, B.C. (1970), *Techniques of Information Retrieval*, pp. 197–200, London: Butterworth. Rowley, J. (1992), 'Current Awareness Service or Competitive Intelligence: a Review of the Options', *Aslib Proceedings*, **44**, 367–72.

42. An example of good practice is the ESRC Data Archive *Bulletin*, University of Essex.

43. Taylor (1984), p. 21.

44. Cook, T. (1980), 'The Tyranny of the Medium: a Comment on "total archives"', *Archivaria*, **9**, 141–50. Also Birrell, A. (1980), 'The Tyranny of Tradition', *Archivaria*, **10**, 249–52. Both cited by Taylor (1984), p. 48. These ideas are further developed by several contributors to Craig, B.L. (ed.) (1992), *The Archival Imagination: Essays in Honour of Hugh A. Taylor*, Ottawa: Association of Canadian Archivists.

45. Cox, R.J. (1996), *Documenting Localities: a Practical Model for American Archivists and Manuscript Curators*, Lanham, MD and London: Society of American Archivists and Scarecrow Press.

BIBLIOGRAPHY

The rapidly changing and developing nature of most of the subjects treated in this book means that many of the relevant reference and source materials are available online or in the form of interim documents. Consequently, this brief bibliography is confined to those complete books (not articles or papers), and some current standards, that are of relatively recent publication and continuing importance. A search for further materials could usefully begin by accessing http://www.archives.org.uk

Aitchison, J. and Gilchrist, A. (1993), *Thesaurus Construction, a Practical Manual*, 2nd edn, London: ASLIB.

Anderson, H. and McIntyre, J. (1985), *Planning Manual for Disaster Control*, Edinburgh: National Library of Scotland.

Archives in the European Union: Report of the Group of Experts on the Coordination of Archives, Luxembourg: European Commission, Secretariat-General.

Archives Nationales du Québec (1992), *Archival Standards and Procedures of the Archives Nationales du Québec*, 4th edn revd, Quebec: Ministère des Affaires Culturelles.

Australian Standard (1996), *AS 4390–1996: Records Management*, Homebush, NSW: Standards Association of Australia.

Bearman, D. (1991), *Archival Methods*, Pittsburgh: Archives and Museums Informatics Technical Report No.9.

Bellotto, H.L. (1991), *Arquivos permanentes: tratamento documental*, São Paulo: T.A. Queiroz.

Bikson, T.K. and Frinking, E.J. (1993), *Preserving the Present: toward Viable Electronic Records*, The Hague: Sdu.

Black, E. (1991), *Authority Control: a Manual for Archivists*, Ottawa: Planning Committee on Descriptive Standards, Bureau of Canadian Archivists.

Bradsher, J.G. (ed.) (1988), *Managing Archives and Archival Institutions*, London: Mansell.

British Standard *BS6529:1984: Recommendations for Examining Documents, Determining their Subjects and Selecting Indexing Terms*, London: BSI.

British Standard *BS1749:1985: Recommendations for the Alphabetical Arrangement and the Filing Order of Numbers and Symbols*, London: BSI.

British Standard *BS5723:1987: Guide to the Establishment and Development of Monolingual Thesauri*, London: BSI.

British Standard *BS3700:1988: Recommendations for Preparing Indexes to Books, Periodicals and Other Documents*, London: BSI.

British Standard *BS5454:1988: Recommendations for Storage and Exhibition of Archival Documents*, London: BSI.

Bureau of Canadian Archivists (1985), *Toward Descriptive Standards: Report and Recommendations of the Canadian Working Group on Archival Descriptive Standards*, Ottawa: Bureau of Canadian Archivists.

Business Archives Council (1992), *Directory of Corporate Archives*, 3rd edn, London: BAC.

Champagne, M. and Chouinard, D. (1987), *Le traitement d'un fonds d'archives: ses documents historiques*, Montreal: Université, de Montréal.

Childs, R.J. (1996), *Health and Safety: a Guide to Good Health and Safety Practice in the Record Office*, Best Practice Guideline 3, London: Society of Archivists.

Cook, M. (1986), *The Management Of Information From Archives,* Aldershot: Gower.

Cook, M. (1993), *Information Management and Archival Data*, London: Library Association Publishing.

Cook, M. and Procter, M. (1989), *Manual of Archival Description*, 2nd edn, Aldershot: Gower.

Cook, T. (1997), 'Interaction of Archival Theory and Practice since the Publication of the Dutch Manual', *Archivum XLIII*, pp. 191[an]214, Munich: K.G. Saur.

Cox, R.J. (1992), *Managing Institutional Archives: Foundational Principles and Practices*, New York: Greenwood Press.

Cox, R.J. (1996), *Documenting Localities: a Practical Model for American Archivists and Manuscript Curators*, Lanham, MD and London: Society of American Archivists and the Scarecrow Press.

Craig, B. (ed.), (1992), *The Archival Imagination: Essays in Honour of Hugh A. Taylor*, Ottawa: Association of Canadian Archivists.

Developing Measures of User Satisfaction for University Archives and Manuscript Repositories, report to JISC.NFF: http://www.kcl.ac.uk/projects/srch/reports/usersat.htm.

Direction des Archives de France (1993), *La pratique archivistique française*, Paris: Archives Nationales.

Dollar, C.M. (1992), *Archival Theory and Information Technologies: the Impact of Information Technologies on Archival Principles and Methods*, Macerata, Italy: University of Macerata Publications.

Dunn, F.I. (1994), *Security*, Best Practice Guideline 2, London: Society of Archivists.

Durance, C.J. (comp.) (1990), *Management of Recorded Information: Converging Disciplines*, London: K.G. Saur, proceedings of the International Council on Archives Symposium on Current Records, National Archives of Canada, May 1989.

Eastwood, T. (ed.) (1992), *The Archival Fonds: from Theory to Practice*, Planning Committee on Descriptive Standards, Ottawa: Bureau of Canadian Archivists.

Ellis, J. (ed.) (1993), *Keeping Archives*, 2nd edn, Sydney: Thorpe, in association with the Australian Society of Archivists.

Emmerson, P. (ed.) (1989), *How to Manage your Records: a Guide to Effective Practice*, Cambridge: ICSA Publishing.

Forbes, H. (1993), *Local Authority Archive Services 1992: a Survey Commissioned by the Royal Commission on Historical Manuscripts and National Council on Archives*, British Library R&D Report 6090, London: HMSO.

Foster, J. (1998), *Subject Indexing Survey and Analysis*, report to JISC.NFF: http://www.kcl.ac.uk/projects/srch/reports/subindex.htm.

Foster, J. and Sheppard, J. (comps) (1995), *British Archives: a Guide to Archive Resources in the United Kingdom*, 3rd edn, London: Macmillan.

Gagnon-Arguin, L. (1989), *An Introduction to Authority Control for Archivists*, Ottawa: Bureau of Canadian Archivists.

Gillman, P. (1998), *National Name Authority File: a Report to the National Council on Archives*, Research and Innovation Report 91, London: British Library.

Gorman, M. and Winkler, P.W. (eds) (1988), *Anglo-American Cataloguing Rules*, 2nd edn revd, London: Library Association Publishing.

Gredley, E. and Hopkinson, A. (1990), *Exchanging Bibliographic Data: MARC and Other International Formats*, London: Library Association.

Ham, F.G. (1993), *Selecting and Appraising Archives and Manuscripts*, Archival Fundamentals Series, Chicago: Society of American Archivists.

Hare, C.E. (1997), *Developing a Records Management Programme*, London: ASLIB.

Helferty, S. and Refaussé, R. (1993), *Directory of Irish Archives*, 2nd edn, Dublin: Irish Academic Press.

Hensen, S.L. (1989), *Archives, Personal Papers and Manuscripts: a Cataloging Manual for Archival Repositories, Historical Societies and Manuscripts Libraries*, 2nd edn, Chicago: Society of American Archivists.

Heredia Herrera, A. (1991), *Archivística General: teoría y práctica*, 5th edn revd and augmented, Seville: Diputación Provincial.

International Council on Archives (1994), *ISAD(G): General International Standard Archival Description*, Ottawa: Secretariat of the ICA Ad Hoc Commission on Descriptive Standards.

International Council on Archives (1996), *ISAAR(CPF): International Standard Archival Authority Record for Corporate Bodies, Persons and Families*, Ottawa: Secretariat of the ICA Ad Hoc Commission on Descriptive Standards.

Ketelaar, E. (1985), *Archival and Records Management Legislation and Regulations*, Paris: Unesco.

Kitching, C. (1993), *Archive Buildings in the United Kingdom 1977–1992*, the Royal Commission on Historical Manuscripts, London: HMSO.

Kitching, C. (1996), *Archives: the Very Essence of our Heritage*, London: Phillimore, for the National Council on Archives.

Maher, W.J. (1992), *The Management Of College And University Archives*, Metuchen, NJ and London: Society of American Archivists and Scarecrow Press.

McKemmish, S. and Piggott, M. (eds) (1994), *The Records Continuum: Ian Maclean and Australian Archives First Fifty Years*, Sydney: Ancora Press in association with Australian Archives.

Mazikana, P. (1990), *Archives and Records Management for Decision-Makers: a RAMP Study*, Paris: Unesco.

Menne-Haritz, A. (ed.) (1993), *Information Handling in Offices and Archives*, London: K.G. Saur.

Methven, P. (1993), *Measuring Performance*, Best Practice Guideline 1, London: Society of Archivists.

Miller, F.M. (1990), *Arranging and Describing Archives and Manuscripts*, Archives Fundamentals Series, Chicago: Society of American Archivists.

National Archives Policy Liaison Group (1996), *An Archives Policy for the UK: Statement of Principles and Policy Objectives*, London: National Council on Archives.

Nesmith, T. (ed.) (1993), *Canadian Archival Studies and the Rediscovery of Provenance*, Metuchen, NJ and London: Society of American Archivists and Association of Canadian Archivists in association with Scarecrow Press.

Nougaret, C. (1997), 'The Impact of Modern Technology on Archives and Archival Work', *Archivum XLIII*, pp. 283–309, Munich: K.G. Saur.

Parker, E. and Smith, C. (1997), *Study of the Archival Records of British Universities*, A report for the Joint Information Systems Committee, Archives Subcommittee, London: TFPL Ltd; www.tfpl.com.

Pickford, C., Rhys-Lewis, J. and Weber, J. (1997), *Preservation and Conservation: a Guide to Policy and Practices in the Preservation of Archives*, Best Practice Guideline 4, London: Society of Archivists.

Piggott, M. and McEwen, C. (eds) (1996), *Archivists: the Image and Future of the Profession,* Sydney: Australian Society of Archivists.

Planning Committee on Descriptive Standards (1992), *Subject Indexing for Archives*, report of the Subject Indexing Working Group, Ottawa: Bureau of Canadian Archivists.

Post, J. and Foster, M. (1992), *Copyright: a Handbook for Archivists*, London: Society of Archivists.

Raspin, A. (1988), *The Transfer of Private Papers to Repositories*, Leaflet 5, London: Society of Archivists.

Ribeiro, F. (1996), *Indexação econtrolo de autoridade em arquivos*, Oporto: Câmara Municipal do Porto.

Royal Commission on Historical Manuscripts (1990), *A Standard for Record Repositories on Constitution and Finance, Staff, Acquisition, Access*, London: HMC.

Samuels, H.W. (1992), *Varsity Letters: Documenting Modern Colleges and Universities*, Metuchen, NJ and London: Society of American Archivists and Scarecrow Press.

Smiraglia, R.P. (ed.) (1990), *Describing Archival Materials: the Use of the MARC AMC Format,* New York and London: Haworth Press.

Society of Archivists (1996), *British Archival Practice: the Society's Archive Diploma Training Manual*, London: Society of Archivists.

Society of Archivists, Irish Region (1997), *Standards for the Development of Archives Services in Ireland*, Dublin: Society of Archivists, Irish Region.

Swedish National Archives (1994), *The Principle of Provenance*, report from the First Stockholm Conference on Archival Theory and the Principle of Provenance, September 1993, Stockholm: Svenska Riksarkivet.

Toronto Area Archivists Group Education Foundation (eds) (1993), *Toward International Descriptive Standards for Archives*, papers presented at the ICA Invitational Meeting of Experts on Descriptive Standards, London: K.G. Saur.

Turton, A. (ed.) (1991), *Managing Business Archives*, London: Butterworth Heinemann in association with the Business Archives Council.

Vaughan, A. (comp.) (1987), *International Reader in the Management Of Library, Information and Archive Services*, Paris: Unesco.

Walch, V.I. for the Working Group on Standards for Archival Description (1994), *Standards for Archival Description: a Handbook*, Chicago: Society of American Archivists.

Walne, P. (comp.) (1985), *Modern Archives Administration and Records Management: a RAMP Reader*, Paris: Unesco.

Wilsted, T. and Nolte, W. (1991), *Managing Archival and Manuscript Repositories,* Archival Fundamentals Series, Chicago: Society of American Archivists.

Your Right to Know: the Government's Proposals for a Freedom of Information Act, (1998), Cmd. 3818, London: HMSO.

Z39.50 for Archival Applications, report to JISC.NFF: http://www.kcl.ac.uk/projects/srch/reports/z3950.htm.

INDEX

Gower Handbook of Library and Information Management

Edited by Ray Prytherch

This *Gower Handbook* is an authoritative guide to both the traditional and newer aspects of library and information management. Edited by Ray Prytherch, it brings together the insight of a range of respected contributors, who offer advice on the management, storage, retrieval, analysis, marketing and delivery of information.

The book begins with Part I analysing the context and trends of the information world. In Part II, Strategy and Planning, the information environment is explored in more detail, with Chapters 3 and 4 presenting the main issues and principles of financial planning and strategic planning. Part III, The Service Infrastructure, looks at customer care, the role of performance measurement and research in service improvement, and the influence of copyright law in the delivery of information products to customers. Part IV, Managing Resources, includes five chapters on strategic management, information auditing, human resource management, preservation and disaster management. The last part of the *Handbook*, Part V, Access and Delivery, focuses on the potential of electronic systems with chapters on subject gateways and Z39.50, electronic publishing, intranets and new models of access and delivery. Each part of the *Handbook* begins with an introduction by the editor and the book concludes with a directory of organizations, including useful URLs, and a glossary.

Flexibility and adaptability are crucial for information professionals if they are to maintain their skills at the right level to provide the services needed by both information-rich and information-poor. In this one book librarians from all backgrounds, information managers and officers, document and records managers, and network and Web specialists will find answers to a wide range of questions that confront them in their working day. The *Handbook* will become a standard reference on best practice for professionals and students. It will be of interest to information analysts, knowledge managers, and others, including publishers, involved in information maintenance and provision.

Gower

Organization of Multimedia Resources

Principles and Practice of Information Retrieval

Mary A Burke

If you want to convert a collection of images into a computer database, organize access to sound recordings through a Web browser or store a company's archives in one searchable computerized structure, the database must be set up so that users can find what they want and make maximum use of the information it holds. Mary Burke provides much-needed guidance on organizing such information for effective retrieval whether from local, stand-alone computers or remote networked databases.

The earlier chapters of the book explain the need for a logical structure for multimedia databases and for consistent description and indexing of their components. Analysing the structure and characteristics of different information items, and the relationship between the original object and surrogate representations of it, the author extends the principles of cataloguing, classification, indexing and database structure to different multimedia products, identifying the difficulties of providing for multimedia retrieval by organizing data according to subject, creator or other characteristics. Theoretical principles and practical guidelines are given for storage of and access to the information content of textual, visual, audio and integrated multimedia databases.

Later chapters of the book analyse electronic data structures and the particular requirements of visual and audio formats. The author also explores future scenarios for multimedia databases in networked environments. Practical assignments throughout the book encourage readers to apply principles to their own individual projects. Examples and illustrations from a variety of systems and formats demonstrate the principles described.

Gower